The European Union
How does it work?

THIRD EDITION

Elizabeth Bomberg, John Peterson, and Richard Corbett

OXFORD
UNIVERSITY PRESS

OXFORD
UNIVERSITY PRESS

Great Clarendon Street, Oxford OX2 6DP

Oxford University Press is a department of the University of Oxford.
It furthers the University's objective of excellence in research, scholarship,
and education by publishing worldwide in

Oxford New York

Auckland   Cape Town   Dar es Salaam   Hong Kong   Karachi
Kuala Lumpur   Madrid   Melbourne   Mexico City   Nairobi
New Delhi   Shanghai   Taipei Toronto

With offices in

Argentina   Austria   Brazil   Chile   Czech Republic   France   Greece
Guatemala   Hungary   Italy   Japan   Poland   Portugal   Singapore
South Korea   Switzerland   Thailand   Turkey   Ukraine   Vietnam

Oxford is a registered trade mark of Oxford University Press in the
UK and in certain other countries

Published in the United States
by Oxford University Press Inc., New York

Typeset by TNQ Books and Journals Pvt. Ltd.
Printed in Great Britain
on acid-free paper by
Ashford Colour Press Ltd, Gosport, Hampshire

ISBN 978-0-19-957080-5

10 9 8 7 6 5 4 3 2

▌ OUTLINE CONTENTS

PART I   Background

PART II   Major Actors

PART III   Policies and Policy-making

■ DETAILED CONTENTS

PART I   Background

PART II   Major Actors

PART III Policies and Policy-making

PART IV   The EU and The Wider World

▌ PREFACE AND ACKNOWLEDGEMENTS

Change is a constant. That is one of the themes of this book and it certainly applies to the EU since we published the second edition of this volume in 2008. At that time, we were in the early days of the new 'EU-27'. The Union had expanded to a population of around 500 million and increased its land mass by 25 per cent as a consequence of adding no fewer than 80 per cent more member states since the first edition of this book was published. Today, arguably, our task is even more daunting. Not only is the EU still expanding, with Croatia due to join in mid-2013, but the EU is involved in a far greater array of policy areas, or involved in existing ones more intensely. It operates under a new (Lisbon) Treaty, which has created a permanent European Council President as well as something like an 'EU Minister of Foreign Affairs', while extending majority voting to a significantly larger number of policies. We and our authors can offer little more than educated guesses about what the precise effects of all of these changes will be. The EU's engagement with the outside world continues to change, often in unexpected ways. What the EU does, how it does it, and with what consequences, have all altered or intensified in some (usually significant) way since our second edition.

We have tried to reflect these changes in this new edition. In addition to updating significantly each individual chapter (five years is a long time in EU affairs), we've altered the book's organization and overall content. First, we've added several entirely new chapters, including one dedicated to some of the EU's fastest developing policy areas: in Chapter 9, John Peterson and Sandra Lavenex consider the EU as a security actor, which extends to issues of peacekeeping, crisis management, immigration, asylum, cross-border crime, and terrorism. A new chapter by Rory Watson and Richard Corbett wrestles with the question of how policies are made in Brussels and Strasbourg. Richard Corbett's chapter on 'democracy in the EU' finds that, by a surprising number of criteria, the Union has much more impressive democratic credentials than any other political system beyond the nation-state. Instead of a separate chapter on the enlargement process, Graham Avery (Chapter 8) looks more generally at EU expansion and the Union's evolving relationship with its neighbours. Finally, we've taken on a new co-editor—Richard Corbett of the *cabinet* of European Council President Herman Von Rompuy—who has given us that insider's eagle eye that Alex Stubb—subsequently Foreign Minister of Finland—contributed to earlier editions.

Even more important is what we have *not* changed. Our core mission remains the same: to produce a clear, concise, truly introductory text for students and the curious general reader. No previous experience required. We know the EU is important; we demonstrate why and how in the next chapters. We also know it can be made both comprehensible and interesting. Our aim is to show how. If we succeed, it is in great part due to our all-star team of contributors, editors, support and publishing staff.

First, the contributors. One of the book's most distinctive and strongest qualities is its blend of academic and practitioner authors. All chapters were either co-authored or reviewed by both an academic and practitioner. We thank our team of authors for working to make this blend workable and even enjoyable. A special thanks to authors or co-authors from the *first* two editions: Laura Cram, Lynn Dobson, Lykke Friis, David Martin, John D. Occhipinti, Michael Shackleton, Michael E. Smith, Albert Weale, and the late, great Sir Neil MacCormick.

A second batch of thanks goes to the editorial and production team. The editorial assistance offered by Andrew Byrne (Universities of Edinburgh and Köln) was tremendous. Andrew reviewed every chapter and helped compile and update the references and glossary—no mean feat in itself. Niklas Helwig—also of the Universities of Edinburgh and Köln—deserves our thanks in advance for editing the online resource centre page that accompanies this volume.

We owe a very special thanks to series editor Helen Wallace, who offered not only excellent substantive guidance but also unflagging and essential encouragement in the production of this and past volumes. Thanks also to the production team at OUP, especially Catherine Page who demonstrated great patience and skill in seeing the project through.

Thirdly, our readers. The real advantage of doing multiple editions is that we are able to benefit from feedback the first ones. We've profited enormously from comments offered by reviewers of the first two editions, by practitioners in Brussels (special thanks to Michael Shackleton of the European Parliament and the late and much missed Ron Asmus of the German Marshall Fund), and by the many EU studies colleagues who have used this book in their teaching. An extremely useful range of comments, criticisms, and suggestions came directly from 'end users' themselves—including students using the earlier editions in their courses at the University of Edinburgh and College of Europe.

Much of the updating of several chapters was done while one of us (John Peterson) was a visiting scholar in Summer 2010 at the Institute of Governmental Studies, University of California, Berkeley. We are immensely grateful for the logistical support, collegiality, and peaceful space offered there. Director Jack Citrin and administrator Jennifer Baires made John's stay especially productive, and we owe them a great deal.

Finally, amidst all the tumultuous change that marks scholarship on EU, one 'constant' most gratefully acknowledged is the support offered by the editors' families. Like last time, but more so: we could not have done it without you.

Elizabeth Bomberg, John Peterson, and Richard Corbett
Edinburgh and Brussels

▌ LIST OF FIGURES

▎ LIST OF BOXES

▋ LIST OF TABLES

ABBREVIATIONS AND ACRONYMS

ACP	African, Caribbean, and Pacific
APEC	Asia Pacific Economic Cooperation
ASEAN	Association of South-East Asian Nations
BEUC	Bureau Européen des Union de Consommateurs (European Consumers Organization)
CAP	Common Agricultural Policy
CEPOL	European Police College
CFSP	Common Foreign and Security Policy
CIA	Central Intelligence Agency (US)
COPA	Committee of Professional Agricultural Organizations
CoR	Committee of the Regions and Local Authorities
COREPER	Committee of Permanent Representatives
DG	Directorate-General (European Commission)
EAW	European Arrest Warrant
EC	European Community
ECAS	European Citizen Action Service
ECB	European Central Bank
ECHO	European Community Humanitarian Office
ECHR	European Convention on Human Rights
ECJ	European Court of Justice
ECOFIN	(Council of) Economic and Finance Ministers
ECSC	European Coal and Steel Community
EDC	European Defence Community
EDF	European Development Fund
EEA	European Economic Area
EEC	European Economic Community
EEW	European Evidence Warrant
EFSF	European Financial Stability Facility
EFTA	European Free Trade Association
EMU	Economic and Monetary Union
EMS	European Monetary System
ENP	European Neighbourhood Policy
EP	European Parliament

EPACA	European Public Affairs Consultancies Association
EPC	European Political Cooperation
ERF	European Refugee Fund
ERM	Exchange Rate Mechanism
ESC	Economic and Social Committee
ESDP	European Security and Defence Policy
ESM	European Stability Mechanism
ESS	European Security Strategy
ETUC	European Trades Union Confederation
EU	European Union
EURATOM	European Atomic Energy Community
FBI	Federal Bureau of Investigation (US)
FD	Framework Decision
FRG	Federal Republic of Germany
FTA	Free Trade Area
FYROM	Former Yugoslav Republic of Macedonia
GAERC	General Affairs and External Relations Council
GATT	General Agreement on Tariffs and Trade
GDP	Gross Domestic Product
GMOs	Genetically Modified Organisms
GNP	Gross National Product
IGC	Intergovernmental Conference
IO	International Organization
IR	International Relations
JHA	Justice and Home Affairs
MEP	Member of the European Parliament
MEPP	Middle East Peace Process
MFA	Minister for Foreign Affairs
NAFTA	North American Free Trade Agreement
NATO	North Atlantic Treaty Organization
NGO	Non-governmental Organization
NSS	National Security Strategy (US)
OEEC	Organization for European Economic Cooperation
OMC	Open Method of Coordination
OSCE	Organization for Security and Cooperation in Europe (formerly CSCE)
PCTF	Police Chiefs Task Force
PNR	Passenger Name Record

PTA	Preferential Trade Agreement
QMV	Qualified Majority Voting
REACH	Registration, Evaluation, Authorization, and Restriction of Chemicals
SAP	Stability and Association Process
SCIFA	Strategic Committee on Immigration, Frontiers, and Asylum
SEA	Single European Act
SGP	Stability and Growth Pact
SIS	Schengen Information System
SME	Small and Medium-sized Enterprise
TEC	Treaty establishing the European Community
TEU	Treaty on European Union
UK	United Kingdom
UN	United Nations
UNICE	Union of Industrial and Employers' Confederations of Europe
US	United States
VIS	Visa Information System
VWP	Visa Waiver Program (US)
WEU	Western European Union
WTO	World Trade Organization
WWF	World Wide Fund for Nature

■ LIST OF CONTRIBUTORS

GRAHAM AVERY	St Antony's College, Oxford
ELIZABETH BOMBERG	University of Edinburgh
RICHARD CORBETT	*Cabinet* of European Council President
DESMOND DINAN	George Mason University
BRIGID LAFFAN	University College Dublin
SANDRA LAVENEX	University of Lucerne
JOHN PETERSON	University of Edinburgh
ALBERTA SBRAGIA	University of Pittsburgh
FRANCESCO STOLFI	University of Sussex
ALEXANDER STUBB	Minister for European Affairs and Foreign Trade, Finland
RORY WATSON	Freelance journalist, Brussels

New to this Edition:

- Richard Corbett, former Member of the European Parliament and currently member of the European Council President's *Cabinet*, joins the editorial team for the third edition to ensure it continues to offer a practitioner's perspective.

- There are new chapters on 'How Policies are Made'—to help clarify what is often viewed as a complex process—and 'The EU as a Security Actor', which spans the full range of internal and external security policies that are a major growth area for EU policy-making.

- The chapter on democracy has been rewritten by Richard Corbett, who focuses specifically on the question of the EU's democratic credentials.

- All chapters have been revised and updated in light of the ratification of the Lisbon Treaty and the effects of the financial crisis on the Eurozone.

FIGURE 0.1 The European Union's Member States

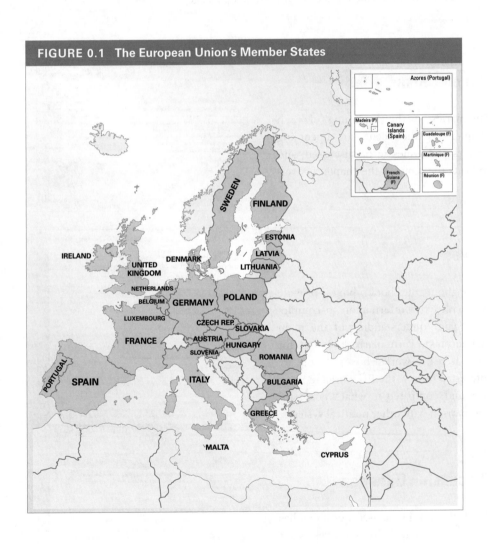

▌ GUIDED TOUR OF TEXTBOOK FEATURES

This book is enriched with a number of learning tools to help you navigate the text and reinforce your knowledge of European Union politics. This guided tour shows you how to get the most out of your textbook package.

Chapter Summaries

Summaries at the beginning of each chapter set the scene for upcoming themes and issues to be discussed, and indicate the scope of the chapter's coverage.

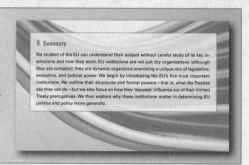

Boxes

Throughout the book, boxes provide you with extra information to complement your understanding of the main chapter text. Particularly look out for 'how it really works' boxes if you are interested in how the EU works in practice, and 'compared to what?' boxes for comparison with other political systems.

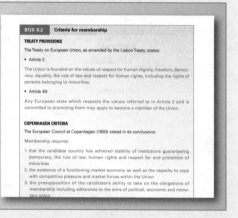

Discussion Questions

A set of carefully devised questions has been provided to help you assess your understanding of core themes, and may also be used as the basis of seminar discussion or coursework.

Further Reading

Take your learning further by using the reading lists at the end of each chapter to find the key literature in the field, or more detailed information on a specific topic.

 FURTHER READING

The definitive guide to policy-making in the EU remains Wallace et al. (2010). Richardson (2005) is also useful. There is also a very wide literature on lobbying in the European Union that can be divided into general texts, specific case studies or analyses, and practical guides and reference works. The most recent general text is Coen and Richardson (2009), but Greenwood (2003) also provides a useful, detailed examination of different interest groups. A special issue of the *Journal of European Public Policy* (2007) is devoted specifically to lobbying. Goergen (2006) offers a very comprehensive practical guide to lobbying, and the regularly updated publication, the stakeholder.eu directory (2011), compiled by the former MEP Frank Schwalba Hoth, offers an overview of the wide range of actors involved. On the European Parliament, including its political groups, see Corbett et al. (2011, Chapter 10) and Judge and Earnshaw (2002).

Coen, D. and Richardson, J. (2009), *Lobbying in the European Union: Institutions, Actors and Issues* (Oxford: Oxford University Press).

Corbett, R., Jacobs, F., and Shackleton, M. (2011), *The European Parliament* 8th edn. (London: Cartermill).

Goergen, P. (2006), *Lobbying in Brussels: A Practical Guide to the European Union for Cities, Regions, Networks and Enterprises* (Brussels, D&P Services).

Greenwood, J. (2003), *Representing Interests in the European Union* (Basingstoke and New York: Palgrave).

Web Links

At the end of each chapter you will find an annotated summary of useful websites to help you with further research.

 WEB LINKS

A good place to start researching the EU's external policy role is the website of the Paris-based Institute for Security Studies http://www.iss.europa.eu/), which formally became an autonomous European Union agency in 2002. Other specific areas of EU policy have their own, dedicated websites:

- External relations (general): http://www.europa.eu/pol/ext/index_en.htm
- Foreign and security policy: http://www.europa.eu/pol/cfsp/index_en.htm
- Humanitarian aid: http://europa.eu/pol/hum/index_en.htm
- Justice/home affairs: http://www.europa.eu/pol/justice/index_en.htm
- Trade: http://europa.eu/pol/comm/index_en.htm
- Development: http://ec.europa.eu/europeaid/index_en.htm

The Commission's site (http://ec.europa.eu/index_en.htm) has general information about EU foreign policy, but the websites of national foreign ministries often reveal more. On the EU's relationship with the US, see http://www.eurunion.org/ and http://www.useu.be/. Web links on the EU's other important relationships include ones devoted to the Cotonou convention (http://www.acpsec.org/), EU–Canadian relations (http://www.canada-europe.org/), and the Union's relationship with Latin America (http://asi.pitt.edu/view/subjects/D002022.html). To see how the EU's

Chronology

In an appendix at the end of the book is a useful chronology of key dates in the history of European integration.

▌ APPENDIX: Chronology of European Integration*

1945 May	End of World War II in Europe
1946 Sept.	Winston Churchill's 'United States of Europe' speech
1947 June	Marshall Plan announced
	Organization for European Economic Cooperation established
1949 Apr.	North Atlantic Treaty signed in Washington
1950 May	Schuman Declaration
1951 Apr.	Treaty establishing the ECSC signed in Paris
1952 May	Treaty establishing the European Defence Community (EDC) signed
Aug.	European Coal and Steel Community launched in Luxembourg
1954 Aug.	French parliament rejects the EDC
Oct.	Western European Union (WEU) established
1955 May	Germany and Italy join NATO
June	EC foreign ministers meet in Messina to relaunch European integration
1956 May	Meeting in Venice, EC foreign ministers recommend establishing the

Glossary Terms

Key terms appear in red in the text and are defined in a glossary at the end of the book to aid your exam revision.

EU's ability to integrate new members into its system.

Accession (see Box 8.1) The process whereby a country joins the EU and becomes a member state.

Acquis communautaire (see Box 4.1) Denotes the rights and obligations derived from the EU treaties, laws, and Court rulings. In principle, new member states joining the EU must accept the entire acquis.

Assent procedure (see Consent Procedure)

Asylum Protection provided by a government to a foreigner who is unable to stay in their country of citizenship/residence for fear of persecution.

Battle groups (see Box 9.3): combine national military resources at the 'hard end' of European capabilities in specialized areas. The EU decided in 2004 to create 20 Battle Groups, which would be deployable at short notice for limited deployments.

Charter of Fundamental Rights (see Box 7.1) Adopted by the Council at the Nice Summit in 2000 but not legally binding, the Charter seeks to strengthen and promote the fundamental human rights of EU citizens.

Civil society (see Box 6.1) The collection of groups and associations (such as private firms and non-governmental organizations) that operate between the individual and state.

Co-decision procedure Under this decision-making procedure the European Parliament formally shares legal responsibility for legislation jointly with the Council of Ministers.

Cohesion policy Introduced after the first enlargement in 1973, its aim has been to reduce inequality among regions and compensate for the costs of economic integration.

Common Foreign and Security Policy (CFSP) (see Box 10.1) Created by the 1992 Maastricht Treaty as a successor to the European Political Cooperation mechanism. It has been embel-

◼ GUIDED TOUR OF THE ONLINE RESOURCE CENTRE

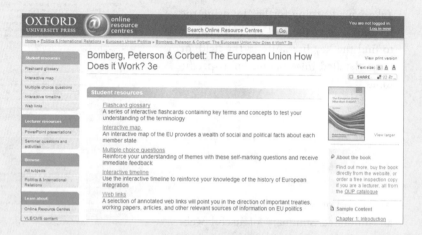

www.oxfordtextbooks.co.uk/orc/bomberg3e/

The Online Resource Centre that accompanies this textbook provides students and lecturers with ready-to-use teaching and learning materials. These resources are free of charge and designed to maximize the learning experience.

The information and exercises on the Online Resource Centre have been updated by Niklas Helwig of the Centre for European Policy Studies, Brussels.

For Students

Flashcard Glossary

A series of interactive flashcards containing key terms allows you to test your knowledge of the terminology of EU politics.

Multiple-choice Questions

A bank of self-marking multiple-choice questions has been provided for each chapter, and includes instant feedback on your answers to aid your revision.

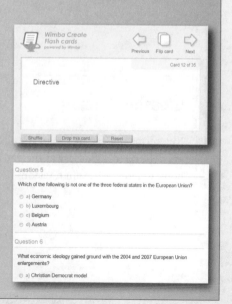

Interactive Map

An interactive map of the EU provides a wealth of social and political facts about each member state. Simply click on the state you are interested in and the information appears in a separate window.

Interactive Timeline

Use the interactive timeline to reinforce your knowledge of the history of European integration. Key events are summarized when you click on each date.

Web Links

A selection of annotated web links will point you in the direction of important treaties, working papers, articles, and other relevant sources of information on EU politics.

EU Publication Office: Includes journals, documents, newsletters, electronic products, and other publications.
www.publications.europa.eu

European Police Office
www.europol.europa.eu

European Council on Refugees and Exiles (ECRE): Promoting the protection and integration of refugees in Europe based on the values of human dignity, human rights, and an ethic of solidarity
www.ecre.org/

European Court of Human Rights: Consisting of a number of judges equal to the number of member States of the **Council of Europe** (www.coe.int/) that have ratified the Convention for the Protection of Human Rights and Fundamental Freedoms.
www.echr.coe.int/

Eurochambres: The Association of European Chambers of Commerce and Industry,

For further online resources about EU politics also visit our European Union Politics resource centre at **www.oxfordtextbooks.co.uk/orc/eupolitics/**

For Registered Adopters of the Textbook

Power Point® Slides

Customizable PowerPoint® slides complement each chapter of the book and are a useful resource for preparing lectures and handouts.

Managing EU Business

- Head of government/ministers
- Minister or State Secretary of European Affairs
- Minister of Foreign Affairs
- Coordination between national ministries
- Permanent Representation in Brussels

OXFORD

Seminar Questions

A suite of seminar questions has been devised to be used in assessment or to stimulate class debate.

Chapter 2

1. In your opinion, which policy (security, agriculture, trade, development the most important in forging European integration?

2. Use historical examples to illustrate how EU policies 'spill over'.

3. Do you think Charles de Gaulle's intergovernmental approach is evide EU?

4. How did wars in the EU's early years (such as the Korean War and th stimulate integration?

PART I

Background

CHAPTER 1

Introduction

Elizabeth Bomberg, Richard Corbett, and John Peterson

▌ Summary

Understanding how the European Union (EU) works is not easy, but it is well worth the effort. This introductory chapter sets out the reasons—both practical and analytical—for studying the European Union. It then introduces some of the main conceptual approaches to understanding this unique organization, how it functions, and why. Finally, the chapter sets out three broad themes that will tie together our analysis of the European Union and how it works.

Studying the EU

In 2007, the European Union celebrated the fiftieth anniversary of its founding Treaty of Rome. Assessments of its state of health varied wildly, from the familiar hand-wringing ('Europe is dead') to the considerably more upbeat ('Europe's golden moment'). Three years later, when member states including Greece and Ireland faced severe economic crises, the result was similarly bipolar analyses: 'the Euro is finished' v. 'the EU always does the right thing in the end' (by aiding its member states when needed). That the EU can elicit such diametrically opposite diagnoses is nothing new. It is an absolutely distinctive creation, varied and complex enough to invite wildly contrasting interpretations of the sort generated by blind men feeling different parts of an elephant and extrapolating about the entire beast (see Puchala 1972). The European Union is indeed not easy to grasp. To the uninitiated, its institutions seem remote, its remit unclear, its actions complex, and its policies perplexing. Such perplexity is understandable. To begin with, the EU defies simple categorization: it combines attributes of a state with those of an international organization, yet it closely resembles neither (see Box 1.1). Its development is shaped by an increasing number of players: 27 member governments, seven EU institutions including a Central Bank, two consultative bodies with legal status, an Investment Bank, a clutch of agencies and almost countless private interests, experts, foreign actors and citizen groups try to influence what the EU does (or does not do). 'What the EU does' has expanded enormously since its origins in the 1950s. Originally narrowly concerned with establishing a common market, at first just for coal and steel, its policy remit has expanded to cover agricultural, monetary, regional, environmental, social, immigration, foreign, and security policy, and the list does not stop there (see Box 1.2).

BOX 1.1	What's in a name?

Even the question of what to call the EU can cause confusion. What became the European Union was originally established as the European Coal and Steel Community in 1951, followed by the main **European Economic Community** (EEC, colloquially known as the Common Market) by the 1957 Treaty of Rome. Its remit was widened and its name shortened to **European Community** (EC) in 1992. The 1992 Maastricht Treaty also created the **European Union**, consisting of the EC as well as two other **'pillars'** of cooperation in the areas of common and foreign policy, and justice and home affairs. The Lisbon Treaty formally merged all three pillars into a single legal entity, called the European Union, in December 2009. We use the label European Community (or EC) to refer to the organization in the pre-Maastricht period (see especially Chapter 2), but 'European Union' to refer to all periods—and the activities of all pillars—thereafter. As we will see, vocabulary in the EU can be a sensitive matter (see Box 11.1).

BOX 1.2	The three pillars of the European Union

The activities of the EU were established in three areas or 'pillars' by the 1992 Maastricht Treaty. When the Lisbon Treaty came into force in 2009, the pillars were collapsed into one common institutional structure and the EU as a whole was given a single legal personality. However, important differences between the 'non-existent' pillars persisted, especially for pillar 2. It remains the case that the EU cannot be fully understood without understanding the previous pillar system.

FIGURE 1.1   The (pre-Lisbon Treaty) 'pillar structure' of the European Union

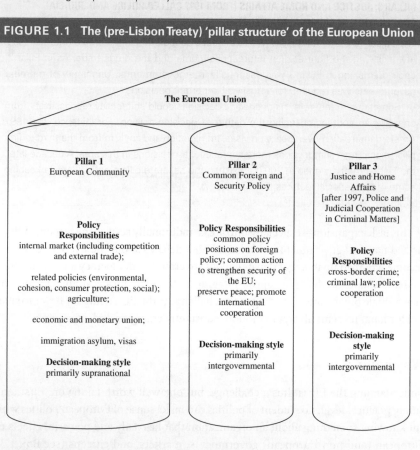

The European Union

Pillar 1
European Community

Policy Responsibilities
internal market (including competition and external trade);

related policies (environmental, cohesion, consumer protection, social); agriculture;

economic and monetary union;

immigration asylum, visas

Decision-making style
primarily supranational

Pillar 2
Common Foreign and Security Policy

Policy Responsibilities
common policy positions on foreign policy; common action to strengthen security of the EU; preserve peace; promote international cooperation

Decision-making style
primarily intergovernmental

Pillar 3
Justice and Home Affairs
[after 1997, Police and Judicial Cooperation in Criminal Matters]

Policy Responsibilities
cross-border crime; criminal law; police cooperation

Decision-making style
primarily intergovernmental

PILLAR 1: EUROPEAN COMMUNITIES

The first pillar was the biggest, incorporating the vast majority of EU responsibilities. It covered internal market policies as well as trade, agriculture and competition policy. Eventually, it was extended to cover most immigration and asylum policy, and economic and monetary union. In this pillar the EU's common institutions (Commission, Council, Court, and Parliament) could act with a significant degree of autonomy from national governments.

Cont. ➤

> **Cont.**
>
> **PILLAR 2: COMMON FOREIGN AND SECURITY POLICY**
>
> In the second pillar, member states attempted to forge common positions and take joint action on foreign and security affairs. Decision-making was primarily intergovernmental (that is, between governments), by unanimity, and without a separate legal framework; neither the Commission nor the European Parliament had much direct influence.
>
> **PILLAR 3: JUSTICE AND HOME AFFAIRS (FROM 1997 CALLED POLICE AND JUDICIAL COOPERATION IN CRIMINAL MATTERS)**
>
> The objective of the third pillar was to increase cooperation in the area of internal security, including the fight against international crime and the drugs trade. As in Pillar 2, decision-making in Pillar 3 was essentially intergovernmental. Unanimity of member governments was required for virtually all important decisions.
>
> Sometimes Treaty reforms or specific decisions could shift policy responsibility from one pillar to another, changing the nature of decision-making. For instance, the 1997 Amsterdam Treaty moved policy on visas, immigration and **asylum** from the third to first pillar, signalling a shift towards more supranational decisions in this area. A decade later, the Lisbon Treaty (signed in 2007) abolished the separate pillars entirely, while keeping some of their special features (see Chapter 7).

This task expansion—especially into areas traditionally seen as the responsibility of elected national governments—has meant that debates about the EU over time have become wrapped up in larger debates about sovereignty, democracy and the future of the nation state. Studying European integration therefore means studying a lot more than a single organization. Adding to the challenge is the EU's tendency never to stand still for long. It seems always in motion, constantly changing and expanding.

Why bother?

Understanding the EU is thus a challenge, but one well worth taking on. First, on a purely practical level, no student of politics can make sense of European politics without knowing something about an organization that has daily and powerful effects on European (and non-European) governments, markets, and citizens (see Box 1.3). What other international body would or could, in a matter of months, issue far-reaching decisions governing: animal welfare, mobile phones, imports of illegally logged timber, caps on carbon emissions, university fees, cross-border policing, and the Middle East peace process? Of course these rules and decisions were not made overnight; most were negotiated and decided over a period stretching into years not months. Not all had immediate or even perceptible impact: in foreign policy, especially, the EU finds it much easier to talk than to act. Nor were these decisions easily reached: they were the result of negotiations amongst an astonishing array of actors across regional, national, even international borders. Yet, however derived, EU decisions frequently have a significant impact on prosperity and peace in Europe and beyond.

BOX 1.3	The practical significance of the EU

The EU's practical impact is felt in a wide range of areas including:

- **Market:** The EU now regulates the world's largest market, including over 500 million consumers, around 60 per cent more than the United States.

- **Legislation:** It is not easy to measure, and estimates vary, but in most years, something between 6 and 35 per cent of the domestic legislation enacted by the Union's member states originates from EU legislation.

- **Currency:** In 2002, 12 national currencies—some dating back 600 years—ceased to be legal tender and were replaced by the euro. By 2011, 17 countries and over 350 million consumers used this single currency.

- **Wealth:** The EU's collective wealth (Gross National Income) accounts for about 30 per cent of the world's total.

- **Trade:** Not counting intra-EU trade, the EU's share of world trade (imports and exports) exceeds that of the United States, accounting for almost 20 per cent of all global trade.

- **Aid:** The EU and its member states are the world's largest donors of development aid, accounting for over 55 per cent. They are also the world's largest importer of goods from less developed countries (see Chapter 10).

While the wisdom or desirability of EU policies and actions are hotly contested, few would deny their practical importance.

Sources: figures available from the websites of Commission, DG Trade:

- http://ec.europa.eu/economy_finance/euro/index_en.htm
- http://ec.europa.eu/economy_finance/index_en.htm
- http://trade.ec.europa.eu/doclib/docs/2006/september/tradoc_122531.pdf;

Eurostat:

- http://epp.eurostat.ec.europa.eu/portal/page/portal/eurostat/home/

and from the World Trade Organization:

- http://stat.wto.org/CountryProfile/WSDBCountryPFView.aspx?Language=E&Country=E27

Second, students of politics, economics, law, and international relations are interested in the EU not just because of its practical relevance, but also because of its analytical significance: it represents the most advanced experiment ever in multilateral cooperation and political integration (see Box 1.5)—the 'process whereby political actors in several distinct national settings are persuaded to shift their loyalties, expectations and political activities toward a new center' (Haas 1958: 16). Thus, understanding the EU helps us frame questions about the future of the nation-state, the prospects for international cooperation, the effects of globalization (see Box 1.5), and the proper role of governments in advanced industrial societies. Put another way, much of what makes the EU challenging to study—its dynamic character, complexity, and expanding activities—also make it fascinating. Rather than avoid these attributes we use them as themes to glue together our analysis (see below).

Finally, the EU fascinates because it represents a political puzzle. On one hand it has been enormously successful. EU governments and institutions have transformed it from a common market of six countries into a peaceful, integrated Union of 27 with a population of close to 500 million. It is the world's largest trading bloc, accounting for over 20 per cent of global trade with a combined economy considerably larger than that of the United States (see Box 1.3). It has its own currency and a fledgling foreign policy. A queue of applicants awaits at its borders.

Yet a growing number of citizens appear disillusioned with the EU, and not just in the traditionally more 'sceptical' states such as the United Kingdom (UK). In 2005 citizens in two founding countries—France and the Netherlands—soundly rejected a Constitutional Treaty designed to make the EU more efficient and bring it closer to its citizens (see Box 1.4). In 2008 Irish voters, albeit narrowly, initially rejected its replacement, the Treaty of Lisbon. 'Brussels bureaucrats' make easy targets for almost every ill and populist parties often gain electoral success through EU-bashing. Voter turnout in European Parliament elections has fallen with each election. EU institutions—the European Commission, the Council of Ministers (representing national governments), and even the directly elected Parliament—are viewed as remote and complex, or just not worth bothering about. The EU certainly is not a well understood body, and it is difficult even for diligent students to see just how (or if) the EU works.

In this book we address the practical question: 'how does it work?': who are the main actors, what are the main processes, dynamics, and explanations for what the EU does, and how it does it? But we also want to address the more rhetorical question: 'how (in the world) does it work?!' How can such a massive, complex, unwieldy amalgam of states, institutions, lobbyists, languages, traditions, legal codes, etc., possibly do much of the governing of Europe? More practically, why have sovereign states agreed to relinquish part of their sovereignty (see Box 1.5)? With what implications? Why do policies emerge looking as they do? Why did the EU develop the way it did and where is it likely to go from here? Why does it elicit such strong demonstrations of support and antipathy? Our main goal is to address these questions in a lively and comprehensible way.

We employ several devices to help us achieve our objective. This book is largely written by experts with either research, teaching, or policy-making experience (some with all three). Many chapters are co-authored by an academic and practitioner to illustrate both how the EU works and how to make sense of it. Students need to understand both the formal 'textbook' rules of EU practice (what the Treaties say; what the legislation stipulates) but also how it 'really' works (how are the Treaties interpreted; what informal rules guide action). We capture this dual dynamic through a series of boxes entitled 'How it Really Works'. They illustrate how a particular actor, policy or process actually works, regardless of the formal rules.

BOX 1.4   Constitutional, Reform, or Lisbon Treaty?

The Constitutional Treaty, the result of a special Convention on the Future of Europe (see Chapter 7), was unanimously endorsed and signed by government leaders in 2004. It was eventually abandoned ... or was it? Debates persist even about the answer to this most basic of questions.

The Constitutional Treaty comprised three basic elements: institutional reform, a charter of fundamental rights and the consolidation of existing treaties. The primary institutional measures (see also Table 3.1) included:

- increased majority voting on the Council of Ministers (where each member state is represented), simplified to represent a double majority based on states and population;

- more legislative powers for the Parliament;

- a full-time president of the European Council (where heads of state and government are represented). This post replaced the previous six-month rotation between Presidents or Prime Ministers of member states;

- a smaller European Commission; and

- a new EU minister of foreign affairs.

The second section of the Treaty codified a **Charter of Fundamental Rights** (a wide-ranging statement of 'rights, freedoms, principles' including the right to life, free expression and the right to strike), binding on the Union's institutions and the field of EU law (see Chapter 7).

The third part (by far the longest) consisted of a consolidated and amended version of all previous treaties. It formally designated the Treaty as a constitution for the first time and gave the Union a single 'legal personality'. However, the term 'Constitutional Treaty' was a typical Eurofudge: yes, it had been prepared by a 'Convention' but it was finally agreed between member states as any treaty would be. At the same time it provided an exit clause for states wishing to leave the Union. Designed to streamline and bring the EU closer to its citizens, the Treaty ended up stretching to 300 pages of text, not all of them comprehensible. (Thus the French government's decision to post copies of the entire text to all voters in advance of France's referendum was not a successful 'vote yes' strategy.)

Treaty change requires ratification by all member states. By mid-2007 18 of the 27 had ratified the Treaty. But voters in two founding member states—France and the Netherlands—had rejected the Treaty in referenda held in 2005. An alternative solution had to be found.

In 2007, European leaders finally agreed to abandon the idea of a 'constitution' and instead amended the pre-existing treaties. They avoided all references to constitutional symbols such as a European flag or anthem, and dropped the idea of giving the title (EU) 'Minister of Foreign Affairs' to a more powerful foreign policy chief. But the new treaty maintained the bulk of the institutional reforms that were contained in the Constitutional Treaty. The treaty was initially referred to as the 'Reform Treaty'—after all, everyone is in favour of reform—but the designation was dropped when, like most

Cont. ➤

> **Cont.**
>
> treaties, it took on the name of the city where it was signed in late 2007: Lisbon. Eventually ratified by all member states by the end of 2009, Lisbon actually leaves the Union with two main treaties. The first is called Treaty on European Union (TEU) and contains the basic aims, principles and instruments of the EU, as well as its provisions on foreign and security policy. The second is called Treaty on the Functioning of the EU (TFEU), which contains detailed policy provisions and procedures. However, the two are often referred to in the singular as the Lisbon Treaty. Its close substantive resemblance to the Constitutional Treaty prompted debates about whether the original was a 'constitution' in anything but name and whether Lisbon was more than an ordinary 'treaty'.

The book also seeks to make the EU more comprehensible by placing its institutions, structures, or policies in a comparative perspective. Most chapters include a 'Compared to what?' box which compares EU institutions, practices or processes with their counterparts inside the member states or outside the EU. The intent is to help students better understand the EU by underlining how it is like—or unlike—other systems of governance (see Box 1.5), and in what ways it is unique. More generally, the book is seasoned throughout with vignettes or other boxes which draw the reader into the substance of the chapter through real life examples or illustrations. Finally, each chapter offers 'key concept' boxes that define important terms, and each also provides guides to further reading and useful internet sites. All these features are designed to achieve our overall aim: to bring the EU to life for our readers.

Understanding the EU: Theory and Conceptual Tools

When studying anything as complex as the European Union we need conceptual tools to guide us. A theory or model simplifies reality and allows us to see relationships between the things we observe. Scholars trying to understand the EU employ different theories developed in the study of international relations, comparative politics, sociology, and public policy. Each theory seeks to explain different developments, episodes and dynamics of EU politics and European integration. Just as there is no single explanation for events, there is no one theory of EU politics. We offer here brief synopses of leading theoretical frameworks or approaches. Our aim is not to present or apply them, with all their nuances, nor to privilege one over the others. We aim to pull out for the reader the key assumptions and insights offered by each. The following chapters will then use these insights to elaborate on and explain their particular topic.

BOX 1.5	Key concepts and terms (listed alphabetically)

globalization is the idea that the world is becoming increasingly interconnected and interdependent because of increasing flows of trade, technology, ideas, people, and capital. Globalization is usually presented as reducing the autonomy of individual states, although whether its impact is essentially positive or negative, inevitable or controllable, are hotly-debated questions.

governance means 'established patterns of rule without an overall ruler'. Even though there is no government, the EU undertakes the sort of activities that governments traditionally have done. The EU is thus said to be a system of governance without a government (or an opposition).

integration is the process whereby sovereign states partially relinquish or pool national sovereignty to maximize their collective power and interests.

intergovernmentalism is a process or condition whereby decisions are reached by specifically defined cooperation between or among governments. Formally, at least, sovereignty is not relinquished. The term intergovernmentalism is usually contrasted with supranationalism.

multilevel governance is often used to describe the EU. It means a system in which power is shared between the supranational, national, and subnational levels. The term also suggests there is a fair bit of interaction and coordination of political actors across those levels. How they interact and with what effect helps determine the shape of European integration (see Hooghe and Marks 2001).

sovereignty refers to the ultimate authority over people and territory. It is sometimes broken down into internal (law-making authority within a territory) and external (international recognition). Opinions vary on whether state sovereignty is 'surrendered' or merely 'shared' or 'pooled' in the context of the EU.

supranationalism means above states or nations. That is, decisions are made by a process or institution that is largely (but never entirely) independent of national governments. The subject governments (in the case of the EU, the member state governments) are then obliged to accept these decisions. The European Court of Justice (see Chapter 3) is a supranational institution. The term supranationalism is usually contrasted with intergovernmentalism.

International relations approaches

Several classic theories of integration draw from international relations theory. They are concerned primarily with explaining the broad development of European integration: that is, how and why nations choose to form European institutions, and who or what determines the shape and speed of the integration process.

One of the earliest theories of European integration was neofunctionalism, which was developed primarily by Ernst Haas in the 1960s to explain the development of the European Coal and Steel Community (ECSC) and the European Economic Community (EEC), the predecessors of the EU. Haas and others were concerned with explaining how a merger of economic activity in specific economic sectors (say, coal and steel) across borders could 'spill over' and provoke wider economic integration in related areas (Haas 1958; 1964; Lindberg and Scheingold 1970). More ambitiously, neofunctionalists believed that this economic integration would produce political integration and the creation of common, integrated supranational institutions to accelerate this process. ('Supranational' here means transcending national borders, interests and powers; see Box 1.5). Finally, according to neofunctionalists, interests and loyalties would gradually shift from the national to supranational level.

Early neofunctionalist theory seemed to explain well the initial successes of European integration, but its uni-directional logic (integration could only go forward) was heavily criticized when European integration appeared to stagnate and even to reverse in the late 1960s and 1970s (Rosamond 2005). Dissatisfaction with neofunctionalism led to the development of alternative theoretical models, especially liberal intergovernmentalism.

Most closely associated with Andrew Moravcsik (1993; 1998), liberal intergovernmentalism builds on the work of international relations scholars and historians who reject the notion that national governments do not control European integration (see Hoffmann 1995; Milward 1992; Moravcsik and Schimmelfennig 2009). Marshalling impressive historical evidence, liberal intergovernmentalists argue that major choices—what Peterson (1995) calls 'history making decisions'—reflect the preferences of national governments rather than supranational organizations. Each state's preferences reflect the balance of their domestic economic interests. The outcomes of EU negotiation are the result of bargaining, that is bargaining between sovereign national governments (see Box 1.5). Any subsequent delegation to supranational institutions is calculated, rational, and circumscribed. In short, national governments are the dominant actors in shaping integration, and they are in control: 'governments first define a set of interests, then bargain among themselves to realize those interests' (Moravcsik 1993: 481).

A comparative politics approach

Analysts drawing on comparative politics approaches have challenged the primacy of the state in shaping European integration and the EU. Foremost among these approaches is the new institutionalism, which emphasizes the importance of institutions in shaping or even determining government preferences and has become perhaps *the* leading theory of EU politics and policy-making (see Cowles and Curtis

2004). In the EU context, institutionalism demonstrates how the EU's common institutions (Commission, Council, Parliament, or Court) are more than impartial arbiters in the policy-making process: they are key players with their own agendas and priorities (Armstrong and Bulmer 1998; Pollack 2009). For *new* institutionalists, 'institutions' refer not only to institutions traditionally defined—executives, parliaments, courts—but also to values, accepted standards, and informal conventions that govern social exchanges between actors. These values affect or 'frame' the way actors perceive the choices open to them. So, for example, the informal rules or practices (say the unwritten goal of seeking consensus whenever possible) can mould the behaviour of national government representatives in ways that governments neither plan nor control.

A second insight of institutionalist analyses is the concept of 'path dependency': the notion that once a particular decision or path is chosen, 'it is very difficult to get back on the rejected path' (Krasner 1984: 225). Path dependency means that it is hard to change policy—such as an expensive Common Agricultural Policy—even when it outlives its usefulness. The 'sunk costs' (time and resources already invested) of agreeing a policy in the first place are often considerable, and the idea of starting again on a long, time-consuming and expensive process of agreeing a new policy is frequently resisted for that reason (see Pierson 1996).

A public policy approach

A third theoretical approach useful to those studying the EU is the policy networks framework (see Jordan and Schout 2006; Peterson 2009). Unlike neofunctionalism or liberal intergovernmentalism, this approach does not tell us much about the policy bargains struck between national governments, nor the history-making decisions (such as treaty reform) that set the broad direction of European integration. But policy network analysis is useful for uncovering the nitty-gritty, behind-the-scenes negotiation and exchange that can shape policies at a day-to-day level. A policy network is 'a cluster of actors, each of which has an interest or stake in a given EU policy sector and the capacity to help determine policy success or failure' (Peterson and Bomberg 1999: 8). Policy networks at the EU level usually bring together institutional actors (from the Commission, Council, Parliament) and other stake-holders such as representatives of private firms, public interest groups, technical or scientific experts and, perhaps above all, national officials. Networks lack hierarchy (there is no one actor in charge) and instead depend on resource exchange. That means participants need to bring to Brussels (or Strasbourg) some valued resource with which to bargain: information, ideas, finances, constitutional-legal power, or political legitimacy. According to network analysts, bargaining and resource exchange among these actors—rather than strictly intergovernmental bargaining—determine the shape of actual EU policies.

A sociological/cultural approach

An increasingly popular conceptual approach that cuts across multiple theories is constructivism, a school drawing on cultural and sociological studies and recent developments in IR theory. It is a strikingly diverse school, but at its core is an attempt to focus attention on the 'social construction' of the collective rules and norms that guide political behaviour (Eilstrup-Sangiovanni 2006: 393). At its most radical, a constructivist approach argues that reality does not exist outside human interpretation or language. In the study of the EU, however, a less radical or abstract form of social constructivism is prevalent.

Above all, constructivists seek to go beyond a rationalist approach to understanding the EU. The latter assumes pre-set and rational interests and identities; political actors (say national representatives) weigh the costs and benefits of actions, and make decisions based on those calculations. Constructivists argue instead that EU political actors' positions and even identities are shaped not (only) by the rational pursuit of national or self interest but by the bargaining process itself, especially the pressure to conform or reach consensus (see Lewis 2003: 99).

Constructivism can and has been coupled with the theories of integration introduced above. Like neo-functionalism, constructivism focuses our attention on socialization, transfers of loyalty, and the process whereby actors redefine their interests as a result of interaction within European institutions (Haas 2001). Similarly, constructivism complements the new institutionalism's emphasis on norms and ideas. Along with institutionalists, social constructivists suggest that informal rules and norms (such as reciprocity or the desire to show 'good will') can shape or even determine political actors' behaviour (Lewis 2003; Checkel 2006).

While most would agree that ideas or norms are important in some way (see especially Chapters 3 and 4), it is extremely difficult to show that abstract ideas or norms actually cause a change in behaviour as many constructivist argue. Constructivists often can correlate ideas with behaviour, but have trouble proving that ideas matter more than interests (Aspinwall and Schneider 2000; Checkel 2004). Thus, constructivism does not offer a theory for understanding the EU as much as it draws our attention to insights that might be missed by other theories.

Each of these approaches has its own assumptions, strengths, and weaknesses (see Table 1.1). No one theory can explain everything treated in this book. But each school introduced here offers different insights about different key features of the EU: how integration evolves; the way policies are made and the role of different actors in this process. Students need not master all these theories to use this book. Rather, these theoretical insights—and their application in subsequent chapters—are meant to encourage students to begin thinking about theory and its role in helping us understand and evaluate European integration and EU politics.

TABLE 1.1	Theories of European integration and the EU		
THEORY/ APPROACH	**PROPONENTS/ MAJOR WORK**	**ASSUMPTIONS**	**SHORTCOMINGS/ CRITICISMS**
Neofunctionalism	Haas 1958	Supranational institutions crucial; spillover drives integration	Cannot explain stagnation
Liberal intergovernmentalism	Moravscik 1998	Member states control European integration	Too state-centric; neglects day-to-day policy-making
New institutionalism	Pollack 2009	Institutions matter; path dependency	Overemphasizes power of the EU's institutions
Policy networks	Peterson 2009	Resource exchange within networks shapes policy	Cannot explain big decisions
Social constructivism	Checkel 2004 Risse 2009	Ideas matter; interests constructed, not predetermined	Methodological weaknesses

Themes

To help the reader make sense of the EU, this text is held together by three common themes. Each highlights a key, distinctive feature of the EU as:

1. an 'experiment in motion', an ongoing process without a clear end-state;
2. a system of shared power characterized by growing complexity and an increasing number of players;
3. an organization with an expanding scope, but limited capacity.

We introduce each of these themes below.

Experimentation and change

Since its conception in the early 1950s, European integration has been an ongoing process without a clear *finalité*, or end-state. In one sense its development has been a functional step-by-step process: integration in one area has led to pressures to integrate in others. As neofunctionalists would point out, the Union has developed from a coal and steel community to a full customs union; from a customs union to single market, and from a single market to an economic and monetary union. This development,

BOX 1.6	The Treaties

When practitioners and academics use the term 'the Treaties', they are referring to the collection of founding treaties and their subsequent revisions. The founding treaties include the Treaty of Paris (signed in 1951, establishing the European Coal and Steel Community) and two Treaties of Rome, 1957, one establishing the European Atomic Energy Community (Euratom), the other the European Economic Community. The ECSC became void in July 2002. The Euratom Treaty never amounted to much. But the **Treaty of Rome** (signed in 1957) establishing the EEC became absolutely central. It has been substantially revised, notably in the:

- **Single European Act** (signed in 1986),
- **Maastricht Treaty** (or Treaty on European Union, signed in 1992),
- **Amsterdam Treaty** (signed in 1997),
- **Nice Treaty** (signed in 2001), and the
- **Lisbon Treaty** (signed 2007).

As Box 1.1 explained, the intergovernmental conference leading up to the Maastricht Treaty not only revised the Treaty of Rome (which it re-named Treaty establishing the European Community) but it also agreed the broader Treaty on European Union (TEU or Maastricht Treaty, 1992) which included two new pillars or areas of activity on foreign policy and justice and home affairs (see Box 1.2). The pillars were subsequently collapsed into a single framework by the Amsterdam and Lisbon Treaties.

The EU's treaties are the basic toolkit of ministers, Commissioners, parliamentarians, and civil servants dealing with EU matters. Each piece of legislation is based on one of these treaty articles (of which there are more than 400). The Treaties have grown increasingly long and complex. To improve the presentation and facilitate the reading of the Treaties, the articles were renumbered in the Amsterdam summit of 1997. But the Treaties are hardly an easy read. Even many legal scholars would agree that the some of their language borders on the incomprehensible. The unratified 2004 Constitutional Treaty was intended to simplify the existing texts and make them more readable. Its successor, the 2007 Lisbon Treaty, made a more modest attempt at simplification, although the term 'constitution' was dropped. Presumably, it will remain a term that dares not speak its name in Brussels for many years to come.

however, has been neither smooth, automatic, nor predetermined. Rather, integration and the EU's development have progressed in fits and starts, the result of constant experimentation, problem-solving, and trial and error. European foreign policy, from failed attempts of the 1950s to the creation of a European Security and Defence Policy (ESDP) in the last decade or so, is a good example of this evolution. With no agreed end goal (such as a 'United States of Europe'), the EU's actors have reacted to immediate problems, but they have done so neither coherently nor predictably.

The nature and intensity of change have also varied. Constitutional change has taken place through Intergovernmental Conferences (IGCs)—special negotiations in which government representatives come together to hammer out agreements to alter the EU's guiding treaties. The first (resulting in the Treaty of Paris, 1951) created the European Coal and Steel Community made up of six states. More recently, the Constitutional Treaty (signed in 2004 but never ratified) or its successor, the Lisbon Treaty (ratified in 2009), were designed to serve an EU of 30 or more (see Box 1.4; 1.6). Less spectacularly, legislative change has taken place through thousands of EU directives and regulations. Finally, the EU's institutions, especially the European Commission and Court of Justice, have themselves acted as instigators of change, and have expanded the powers of the Union throughout its history. The point is that change is a constant in the EU. This book will explore its main sources and implications.

Power-sharing and consensus

Our second theme concerns power and how it is shared between different actors and across layers of government. The EU policy-making system lacks a clear nexus of power: there is no 'EU government' in the traditional sense of the term. Instead, power is dispersed across a range of actors and levels of governance (regional, national, and supranational). Deciding which actors should do what, and at what level of governance, is a matter of ongoing debate within the EU.

The three most important sets of actors are the member states, institutions, and organized interests. Certainly, much about the evolution of the EU has been determined by the member states themselves, and in particular their different approaches to integration. Some member states want deeper integration, others do not, and this division continues to shape the speed and form of the integration process. Meanwhile, EU institutions have shaped the EU's development as they vie for power with the member states, as well as among themselves. Finally organized interests—including representatives of sub-national levels of governance, private interests, citizens groups—now play an increasing role.

Part of what makes the EU unique—and certainly different from its member states—is that these actors exist in a complex web where there are established patterns of interaction but no overall 'ruler', government, or even dominant actor. Instead, actors must bargain and share power in an effort to reach an agreement acceptable to all, or at least most. This dynamic has been captured in the term multi level governance (see Box 1.5), which suggests a system of overlapping and shared powers between actors on the regional, national, and supranational levels (Hooghe and Marks 2001). EU governance is thus an exercise in sharing power between states and institutions, and seeking consensus across different levels of governance. Coming to grips with this unique distribution of power is a key task of this book.

Scope and capacity

Our final theme concerns the expanding remit of the EU, and its ability to cope with it. The EU has undergone continuous (in a phrase used by insiders) 'widening and deepening'. The widening of its membership has been astonishing. It has grown from a comfortable club of six member states (Germany, France, Italy, the Netherlands, Belgium, and Luxembourg) to nine (UK, Denmark, and Ireland joined in 1973), to 12 (Greece in 1981; Portugal and Spain in 1986) to 15 (Austria, Finland, and Sweden joined in 1995). Then in 2004 the EU jumped to 25 following the accession of 10 mainly central and eastern states. The accession of Bulgaria and Romania in 2007 took the EU to 27 with additional candidates, including Turkey, knocking on the door. The institutional, political, economic, and even linguistic challenges this enlargement poses are immense (see Box 1.7).

The EU has also 'deepened' in the sense that the member states have decided to pool sovereignty in an increasing number of policy areas, including, most dramatically in the sensitive area of justice and home affairs (see Chapter 9). This robust policy development has meant that the EU is managing tasks that have traditionally been the exclusive preserve of the nation-state. At the same time the EU continues to try to dispose of its image as an 'economic giant, but a political dwarf'. The Union is trying to stamp its authority on the international scene through its leadership on

---

BOX 1.7   Lost in interpretation?

With the addition of Irish as an official language in 2007, the EU boasted 23 official languages:

- Bulgarian, Czech, Danish, Dutch, English, Estonian, Finnish, French,
- German, Greek, Irish, Hungarian, Italian, Latvian, Lithuanian, Maltese,
- Polish, Portuguese, Romanian, Slovak, Slovene, Spanish, and Swedish.

The EU's translation service is the largest in the world by far (over twice the size of the UN's) and the cost of translation and interpretation is over €850m a year, or around €1.70 for every person in the EU. In Parliament alone, where interpreters in soundproof boxes attempt to translate words such as gobbledygook (the word doesn't exist in Polish), and avoid confusing frozen semen with seamen (as occurred in one parliamentary debate), the cost and potential confusion is immense. But being able to communicate with your electors and fellow representatives in your own language is also seen as a fundamental right. After all, it is difficult for EU citizens to feel close to an institution which does not operate—at least officially—in their own language. In practice, most work of the EU is carried out in just three languages, English, French, and German. Meanwhile, the rising cost of translation has had one positive effect—it has forced practitioners to limit official texts to under 15 pages.

Sources: Commission 2007b; 2011; query to Commission DG Translation

issues such as climate action, or the development of a Common Foreign and Security Policy (CFSP), which, according to the Treaties, 'might in time lead to a common defence'. These developments have challenged the EU's 'capacity'—its practical and political ability to realize its ambitions. While the Union has taken on more members and more tasks, its institutional and political development has not kept pace. This mismatch—between the EU's ambitions on one hand and its institutional and political capacity on the other—raises questions about the EU's future and ability to adapt. It also represents the third theme of the volume.

Taken together these three themes address:

1. how the EU has developed and why (experimentation and change);
2. who are the main players and how do they interact (power-sharing and consensus);
3. what the EU does, and how it does it (scope and capabilities).

These three themes provide the glue necessary to hold together our investigation of the EU and how it works.

Chapter Layout

Any book on European integration that aims to be at all comprehensive is bound to cover a lot of ground, both theoretical and practical. In explaining how the EU works, it is necessary to look at the historical background of European integration, the major actors involved, the key policies and their impact, and the EU's global presence. The book's layout reflects this logic. Chapter 2 tells us 'how we got here' by providing a concise historical overview of the EU's development. The next section (see Chapters 3–4) focuses on the major actors: the EU's institutions and member states. Section III focuses on policy and process. It provides an expert overview of key economic and related policies (see Chapter 5), how policies are made (see Chapter 6), and the wider constitutional issues arising from these policy processes (see Chapter 7). Chapters in the last section examine the EU's relations with the wider world. Chapter 8 covers EU enlargement and its policy towards states in its geographical neighbourhood. Chapter 9 focuses on the EU's foray into the sensitive areas of internal and external security policy. Chapter 10 explores the EU's growing role as a global actor. A conclusion draws together the main themes of the volume and ponders how the EU might work in the future.

DISCUSSION QUESTIONS

1. The EU can be seen as one of the most successful modern experiments in international cooperation, yet it is increasingly unpopular amongst its citizens. Why?

2. Which theory appears to offer the most compelling account of recent developments in European integration?

FURTHER READING

Some of the key themes introduced in this chapter are inspired by leading general broad studies of the EU including Hooghe and Marks (2001), Scharpf (1999), Wallace *et al.* (2010) and Weiler (1999). Nelsen and Stubb (2003) feature a collection of seminal works on European integration theory and practice. Holmes (2001) provides a collection of 'Eurosceptical' readings while Leonard and Leonard (2002) counter with their 'Pro-European Reader'. An excellent and comprehensive overview of key perspectives, works and theories is provided by Jørgensen *et al.* (2006). A useful summary and overview of different theoretical approaches is offered by Eilstrup-Sangiovanni's collection (2006). For an incisive survey of these different theories applied to the EU, see Pollack (2010). To explore in more depth some of the key theoretical approaches, see Haas (1958; 2001) on neofunctionalism; Milward (1992) and Moravcsik (1998) on liberal intergovernmentalism; Armstrong and Bulmer (1998), Pollack (2009) or Meunier and McNamara (2007) on new institutionalism; Peterson (2009) on policy networks; and Checkel (2006) on constructivism.

Armstrong, K. and Bulmer, S. (1998) *The Governance of the Single European Market* (Manchester and New York: Manchester University Press).

Checkel, J. (2006), 'Constructivism and EU Politics' in K. E. Jørgensen, M. Pollack, and B. Rosamond (eds.), *Handbook of European Union Politics* (London: Sage): 57–76.

Eilstrup-Sangiovanni, M. (ed.) (2006), *Debates on European Integration. A Reader* (Basingstoke and New York: Palgrave).

Haas, E. (1958), *The Uniting of Europe: Political, Social, and Economic Forces, 1950–7* (Stanford: Stanford University Press).

Haas, E. (2001), 'Does Constructivism Subsume Neo-functionalism?' in T. Christiansen, K. E. Jørgensen, and A. Weiner, *The Social Construction of Europe* (London and Thousand Oaks CA: Sage): 22–31.

Holmes, M. (ed.) (2001), *The Eurosceptical Reader 2* (Basingstoke and New York: Palgrave).

Hooghe, L. and Marks, G. (2001), *Multi-Level Governance and European Integration* (Lanham and Oxford: Rowman and Littlefield Publishers Inc).

Jørgensen, K. E., Pollack, M., and Rosamond, B. (2006), *Handbook of European Union Politics* (London: Sage).

Leonard, D. and Leonard, M. (eds.) (2002), *The Pro-European Reader* (Basingstoke and New York: Palgrave).

Meunier, S. and McNamara, K. (eds.) (2007), *Making History. European Integration and Institutional Change at Fifty* (Oxford and New York: Oxford University Press).

Milward, A. (1992), *The European Rescue of the Nation-State* (London: Routledge).

Moravcsik, A. (1998), *The Choice for Europe* (Ithaca NY: Cornell University Press).

Nelsen, B. and Stubb, A. (eds.) (2003), *The European Union: Readings on the Theory and Practice of European Integration,* 3rd edn. (Boulder CO and Basingstoke: Lynne Rienner and Palgrave).

Peterson, J. (2009), 'Policy Networks' in A. Wiener and T. Diez (2009) *European Integration Theory,* 2nd edn. (Oxford and New York: Oxford University Press): 105–24.

Pollack, M. (2009), 'New Institutionalism' in A. Wiener and T. Diez, *European Integration Theory,* 2nd edn. (Oxford and New York: Oxford University Press): 125–43.

Pollack, M. (2010), 'Theorizing EU Policy-Making' in H. Wallace, M. Pollack, and A. Young (eds.), *Policy-Making in the European Union,* 6th edn. (Oxford and New York: Oxford University Press): 15–44.

Scharpf, F. W. (1999), *Governing in Europe: Effective and Democratic?* (Oxford and New York: Oxford University Press).

Wallace, H., Pollack, M., and Young, A. (eds.) (2010), *Policy-Making in the European Union,* 6th edn. (Oxford and New York: Oxford University Press).

WEB LINKS

- The EU's official website 'The European Union online' (**http://europa.eu/**) is a valuable starting point. It provides further links to wide variety of official sites on EU policies, institutions, legislation, treaties, and current debates.

- Precisely because the EU's website is so large, the Europa—Information Services website provides a nice index of where to find answers on the Europa website (**http://europa.eu/geninfo/info/guide/index_en.htm**).

- You can also use the web to access the *Official Journal* (OJ) which is updated daily in several languages. The OJ is the authoritative and formal source for information on EU legislation, case law, parliamentary questions, and documents of public interest (**http://eur-lex.europa.eu/**).

- For pithier reporting, the *Economist* (**http://www.economist.com/**) provides useful general articles, while *European Voice* (**http://www.european-voice.com/**) offers insider coverage of EU policies and news.

- To follow current events and developments within the EU, the following sites are useful:

  - EurActiv reports EU current affairs with analysis, and has an easy to navigate system of 'dossiers' which provide an overview of different policy areas (**http://www.euractiv.com/en/HomePage**); while the

  - EUobserver offers coverage of EU current affairs with a very useful email bulletin service (**http://euobserver.com/**).

- Current debates and topics are also addressed in series of think tank websites. Some of the better known include the Centre for European Policy Studies (**http://www.ceps.eu/**); the European Policy Centre (**http://www.epc.eu/**); the Centre for European Reform (**http://www.cer.org.uk/**), and the Trans European Policy Studies Association (**http://www.tepsa.be/**).

- The Institute for European Politics' (Berlin) website offers an overview of current thinking on EU policies and issues in all the member states (**http://www.iep-berlin.de/index.php?id=publikationen&L=1**).

 Visit the Online Resource Centre that accompanies this book for additional material: **www.oxfordtextbooks.co.uk/orc/bomberg3e/**

CHAPTER 2

How Did We Get Here?

Desmond Dinan

▌ Summary

European countries responded to a series of domestic, regional, and global challenges after the Second World War by integrating economically and politically. These challenges ranged from post-war reconstruction, to international financial turmoil, to the consequences of the end of the Cold War. Driven largely by national interests, Franco-German bargains, and American influence, Europeans responded by establishing the European Community and later the European Union. Deeper integration clashed with cherished concepts of national identity, sovereignty, and legitimacy. Successive rounds of enlargement, which saw the EU grow in size from its original six member states, also generated institutional and policy challenges that have shaped the contours of European integration.

Introduction

The history of the European Union presents a fascinating puzzle: why did European states, traditionally jealous of their independence, pool sovereignty in an international organization that increasingly acquired federal attributes? This chapter argues that the answer is as simple as it is paradoxical: because it was in their national interests to do so. Political parties and interest groups did not always agree on what constituted the national interest, and governments themselves were sometimes divided. But at critical junctures in the post-war period, for various strategic and/or economic reasons, national leaders opted for closer integration.

This chapter aims to outline the history of European integration by focusing on national responses to major domestic and international challenges since the end of the Second World War. These responses gave rise to the European Community (EC) and later the European Union (EU). France and Germany played key roles. The EC was a bargain struck (primarily) between them for mutual economic gain. In strengthening post-war Franco-German ties, the EC also had an important political dimension. Indeed, Germany conceded a lot to France in the negotiations that led to the EC in order to deepen Franco-German solidarity, a key step towards binding the Federal Republic to the West. Subsequent milestones in the history of European integration also hinged on Franco-German bargaining.

Ideology—the quest for a united Europe—was not a major motive for European integration (see Box 2.1). The Preamble of the Rome Treaty, the EC's charter, called for an 'ever closer union' among the peoples of Europe. This assertion of the popular aspiration for European unity was vague and hardly constituted a guiding principle for the EC. Some national and supranational leaders were strongly committed to

---

BOX 2.1   Interpreting European integration

Historians have offered different interpretations of how European integration has developed and why. Alan Milward (1984; 2000) was the foremost historian of European integration. He argued that economic interests impelled Western European countries to integrate, but that national governments shared sovereignty only to the extent necessary to resolve problems that would otherwise have undermined their legitimacy and credibility. Paradoxically, European states rescued themselves through limited **supranationalism**. Andrew Moravcsik (1998) has complemented Milward's thesis by claiming that national governments, not supranational institutions, controlled the pace and scope of integration. Moravcsik uses historical insights from a series of case studies from the 1950s to the 1990s to develop **liberal intergovernmentalism** as a theory of European integration. Intergovernmentalism generally is in the ascendant in the historiography of European integration, in contrast to the early years of the EC when the arguments of neofunctionalist scholars such as Ernst Haas (1958) and Leon Lindberg (1963) dominated academic discourse on the EC (see Chapter 1).

federalism. But they succeeded in moving Europe in a federal direction only when ideological ambition coincided with national political and economic preferences. The language of European integration, redolent of peace and reconciliation, provided convenient camouflage for the pursuit of national interests based on rational calculations of costs and benefits.

This chapter also argues that the United States (US) has been a major player in the integration process, both positively (as a promoter of integration) and negatively (as an entity against which Europe has integrated). Globalization (see Box 1.5) and its presumed association with Americanization has driven European integration in recent years. Since the late 1980s, the EU has been in search of strategies to compete globally against the US while retaining a social structure that is relatively egalitarian and distinctly not American.

Post-war Settlement

The most pressing question at the end of the Second World War was what to do about Germany. The question became acute with the onset of the Cold War. As the Soviet Union consolidated its control over the eastern part of the country, the Western Powers—the United Kingdom (UK), France, and the US—facilitated the establishment of democratic and free market institutions in what became the Federal Republic of Germany (FRG). The German question then became how to maximize the economic and military potential of the FRG for the benefit of the West while allaying the understandable concerns of Germany's neighbours, especially France. France accepted a supranational solution to the problem of German economic recovery, but not to the problem of German remilitarization.

The US championed integration as a means of reconciling old enemies, promoting prosperity, and strengthening Western Europe's resistance to communism. The Marshall Plan (see Box 2.2) was the main instrument of American policy. European governments wanted American dollars for post-war reconstruction, but without any strings attached. For their part, the Americans insisted that European recipients coordinate their plans for using the aid. That was the extent of European integration in the late 1940s. The UK had no interest in sharing sovereignty. France wanted to keep the old enemy down and keep Germany's coal-rich Ruhr region from becoming a springboard to remilitarization. Few countries were willing to liberalize trade. Winston Churchill's famous call in 1946 for a United States of Europe belied the reality of politicians' unwillingness to change the international status quo.

It was Germany's rapid economic recovery, thanks in part to the Marshall Plan, that made the status quo untenable. The US wanted to accelerate German recovery in order to reduce occupation costs and promote recovery throughout Europe. A weak West Germany, the Americans argued, meant a weak Western Europe. France agreed, but urged caution. France wanted to modernize its own economy before allowing Germany's economy to rebound. Indeed, France agreed to the establishment of the FRG only on condition that German coal production (a key material for warmaking) remained under international control.

German expressions of resentment of French policy fell on receptive American ears. As the Cold War deepened, the US intensified pressure on France to relax its policy towards the FRG so that German economic potential could be put at the disposal of the West. Yet the US was not insensitive to French economic and security

---

BOX 2.2   Key concepts and terms

The **Empty Chair Crisis** was prompted by French President Charles de Gaulle's decision to pull France out of all Council meetings in 1965, thereby leaving one chair empty. De Gaulle staunchly opposed the Commission's plans to extend the EC's powers generally and the application of the treaty provisions on the extension of **qualified majority voting (QMV)**.

The **Luxembourg Compromise** resolved the empty chair crisis. Reached during a foreign ministers' meeting in 1966, the Compromise was an informal agreement (issued only in the form of a press release) stating that when a decision was subject to QMV, the Council would postpone a decision if any member states felt 'very important interests' were under threat, and would 'endeavour, within a reasonable time' to find a solution acceptable to all. Although France and the Five disagreed on what would happen if no such solutions were found within a reasonable time (continue discussions or proceed to a vote), in practice the compromise meant QMV was used far less often, and unanimity became the norm.

The **Marshall Plan** (1947) was an aid package from the US of $13 billion (a lot of money in 1947, equivalent to 5 per cent of US GNP) to help rebuild West European economies after the war. The aid was given on the condition that European states cooperate and jointly administer these funds.

Qualified Majority Voting (QMV) is the voting system most commonly used in the Council. Decisions require a high level of support but do not need unanimity. The formula used, revised by the Lisbon Treaty, can be found in Table 3.2

The **Schengen Agreement** was signed by five member states in 1985 (Belgium, France, Germany, Luxembourg, and the Netherlands) and came into effect 10 years later. It removed all border controls among its signatories, which now includes most member states as well as Switzerland, Norway, and Iceland. Ireland and the UK are not full participants.

Subsidiarity is the idea that action should be taken at the level of government which is best able to achieve policy goals, but as close to the citizens as possible.

interests. Instead of imposing a solution, Washington pressed Paris to devise a policy that would allay French concerns about the Ruhr region, without endangering Germany's full recovery. Given its preference for European integration, the US hoped that France would take a supranational tack.

Originally, the US wanted the UK to lead on the German question. The UK had already taken the initiative on military security in Europe, having pressed the US to negotiate the Washington Treaty (which founded NATO, the North Atlantic Treaty Organization). Yet the UK was reluctant for reasons of history, national sovereignty, and economic policy to go beyond anything but intergovernmental cooperation. The UK's prestige in Europe was then at its height. Continental countries looked to the UK for leadership. Such leadership, however, was absent. Under mounting American pressure, France came up with a novel idea to reconcile Franco-German interests by pooling coal and steel resources under a supranational High Authority.

Schuman Plan

This idea became the Schuman Plan, drafted by Jean Monnet, a senior French civil servant with extensive international experience. Monnet faced intense American pressure to devise a new policy towards Germany but also believed in European unity and saw the Schuman Plan as a first step in that direction. More immediately, it would protect French interests by ensuring continued access to German resources, although on the basis of cooperation rather than coercion. The new plan bore the name of the French Foreign Minister, Robert Schuman, who risked his political life promoting it at a time when most French people deeply distrusted Germany.

Naturally, German Chancellor Konrad Adenauer endorsed the plan, which provided a means of resolving the Ruhr problem and rehabilitating Germany internationally. Schuman and Adenauer trusted each other. They were both Christian Democrats, came from the Franco-German borderlands, and spoke German together. Aware of the UK's attitude towards integration, Schuman did not bother to inform London of the plan. By contrast, the Americans were in on it from the beginning.

The Schuman Plan was a major reversal of French foreign policy. Having tried to keep Germany down since the war, France now sought to turn the inevitability of Germany's economic recovery to its own advantage through the establishment of a common market in coal and steel. The Schuman Declaration of 9 May 1950, announcing the plan, was couched in the language of reconciliation rather than *realpolitik*. In fact the initiative cleverly combined national and European interests. It represented a dramatic new departure in European as well as in French and German affairs (see Box 2.3).

Participation in the plan was supposedly open to all the countries of Europe. In fact, the list of likely partners was far shorter. The Cold War excluded Central and Eastern Europe from the plan. In Western Europe, the UK and the Scandinavian countries had already rejected supranationalism. Ireland was isolationist; Spain and Portugal, under dictatorial regimes, were international outcasts; and Switzerland was resolutely neutral. That left the Benelux countries (Belgium, the Netherlands, and Luxembourg), which were economically tied to France and Germany, and Italy, which saw integration primarily as a means of combating domestic communism and restoring international legitimacy. Consequently the European Coal and Steel Community (ECSC), launched in 1952, included only six countries. The ECSC soon established a common market in coal and steel products, with generous provisions for workers' rights.

BOX 2.3	How it really works

Rhetoric versus reality in the Schuman Plan

Jean Monnet's drafting of the Schuman Plan in 1950 marked a diplomatic breakthrough on the contentious German question. More generally, the plan's proposal for a coal and steel community also advanced the goal of European unity. When outlining the proposal in the Schuman Declaration, a highly publicized initiative, Monnet emphasized the European and idealistic dimension of the proposal. Issued on 9 May, the Schuman Declaration proclaimed that:

World peace can only be safeguarded if constructive efforts are made proportionate to the dangers that threaten it . . . France, by advocating for more than twenty years the idea of a united Europe, has always regarded it as an essential objective to serve the purpose of peace . . . With this aim in view, the French government proposes to take immediate action on one limited but decisive point. The French government proposes that Franco-German production of coal and steel be placed under a common 'high authority' within an organization open to the participation of the other European nations . . . [This step] will lay the first concrete foundation for a European federation, which is so indispensable for the preservation of peace.

But Monnet was also concerned to defend French national interests. He wanted to ensure French access to German raw materials and European markets despite Germany's economic resurgence. In a private note to Schuman some days before the Declaration's release, Monnet explained that France had little choice but to safeguard its interests by taking a new approach. On 1 May Monnet informed Schuman that:

Germany has already asked to be allowed to increase its output [of steel] from 10 to 14 million tons [French output was 9 million tons at the time]. We will refuse but the Americans will insist. Finally, we will make reservations and give way . . . There is no need to describe the consequences [of not giving way] in any detail

(quoted in Duchêne 1994: 198).

Instead of trying to block Germany's advance, Monnet advocated a European initiative—the Schuman Plan—which also catered for French interests.

European Defence Community

The same six countries ('the Six') signed a treaty to establish a defence community in 1952. The rationale for both communities was the same: supranational institutions provided the best means of managing German recovery. In this case, the outbreak of the Korean War in June 1950, perceived as a possible precursor to a Soviet attack on Western Europe, made German remilitarization imperative. France at first resisted, and then acquiesced on condition that German military units were subsumed into a new European Defence Community (EDC). Like the Schuman Plan, the plan for the EDC sought to make a virtue (European integration) out of necessity (German remilitarization). Although the EDC was a French proposal, most French people fiercely opposed German remilitarization. The EDC became the most divisive issue in the country. In view of the treaty's unpopularity the government delayed ratification for two years. The French parliament ignominiously defeated the treaty in 1954.

Ironically, Germany formed an army anyway, under the auspices of the Western European Union (WEU), an intergovernmental organization comprising the UK and the Six and established in 1954. Germany joined NATO via the WEU in May 1955 and effectively regained full formal sovereignty. Whereas the intergovernmental WEU endured (until it was folded into the EU, beginning in 2000), the European Defence Community was a bridge too far for European integration. At a time when the Six were setting up the ECSC, the launch of a similar supranational initiative in the much more sensitive defence sector was too ambitious. Even if it had come into existence, in all likelihood the EDC would have been unworkable. Resistance to its implementation, especially from the far left and far right, would have been intense. Although ratified by the others, the EDC brought the idea of supranationalism into disrepute in France. The end of the affair allowed supporters of supranationalism to jettison the baggage of German remilitarization and concentrate on first principles: economic integration.

It is remarkable how quickly the idea of European integration bounced back to life. The ECSC was operating fully, but its political and economic impact was slight. Despite what some observers (and neofunctionalist theorists) predicted, there was little 'spillover' from supranational cooperation in coal and steel to other sectors. Monnet, who became President of the High Authority, was bored in Luxembourg, the ECSC's capital. He left office and returned to Paris in 1955, where he set up a transnational organization, the Action Committee for the United States of Europe, to advocate further integration. His pet scheme was for an Atomic Energy Community (Euratom), along the same lines as the ECSC. The French government was interested, but not for the same reasons as Monnet. Whereas Monnet saw Euratom as a further step towards European unity, the government saw it as a means of bolstering France's nuclear programme for civil and military purposes. Not surprisingly, this idea held little appeal for France's partners.

European Community

The relaunch of European integration after the EDC's collapse was due not to Monnet nor support for Euratom, but to changes in international trade relations in the mid-1950s. Thanks largely to liberalization measures in the Organization for European Economic Cooperation (OEEC) and the General Agreement on Tariffs and Trade (GATT), intra-European trade was on the rise. With it, prosperity increased. European governments wanted more trade, but disagreed on the rate and range of liberalization. The British favoured further liberalization through the OEEC and the GATT, as did influential elements in the German government (notably Ludwig Erhard, the economics minister). The French were instinctively protectionist, although some influential politicians advocated openness. The Dutch, with a small and open economy, wanted full liberalization and were impatient with progress in the OEEC and the GATT, where intergovernmentalism constrained decision-making.

The Dutch had proposed a common market for all industrial sectors in the early 1950s. The idea was to combine a customs union (the phased abolition of tariffs among member states and erection of a common external tariff, see Box 2.4) with the free movement of goods, people, services, and capital, as well as supranational decision-making in areas such as competition policy. The Netherlands revived the proposal in 1955, arguing that the international economic climate was more propitious than ever for the launch of a common market.

Successful negotiations to establish the European Economic Community (EEC or EC) in 1956, so soon after the collapse of the EDC, owed much to the leadership of politicians such as Paul-Henri Spaak in Belgium, Guy Mollet and Christian Pineau in France, and Konrad Adenauer in Germany. Because of France's political weight in Europe and traditional protectionism, Mollet and Pineau played crucial roles. But their advocacy of the EC came with a price for the other prospective member states. In order to win domestic support they insisted on a special regime for agriculture in the common market, assistance for French overseas territories (France was then in the painful process of decolonization), and the establishment of Euratom.

The negotiations that resulted in the two Rome treaties, one for the EC and the other for Euratom, were arduous. Because the UK opposed supranationalism and the proposed agricultural regime, it did not participate. Germany succeeded in emasculating Euratom and grudgingly accepted the EC's overseas territories provisions. In the meantime, Adenauer resisted Erhard's efforts to jettison the common market in favour of looser free trade arrangements, arguing that the EC was necessary for geopolitical as well as economic reasons. French negotiators fought what they called the 'Battle of Paris', trying to assuage domestic criticism of the proposed common market while simultaneously driving a hard bargain in the negotiations in Brussels.

The ensuing Treaty of Rome establishing the EC was a typical political compromise. Its provisions ranged from the general to the specific, from the mundane to the arcane. Those on the customs union, calling for the phased abolition of tariffs (a tax on trade) between member states and erection of a common external tariff, were the

| BOX 2.4 | Compared to what? |

Regional and economic integration

Economic integration in Europe has proceeded through a number of steps or stages. A similar trajectory has occurred in other regions of the world, although nowhere has the level of economic cooperation matched that found in the EU.

In a **free trade area (FTA)** goods travel freely among member states, but these states retain the authority to establish their own external trade policy (tariffs, quotas, and non-tariff barriers) towards third countries. By allowing free access to each other's markets and discriminating favourably towards them, a free trade area stimulates internal trade and can lower consumer costs. But the lack of a common external tariff means complicated rules of origin are required to regulate the import of goods. One example of an FTA outside the EU is the European Free Trade Association (EFTA) which was established under British leadership in 1960 to promote expansion of free trade in non-EC western European countries. The UK left EFTA to join the EC in 1973, but Iceland, Liechtenstein, Norway, and Switzerland are still members. Canada, Mexico, and the US signed the North American Free Trade Agreement (NAFTA) in 1992.

Regional organizations elsewhere have created closer economic ties which may develop into FTAs. For instance the Association of South-East Asian Nations (ASEAN) was established in 1967 to provide economic as well as social cooperation among non-communist countries in the area. A wider forum for regional economic cooperation is found among Pacific Rim countries within APEC (Asia Pacific Economic Cooperation) which includes Australia, China, Indonesia, Japan, Mexico, the Philippines, and the US.

A customs union requires more economic and political cooperation than an FTA. In addition to ensuring free trade among its members, a customs union has a common external tariff and quota system, and a common commercial policy. No member of a customs union may have a separate preferential trading relationship with a third country or group of third countries. A supranational institutional framework is required to ensure its functioning. Customs unions generally create more internal trade and divert more external trade than do free trade areas. The six founding members of the EC agreed to form a customs union, which came into being in 1968, two years ahead of schedule. A customs union also exists in South America. Mercosur (Southern Cone Common Market) was established in 1991 by Argentina, Brazil, Paraguay, and Uruguay.

A common market represents a further step in economic integration by providing for the free movement of services, capital, and labour in addition to the free movement of goods. For various economic and political reasons the Six decided to go beyond a common market (the colloquial name for the EC) by establishing additionally a common competition policy; monetary and fiscal policy coordination; a common agricultural policy (CAP); a common transport policy; and a preferential trade and aid agreement with member states' ex-colonies. Not all of these elements were fully implemented. By the 1980s it was clear that the movement of labour and capital was not entirely free, and a host of non-tariff barriers still stymied intra-Community trade in goods and services. The '1992 project' or single market programme was designed to achieve a true internal market in goods, services, labour, and capital.

Cont. ➤

> **Cont.**
>
> An **economic and monetary union (EMU)** is far more ambitious. It includes a single currency and the unification of monetary and fiscal policy. In the EU, plans to introduce EMU, outlined in the Maastricht Treaty, were successfully implemented in January 1999, with euro notes and coins circulating by January 2002. No other region in modern times has come close to this level of economic cooperation.

most concrete. The treaty did not outline an agricultural policy, but contained a commitment to negotiate one in the near future. Institutionally, the treaty established a potentially powerful Commission, an Assembly (of appointed, not elected, members) with limited powers, a Council to represent national interests directly in the decision-making process, and a Court of Justice (see Chapter 3).

The Rome treaties were signed on 25 March 1957, and the EC came into being on 1 January 1958. Most Europeans were unaware of either event. Apart from the EDC, European integration had not impinged much on public opinion. Yet the ECSC and EC were highly significant developments. The Coal and Steel Community represented a revolution in Franco-German relations and international organization; the so-called Common Market had the potential to reorder economic and political relations among its member states.

Consolidating the European Community

The big news in Europe in 1958 was not the launch of the EC but the collapse of the French Fourth Republic and the return to power of General Charles de Gaulle. Events in France had a direct bearing on the EC. De Gaulle helped consolidate the new Community by stabilizing France politically (through the construction of the Fifth Republic) and financially (by devaluing the franc). On the basis of renewed domestic confidence, France participated fully in the phased introduction of the customs union, so much so that it came into existence in 1968, 18 months ahead of schedule.

De Gaulle also pushed for completion of the Common Agricultural Policy (CAP). With a larger farming sector than any other member state, France had most to gain from establishing a single agricultural market, based on guaranteed prices and export subsidies funded by the Community. France pressed for a generous CAP and had the political weight to prevail. Nevertheless the construction of the CAP, in a series of legendary negotiations in the early 1960s, proved onerous. What emerged was a complicated policy based on protectionist principles, in contrast to the liberalizing ethos of Community policies in most other sectors (see Chapter 5). The contrast represented the competing visions of the EC held by its members, potential members, and the wider international community (see Box 2.5).

Implementation of the customs union and construction of the CAP signalled the Community's initial success, obscuring setbacks in other areas such as the failure to implement a common transport policy. The customs union and the CAP had a major international impact. For instance, as part of its emerging customs union the EC developed a common commercial policy, which authorized the Commission to represent the Community in international trade talks, notably the GATT. The CAP tended to distort international trade and irritate the EC's partners. It is no coincidence that the first transatlantic trade dispute was over the CAP (the so-called 'Chicken War' of 1962–3, sparked by higher tariffs on US chicken imports).

The EC's fledgling institutions also began to consolidate during this period. The Commission organized itself in Brussels under the presidency of Walter Hallstein, a former top official in the German foreign ministry and a close colleague of Adenauer's. There were nine Commissioners, two each from the large member states and one each from the small member states (this formula would remain unchanged for nearly 50 years). The Commission's staff came initially from national civil services and from the ECSC's High Authority, which continued to exist until it merged into the Commission in 1967. In the Council of Ministers, foreign ministers met most often, indicating the EC's growing political as well as economic nature. The Council

---

BOX 2.5	How it really works

British accession and competing visions of Europe

The integration of Europe is sometimes portrayed (not least in the popular press) as an inexorable process following some overarching agreed plan. But in practice integration has proceeded in fits and starts, the result of domestic and international pressures and competing visions of what the EU is or should be. The debates surrounding the UK's first application to join the EC illustrate very different visions of Europe competing for dominance during the Community's early years.

In a remarkable reversal of policy, the UK applied to join the EC in 1961. The UK wanted unfettered access to EC industrial markets, but also wanted to protect trade preferences for Commonwealth countries (former British colonies) and turn the CAP in a more liberal direction. De Gaulle was unsympathetic to the UK's application. Economically, he wanted a protectionist CAP. Politically, he espoused a 'European Europe', allied to the United States but independent of it. By contrast, the UK acquiesced in America's Grand Design for a more equitable transatlantic relationship built on the twin pillars of the US and a united Europe centred on the EC, a design that arguably disguised America's quest for continued hegemony in NATO. The US supported British membership in the EC as part of its Grand Design. By vetoing the UK's application in January 1963, de Gaulle defended the CAP and thwarted American ambitions in Europe. The episode suggests how international pressure, domestic politics, and competing visions of Europe have shaped the evolution of European integration.

formed a permanent secretariat in Brussels to assist its work. Member states also established permanent representations of national civil servants in Brussels, whose heads formed the Committee of Permanent Representatives (Coreper), which soon became one of the Community's most powerful bodies. The Assembly, later known as the European Parliament (EP), tried to assert itself from the beginning, demanding for instance that its members be directly elected rather than appointed from national parliaments. But the EP lacked political support from powerful member states. Working quietly in Luxembourg, the Court of Justice began in the 1960s to generate an impressive corpus of case law. In several landmark decisions, the Court developed the essential rules on which the EU legal order now rests, including the supremacy of Community law (see Chapter 3).

Crisis and compromise

De Gaulle's arrival had a negative as well as a positive effect on the consolidation of the nascent EC. De Gaulle openly opposed supranationalism. He and his supporters (Gaullists) had resisted the ECSC and the EDC; they tolerated the EC, but primarily because of its economic potential for France. In de Gaulle's view, the nation-state was supreme. States could and should form alliances and collaborate closely, but only on the basis of intergovernmentalism, not shared sovereignty. Yet de Gaulle thought that the Community could be useful politically as the basis of an intergovernmental organization of European states.

A clash over supranationalism was likely to arise in 1965 as, under the terms of the Rome Treaty, a number of decisions in key policy areas, including agriculture, were due to become subject to qualified majority voting (QMV) (see Box 2.2). Majority voting is a key instrument of supranationalism because member states on the losing side agree to abide by the majority's decision. De Gaulle rejected this idea in principle, seeing QMV as an unacceptable abrogation of national sovereignty. The looming confrontation erupted in June 1965, when de Gaulle triggered the so-called Empty Chair Crisis (see Box 2.2) by withdrawing French representation in the Council ostensibly in protest against Commission proposals to strengthen the EC's budgetary powers, but really in an effort to force other member states to agree not to extend the use of QMV. De Gaulle had a compelling practical reason to resist QMV: he wanted to protect the CAP against a voting coalition of liberal member states.

The crisis ended in January 1966 with the so-called Luxembourg Compromise (see Box 2.2). The Treaty's provisions on QMV would stand, but the Council would not take a vote if a member state insisted that very important interests were at stake. The Luxembourg Compromise tipped the balance toward intergovernmentalism in the Community's decision-making process, with unanimity becoming the norm. This development had a detrimental effect on decision-making until the Single European Act took effect in 1987.

The EC after De Gaulle

By 1969, when de Gaulle resigned, the EC was economically strong but politically weak. Supranationalism was in the doldrums. The Commission and Parliament were relatively powerless, and unanimity hobbled effective decision-making in the Council. De Gaulle had twice rebuffed the UK's application for EC membership, in 1963 and in 1967, Britain having decided by the early 1960s that, for economic reasons, it was better off inside the common market. Following de Gaulle's departure, British membership became inevitable, although accession negotiations were nonetheless difficult. Ireland, Denmark, and Norway negotiated alongside the UK, but a majority of Norwegian voters rejected membership in a referendum in 1972. The UK, Ireland, and Denmark joined the following year.

The EC's first enlargement was a milestone in the organization's history. Unfortunately it coincided with international financial turmoil and a severe economic downturn that slowed momentum for further integration. Moreover, the UK's early membership was troublesome. A new Labour government insisted on renegotiating the country's accession terms. The renegotiations alienated many of the UK's partners in the EC, especially France and Germany. At the end of the 1970s a new Conservative government, under Margaret Thatcher, demanded a huge budgetary rebate. The UK had a point, but Thatcher's strident manner when pushing her case incensed other member states. The British budgetary question dragged on until 1984, overshadowing a turnaround in the Community's fortunes after a decade of poor economic performance.

Difficult decade

Because of the UK's early difficulties in the EC and prevailing stagflation in Europe (weak economic growth combined with high inflation and unemployment), the 1970s is generally seen as a dismal decade in the history of integration. Yet a number of important institutional and policy developments occurred at that time. On the policy side, the 1979 launch of the European Monetary System (EMS), the precursor to the single currency, was especially significant. Concerned about America's seeming abdication of international financial leadership, and eager to curb inflation and exchange rate fluctuations in the EC, French and German leaders devised the EMS, with the Exchange Rate Mechanism (ERM) designed to regulate currency fluctuations at its core. The sovereignty-conscious UK declined to participate. By the mid-1980s, the inflation and exchange rates of ERM members began to converge, thus helping to keep their economies stable. The Lomé agreement of 1975, providing preferential trade and development assistance to scores of African, Caribbean, and Pacific countries, was another important achievement for the beleaguered Community, as was the launch of European Political Cooperation (EPC), a mechanism to coordinate member states' foreign policies (see Chapter 10). In terms of closer European integration, the development of EC environmental policy in the 1970s was even more important.

Institutionally, the 1970s saw a gradual improvement in the Commission's political fortunes, especially later in the decade under the presidency of Roy Jenkins. The first direct elections to the EP took place in 1979, raising the institution's political profile and enhancing the EC's formal legitimacy. The inauguration of the European Council (regular meetings of the heads of state and government) in 1975 strengthened intergovernmental cooperation. The European Council soon became the EC's most important agenda-setting body (see Chapter 3), while direct elections laid the basis for the European Parliament's institutional ascension in the 1980s and 1990s. The Court of Justice continued in the 1970s to build an impressive body of case law that maintained the momentum for deeper integration.

By the early 1980s, the EC had weathered the storm of recession and the challenge of British accession. The end of dictatorial regimes in Greece, Portugal, and Spain in the mid-1970s presaged the EC's Mediterranean enlargement (Greece joined in 1981, Portugal and Spain in 1986). By that time the EC was more than a customs union but still less than a full-fledged common market. A plethora of non-tariff barriers (such as divergent technical standards) hobbled intra-Community trade in goods and services, and the movement of people and capital was not entirely free. Intensive foreign competition, especially from the US and Japan, began to focus the attention of political and business leaders on the EC's ability to boost member states' economic growth and international competitiveness. This focus became the genesis of the single market programme, which spearheaded the EC's response to globalization and ushered in the EU.

The Emerging European Union

The single market programme for the free movement of goods, services, capital, and people emerged as a result of collaboration between big business, the Commission, the Parliament and national leaders in the early 1980s. Several European Councils endorsed the idea. But the initiative only took off when the Commission, under the new presidency of Jacques Delors, unveiled a legislative roadmap (a White Paper on the 'completion' of the internal market) in 1985. To ensure the programme's success, the European Council decided to convene an Intergovernmental Conference (IGC) to make the necessary treaty changes. Chief among them was a commitment to use qualified majority voting for most of the White Paper's proposals, thereby ending the legislative gridlock that had hamstrung earlier efforts for full market liberalization.

As well as covering the single market programme, the Single European Act (SEA) of 1986 brought environmental policy into the treaty, strengthened Community policy in research and technological development, and included a section on foreign policy cooperation. It also committed the EC to higher expenditure on regional development (cohesion policy), partly as a side payment to the poorer member states, including new entrants Portugal, Spain, and Greece, which were unlikely to benefit as much from market integration as were their richer counterparts. Institutionally, the SEA's most important provisions enhanced the EP's legislative role through the introduction of the cooperation procedure. This procedure was intended to improve democratic accountability at a time when the EC's remit and visibility were about to increase dramatically.

The single market programme, with a target date of 1992, was a success. Business responded enthusiastically to the prospect of a fully integrated European marketplace. '1992' unleashed a wave of Europhoria. The EC was more popular than at any time before or since. Eager to remove barriers to the free movement of people even before implementation of the single market programme, France and Germany agreed in 1984 to press ahead with the abolition of border checks. This pledge led to the Schengen Agreement (see Box 2.2) for the free movement of people, which gradually added other member states and formally became part of the EU under the terms of the 1997 Amsterdam Treaty.

Economic and Monetary Union

The popularity of the single market programme emboldened Commission President Delors to advocate Economic and Monetary Union (EMU). He had the strong support of German Chancellor Helmut Kohl, an avowed 'Euro-federalist'. The Commission publicly justified EMU on economic grounds, as the corollary of the single market programme. But Delors and Kohl saw it primarily as a political undertaking. French President François Mitterrand also supported EMU, for both political and economic reasons. Thatcher opposed EMU vehemently, seeing it as economically unnecessary and politically unwise. Not only did Thatcher fail to turn the tide against EMU; her strident opposition to it contributed to her loss of the leadership of the Conservative Party and thus her prime ministership.

The European Council authorized Delors to set up a committee to explore the road to EMU. The Delors Report of 1989 proposed a three-stage programme, including strict convergence criteria for potential participants and the establishment of a European Central Bank with responsibility primarily for price stability. The report reflected German preferences for EMU. That was understandable, given Germany's economic weight and German obsession with inflation. Even so, opinion in Germany remained sceptical about EMU, with the politically influential German central bank (Bundesbank) opposed to it.

Planning for EMU was well on track by the time the Berlin Wall came down in November 1989. By raising again the spectre of the German question, the end of the Cold War increased the momentum for EMU. Fearful of the prospect, however remote, of a rootless Germany in the post-Cold War world, other Community leaders determined to bind Germany fully into the new Europe, largely through EMU.

Kohl was more than happy to oblige and cleverly exploited the concerns of Germany's neighbours to overcome domestic opposition to EMU, especially in the Bundesbank.

Maastricht and beyond

EC leaders convened two Intergovernmental Conferences in 1990, one on EMU and the other on political union, meaning institutional and non-EMU policy reforms. Both conferences converged in the Maastricht Treaty of 1992, which established the European Union with its three-pillar structure (see Box 1.2). The first pillar comprised the EC, including EMU; the second comprised the Common Foreign and Security Policy (CFSP), a direct response to the external challenges of the post-Cold War period; the third covered cooperation on justice and home affairs, notably immigration, asylum, and criminal matters. This awkward structure reflected most member states' unwillingness to subject internal security and foreign policy to supranational decision-making. Thus the Commission and the EP were merely associated with Pillar 2 and 3 activities. Within Pillar 1, by contrast, the Maastricht Treaty extended the EP's legislative power by introducing the far-reaching co-decision procedure, which made the Parliament a legally and politically equal co-legislator with the Council of Ministers (see Chapter 3).

The further extension of the EP's legislative authority, and the introduction of the principle of subsidiarity (whereby decisions should be taken as closely as possible to the people compatible with effective policy delivery; see Box 2.2), demonstrated EU leaders' concerns about the organization's legitimacy. Those concerns were fully vindicated in tough ratification battles in several member states, including the UK, France, and Germany, but especially in Denmark, where a narrow majority rejected the treaty in a referendum in June 1992. Voters approved the treaty, with special concessions for Denmark, in a second referendum, in May 1993. Thus the EU came into being six months later.

At issue in Denmark and elsewhere was the so-called democratic deficit: the EU's perceived remoteness and lack of accountability (see Chapter 8). This issue remained a major challenge for the EU into the twenty-first century. The resignation of the Commission under the Presidency of Jacques Santer in March 1999, amid allegations of fraud and mismanagement, increased popular scepticism, although it also demonstrated the Commission's accountability to the EP (the Commission resigned to avoid being sacked by the Parliament). Yet many Europeans saw the EP as part of the problem: few understood exactly its role, and the turnout in EP elections declined yet again in 1999, 2004, and 2009. For its part, the Commission launched successive rounds of reform, while EU leaders attempted to improve transparency and efficiency in the decision-making process. Nevertheless, as illustrated by the negative results of the first Irish referendum on the Nice Treaty in 2001, the Dutch and French referenda on the Constitutional Treaty in 2005, and the first Irish referendum on the Lisbon Treaty in 2008, public opinion in some member states remained highly sceptical of the EU.

Despite considerable public disquiet, the post-Maastricht period saw substantial policy development. The launch of the final stage of EMU in January 1999, in keeping with the Maastricht timetable, was one of the EU's most striking achievements. Euro notes and coins came into circulation in January 2002. The strengthening of the CFSP and the initiation of a European Security and Defence Policy, largely in response to the Balkan wars and uncertainty about US involvement in future European conflicts, was another important policy development. Reform of CFSP was the main outcome of the Amsterdam Treaty, which nevertheless ducked increasingly pressing questions of institutional reform necessitated by impending enlargement.

Post-Cold war enlargement and constitution building

Enlargement was a major challenge for the new EU. As a result of the end of the Cold War, three militarily-neutral European states (Austria, Finland, and Sweden) joined in 1995. (Norway, a non-neutral, again chose not to join in another referendum held in 1994.) The newly independent states of Central and Eastern Europe also applied for EU membership soon after the end of the Cold War (as did Cyprus and Malta). For the Central and Eastern European states the road to membership would be long and difficult, involving major political, economic, and administrative reforms. The slow pace of enlargement disappointed the applicant countries and their supporters in the US, who criticized the EU for being too cautious. The EU countered that enlargement, an inherently complicated process, was even more complex in view of the applicants' history, political culture, and low level of economic development. The EU's approach reflected a widespread lack of enthusiasm for enlargement among politicians and the public in existing member states. Even so, negotiations with the Central and Eastern European applicants eventually began in 1998 (with the five front-runners) and in 2000 (with the five others). Cyprus also began accession negotiations in 1998 and Malta in 2000.

Eight of the Central and Eastern European counties joined in 2004, together with Cyprus and Malta. The other two Eastern European countries, Bulgaria and Romania, joined in 2007. The EU reluctantly acknowledged Turkey as a candidate in December 1999 and, no less reluctantly, opened formal accession negotiations with it in October 2005. However, persistent popular antipathy towards Turkey, as well as specific issues such as the unresolved Cypriot question, bedevilled the country's membership prospects. The EU also began accession negotiations with Croatia in October 2005 and granted candidate status to the Former Yugoslav Republic of Macedonia at the end of the year. Earlier, the EU had acknowledged the 'European perspective' of the Western Balkans, meaning that every country in the region stood a reasonable chance of eventually becoming a member. At the other end of Europe, Iceland applied for EU membership in July 2009, in response to the devastating impact of the global financial crisis. The EU granted candidate status to Iceland in June 2010; membership negotiations began a month later.

As Chapter 8 explains, enlargement has greatly altered the EU. The accession of so many relatively poor countries, with comparatively large agricultural sectors, will continue to have a profound effect on the CAP and cohesion policy. The EU reformed both policies as part of its Agenda 2000 initiative, in anticipation of enlargement, but the results were patently inadequate. Further reform is inevitable and is bound to fuel bitter budgetary disputes, such as the one on the new multi-annual financial framework for the period beginning in 2014.

The EU's institutions also required reform because of enlargement. Member states avoided the contentious question of institutional reform in the Amsterdam Treaty, agreeing instead to undertake an institutional overhaul in another IGC in 2000. That conference resulted in the Nice Treaty of 2001, which changed the modalities of QMV in anticipation of enlargement, but in a way that complicated rather than clarified legislative decision-making. In other institutional areas the outcomes of the 2000 IGC were equally disappointing. The messy compromises that were struck illustrated the growing difficulty of reaching agreement among member states on institutional issues, especially those which tended to drive a wedge between France and Germany, or between the small and large member states.

Appreciating the inadequacies of the Nice Treaty, the European Council decided in December 2001 to hold a convention of national and EU-level politicians to draft a new treaty that would supersede and supposedly simplify the existing treaties. That was the genesis of the Convention on the Future of Europe of 2002–3 and ensuing IGC, which resulted in the Constitutional Treaty of June 2004. Amongst other things, the Constitutional Treaty altered the system of QMV, giving more power to the big member states; incorporated the previously negotiated Charter of Fundamental Rights into the EU's legal system; called for a standing president of the European Council; and provided for an EU foreign minister. Although ratified by a majority of member states, voters in the Netherlands and France, two of the EU's founding member states, rejected the Constitutional Treaty in spring 2005, for a variety of reasons mostly unrelated to the treaty itself, ranging from domestic political considerations to concerns about the consequences of globalization and fear of further enlargement. The results of the Dutch and French referenda were a severe blow to the image and prestige of the EU. But they did not derail the process of European integration, to which most European politicians (if not all their publics) remained committed, as was revealed in December 2007 when EU leaders signed the Lisbon Treaty, which incorporated most of the changes in the unratified Constitutional Treaty. While apparently less far-reaching than the Constitutional Treaty, in fact the Lisbon Treaty marked another historically significant step towards 'ever closer union' (see Box 1.4).

Conclusion

The history of European integration demonstrates the importance of opportunistic political leadership against a backdrop of fluctuating economic and political fortunes. Early post-war Europe threw up a number of challenges to which European leaders responded with an initiative for limited integration, with strong US support. The ECSC was far from the grand design for European integration that the US had envisioned at the time of the Marshall Plan, but it fostered reconciliation in Franco-German relations and laid an economic foundation for further European integration.

The launch of the European Community in 1958 owed more to economic necessity (potential greater trade among the Six) than geopolitical concerns (the German question), and more to European initiative than American prompting. National interests and individual initiatives also played a definitive part. Despite his aversion to supranationalism, de Gaulle appreciated the EC's economic potential and ensured the organization's initial success. De Gaulle's support for the EC, however qualified, reassured Adenauer and strengthened Franco-German relations.

The Single European Act of 1986, which revitalized the EC, and the Maastricht Treaty of 1992, which gave rise to the EU, were also products of Franco-German bargaining. In both cases France and Germany sought to boost European competitiveness in a globalizing economic system while retaining Europe's distinctive social structure, in contrast to that of the United States. The Commission, under the energetic leadership of Jacques Delors, contributed to these developments, but only in association with France and Germany.

The dynamics of Franco-German relations and leadership in the EU are changing, not least because of enlargement. As recent treaty negotiations have shown, France and Germany are often far apart on institutional issues such as the modalities of QMV, the size and role of the Commission, and the composition of the EP. United Germany is showing signs of greater political assertiveness in the EU. Unsure of its place in the post-Cold War, rapidly-globalizing world, France often seems to lack confidence and direction. Meanwhile, enlargement is shifting the geopolitical balance of the EU eastward, in favour of Germany.

Yet the history of European integration shows how countries can overcome institutional and policy differences for the sake of common economic and political interests. The end of the Cold War changed the context of European integration but not necessarily its substance. With the challenge of globalization greater than ever before, it is in the national interest of all member states to manage the single market and monetary union, and make a success of enlargement. In a sense, they have little choice but to perpetuate European integration.

DISCUSSION QUESTIONS

1. Are France and Germany bound to lead in Europe?

2. How significant have federalist aspirations been in the history of European integration?

3. Is the United States a 'federator' of Europe?

4. What economic factors impelled European integration during various stages of its history?

5. What impact have the controversies over the Constitutional and Lisbon Treaties had on the process of European integration?

FURTHER READING

Dinan (2004) provides a thorough history of the EU. Dinan (2006) examines key developments in EU history and includes a chapter on the historiography of European integration. For a neofunctionalist analysis of the EC's development, see Haas (1958) and Lindberg (1963). Milward (1984, 2000) was the most influential historian of European integration. Moravcsik (1998) blends political science and historical analysis to produce liberal intergovernmentalism and explain major developments in the history of the EU. Duchêne (1994) is excellent on Jean Monnet, and Gillingham (1991) provides an authoritative account of the origins of the ECSC. Gillingham (2003) describes the history of European integration as a struggle between economic liberalism and centralization, personified in the 1980s by Delors and Thatcher. Vanke (2010) provides an excellent counterpoint to Milward and Moravcsik by emphasizing the importance of ideas and emotions—'Europeanism'—and not just economic interests in the history of European integration.

Dinan, D. (2004), *Europe Recast: A History of European Union* (Boulder CO and Basingstoke: Lynne Rienner Publishers and Palgrave).

_____ (ed.) (2006), *Origins and Evolution of the European Union* (Oxford and New York: Oxford University Press).

Duchêne, F. (1994), *Jean Monnet: The First Statesman of Interdependence* (New York: Norton).

Gillingham, J. (1991), *Coal, Steel and the Rebirth of Europe, 1945–1955* (Cambridge and New York: Cambridge University Press).

_____ (2003), *European Integration, 1950–2003* (Cambridge and New York: Cambridge University Press).

Haas, E. (1958), *The Uniting of Europe: Political, Social, and Economic Forces* (Stanford CA: Stanford University Press).

Lindberg, L. (1963), *The Political Dynamics of European Economic Integration* (Stanford CA: Stanford University Press).

Milward, A. (1984), *The Reconstruction of Western Europe, 1945–51* (Berkeley: University of California Press).

_____ (2000), *The European Rescue of the Nation-State,* 2nd edn. (London: Routledge).

Moravcsik, A. (1998), *The Choice for Europe: Social Purpose and State Power from Messina to Maastricht* (Ithaca NY and London: Cornell University Press and UCL Press).

Vanke, J. (2010), *Europeanism and European Union: Interests, Emotions, and Systemic Integration in the Early European Economic Community* (Palo Alto CA: Academica Press).

 WEB LINKS

The EU's official portal site has its own useful history page: **http://europa.eu/abc/ history/index_en.htm**

The Florence-based European University Institute (EUI)'s European Integration History Index provides internet resources (in all languages) on post-war European history, with a particular emphasis on the EU: **http://vlib.iue.it/hist-eur-integration/Index.html**

 Visit the Online Resource Centre that accompanies this book for additional material: **www.oxfordtextbooks.co.uk/orc/bomberg3e/**

PART II

Major Actors

CHAPTER 3

The EU's Institutions

Richard Corbett, John Peterson, and Elizabeth Bomberg

▌ Summary

No student of the EU can understand their subject without careful study of its key institutions and how they work. EU institutions are not just dry organizations (although they are complex); they are dynamic organisms exercising a unique mix of legislative, executive, and judicial power. We begin by introducing the EU's five most important institutions. We outline their structures and formal powers—that is, what the Treaties say they can do—but we also focus on how they 'squeeze' influence out of their limited Treaty prerogatives. We then explore why these institutions matter in determining EU politics and policy more generally.

Institutions in Treaties and in Practice

What makes the EU unique, perhaps above all, is its institutions. This chapter explores the five that exercise the most power and influence: the European Commission, the Council (of Ministers), the European Council, the European Parliament, and the European Court of Justice. We draw analogies to their counterparts at the national level, but also show how they are distinct and unique. Table 3.1 summarizes the formal powers conferred on each by major Treaty reforms. It does not, however, convey how informal powers have accrued over time, nor the incremental power shifts that may occur between rounds of Treaty reform. The informal institutional politics of European integration are lively and important. A diligent student of the EU would be wise not to ignore them.

The European Commission

One of the EU's most powerful and controversial institutions is the European Commission. The EU's founding fathers were faced with a challenge. If the member states wanted to pursue common policies in certain fields, should they hand over responsibilities to a common institution, and leave it to get on with it, which would pose major questions of democratic accountability? Or should policies be settled by agreement between national governments, thus risking endless intergovernmental negotiations and lowest common denominator agreements?

In the end they opted for a compromise: a common institution—the European Commission—was charged with drafting policy proposals and implementing policies once agreed. But a separate institution—the Council of Ministers—consisting of representatives of national governments would take most decisions on the basis of those proposals. This interplay of an institution charged with representing the common interest and those composed of representatives of national governments (Council) or citizens (Parliament) is the essence of what became known as the 'Community method'.

Tasks and powers

The Treaties allocated to the Commission other important tasks besides the right to propose policies. The Commission does a variety of jobs:

- it represents the general interest of the European Union;
- it also acts as guardian of the Treaties (to defend both their letter and spirit);
- it ensures the correct application of EU legislation; and
- it manages and negotiates international trade and cooperation agreements.

In practical terms, the Commission's power is exercised most dramatically in four areas: its exclusive right to propose policy, its lead in international trade talks, its role in competition policy (it has powers to vet and veto mergers—even of companies based outside the EU) and its duty to ensure compliance with European law. Simply put, the Commission is the most powerful international administration in existence, and many of its decisions are contentious. Perhaps controversy is unavoidable for an institution that is designed to act independently of the EU's member states, and in the general, supranational interest of the Union as a whole.

The Commission's powers are not far short of those enjoyed, in the economic field, by national governments. But its capacity to act autonomously is more limited than that of a government in a national context. It does not have the powers that national governments have over armed forces, police, and the nomination of judges or foreign policy. The Commission's powers and autonomy are limited by the Treaties.

How the Commission is organized

'The Commission' rather confusingly refers to two separate arms of the same body: the College of Commissioners (or executive Commission) and the administrative Commission (its permanent 'services'). The College is the powerhouse of the Commission. Individually, each of the 27 Commissioners—one from each member state—is, like a minister in a national government, nominated by the prime minister or president of their country. Commissioners are not directly elected, but they are more like politicians than civil servants (most held high office in national politics before becoming Commissioners) and hold office only with parliamentary approval. The permanent civil servants (in French, the *fonctionaires*), who are recruited normally through competitive examination, work under the College's authority. Here we find a unique feature of the EU: its institutions recruit their own civil servants and do not rely (much) on national appointees.

The Commission President is elected by the European Parliament (EP) on a proposal of the European Council, which itself is obliged to take account of EP election results in making that nomination. In other words, heads of government have to choose a candidate capable of commanding a parliamentary majority much in the same way that a head of state in a national context has to when nominating a prime minister. Once elected by the EP, the President must then agree with each head of government on the nomination from each country for the remaining members of the Commission. It is then up to the President to distribute policy responsibilities— known as 'portfolios'—to individual Commissioners (for Transport, Agriculture, and so on). The one exception is the Vice President of the Commission, who is the Union's High Representative for foreign policy (see below).

The prospective Commission must then present itself to the Parliament for a vote of confidence. This vote is on the Commission as a whole—again, much in the same

TABLE 3.1 The institutions: Treaty reform and power

	Rome (1957)	SEA (1986)	Maastricht (1992)	Amsterdam (1997)	Nice (2001)	Lisbon Treaty (2009)
European Commission	Right to propose legislation; draft budget; act as guardian of Treaty; negotiate international trade agreements.	Right of initiative expands to new areas related to the completion of the single market.	Powers enhanced in economic and monetary union and in foreign policy; further extension of the right of initiative.	President's role strengthened and right of initiative broadened in line with increase in EU's competences.	President's powers (to reshuffle portfolios) enhanced; size stabilized to one Commissioner per member state up to 27 states; then reduced on basis of equal rotation.	High Representative for Foreign and Security Policy (shared with Council) established.
Council of Ministers	Power to pass legislation; agree budget.	Increased use of Qualified Majority Voting (QMV) in areas relating to the single market.	Further extension of QMV; right to propose legislation in justice and foreign affairs pillars together with the Commission.	Further extension of QMV and co-decision with the Parliament.	Continued expansion of QMV, re-weighting of votes between large and small member states.	QMV set at double majority (55% of member states, 65% of population); a High Representative of the Union for Foreign Affairs and Security Policy (shared with Commission) established.
European Council	Not mentioned in Treaty.	Granted legal status.	Assigned responsibility of defining the general political guidelines of the Union.	Confirmed role in EMU and strengthened position in respect of CFSP.	Seat fixed in Brussels.	Becomes an official EU institution; a permanent president replaces rotating presidency.

European Parliament	Right to be consulted on legislation; right to dismiss the Commission.	Extension of legislative authority through the introduction of the cooperation procedure.	Right to pass legislation jointly with Council in limited range of areas (co-decision procedure); greater role in appointing Commission.	Co-decision extended; right to approve appointment of Commission President and Commission as a whole.	Further extension of co-decision procedure; strengthened right to place matters before the Court; legal base established for party funding at European level.	Further extension of co-decision procedure (renamed 'ordinary legislative procedure'); power to elect President of the Commission; maximum number of seats set at 750 plus the President.
European Court of Justice	Guardian of Treaties and EC Law.	Creation of Court of First Instance.	Power to impose fines against member states (but excluded from two inter-governmental pillars).	Increased jurisdiction in third-pillar matters.	Further sharing of tasks with Court of First Instance; creation of more specialized Chambers; number of judges limited to one per member state.	Name changed to 'Court of Justice of the European Union'; more specialized courts attached.

way as a vote of confidence in a government in a national context. However, prior to this vote, the EP holds public hearings for each Commissioner before the parliamentary committee corresponding to their portfolio (which does not happen to government ministers in most European countries). The Commission's fixed, five-year term is linked to that of the European Parliament, which is elected every five years. The Parliament—and only the Parliament—can dismiss the Commission earlier in a vote of no confidence.

The distribution of portfolios can be controversial. Portfolios dealing with international trade, the internal market, competition policy, agriculture, regional development funds and, in recent times, environment and energy are particularly sought after. The 2009 appointment of the Frenchman, Michel Barnier, as Internal Market Commissioner (including financial regulation) was seen by some as a move by France to gain regulatory powers over the City of London. In reality, how much an individual Commissioner can shape policy is limited by the principle of collegiality: all policy proposals are agreed collectively by the entire College. Once it takes a decision, if necessary by majority vote (but nearly always by consensus), it becomes the policy of all of the Commission. Each Commissioner must support it or (in principle) resign. Moreover, key legislation and policy decisions have to be agreed with the other EU institutions. The Commission illustrates one of the ironies of the EU: its institutions are more powerful than they are autonomous.

The growing size of the Commission with successive enlargements has risked turning it from a compact executive into a miniature assembly. The 2009 Lisbon Treaty had provisions for a smaller Commission but also allowed member states to vary its size, leading to a decision to stick with one Commissioner per country. The move shows that there remains more concern for the Commission's legitimacy—with, for instance, one member of the College who speaks each country's language and can appear in the national media—than with its efficiency.

Commissioners each have their own private office—or (in French) cabinet—of around seven personal advisers. These officials are chosen by the Commissioner and may be drawn from inside or outside the Commission. They perform a very demanding and important role, keeping the Commissioner informed about their own policy area(s) as well as wider developments in the Commission and Europe more generally. Most cabinets are composed largely of members of staff of the same nationality as the Commissioner, but the Head or Deputy Head of each must hail from a member state different from that of the Commissioner. Member states are often accused of seeking to appoint their own national officials to Commission cabinets to ensure that their interests are not overlooked. However, after new rules were imposed by President Romano Prodi (1999–2004), cabinets became more 'European'—with nearly all having at least three nationalities—and less male-dominated, with around 40 per cent of appointees being women (see Peterson 2012a).

Controversy surrounding portfolio assignments and cabinet appointments shows that the defence of national interests in the Commission can never be entirely removed. Commissioners take an oath of independence when they are appointed, but never abandon their national identities. Indeed, many consider it to be an advantage that they bring knowledge of their respective countries to the Commission, even if they are not there to represent them—that job belongs to ministers in the Council.

The independence of Commissioners can sometimes be a matter of contention. A Commissioner who simply parrots the position of her national government would soon lose credibility within the Commission. However, one that too obviously ignores major national interests may be liable for criticism at home. Famously, the UK Prime Minister, Margaret Thatcher, despaired at the alleged failure of 'her' Commissioner—Lord Cockfield—to defend the interests of the Thatcher government. Thus Commissioners face a tough balancing act: they must be sensitive to the interests of the member state that (in Brussels speak) 'they know best', but must not undermine the independence of the Commission.

Each Commissioner is responsible for one or more Directorate General (DGs)—or services—which relate to their portfolio. These DGs, the equivalent of national ministries, cover the EU's main policy areas such as competition, the environment, or agriculture. Each is headed by a Director General who reports directly to the relevant Commissioner. There are about 30 or so services that together make up the administration of the Commission.

The Commission is far smaller than is often portrayed in the popular press, where it is frequently characterized as an enormous body intent on taking over Europe. In fact, it has roughly as many officials (in policy-making posts) as work for a medium-sized national government department, such as the French Ministry of Culture, or for a medium-sized city council. Of the Commission's approximately 28,000 officials, only about one-fifth are in policy-making posts, with a huge proportion involved in translating or interpreting into the Union's 23 official languages.

In day-to-day work, the dividing line between administrative civil servants and Commissioners is not always self-evident. While the College is ultimately responsible for any decisions that emanate from the institution, in practice many matters are handled much further down in the administration and much of the Commission's agenda is set for it by the EU's Treaties or other commitments (see Box 3.1). In turn, some Commissioners are more interventionist than others in seeking to influence the day to day functioning of 'their' Directorate General, in much the same way as occurs in relations between ministers and civil servants in a national context.

The major challenge for the Commission is stretching its limited resources to cover the wide range of tasks that member states have conferred upon it. At times, the Commission can be adept at making the most of the powers given to it. For example, the Commission was among the first institutions to conduct detailed research on climate change, which highlighted the necessity of new initiatives such as an emissions trading scheme and a stronger role for the EU. Thus, the Commission is not simply the servant of the member states but can sometimes 'squeeze' more prerogatives despite its limited competence.

> ### BOX 3.1   How it really works: who initiates policy?
>
> The formal right to initiate policies is one of the Commission's most precious and funda-
> mental powers. But the origins of its initiatives are diverse. In practice, most initiatives
> emanating from the Commission are a response to ideas, suggestions, or pressures
> from other sources. While figures vary from year to year, the Commission has estimated
> that only about one-fifth of its proposals are entirely of its own initiative. Of course, it
> decides the shape and form of all of its proposals. However, an ever greater proportion
> amend existing EU law, rather than legislating in new fields. For example, of all (416)
> Commission proposals in the year 2008:
>
> - 52 per cent were to amend, replace, codify, or recast existing EU laws;
> - 8 per cent were further measures arising from existing law;
> - 21 per cent arose from the EU's international obligations;
> - 10 per cent were proposals for trade defence measures (such as anti-dumping
>   duties); and
> - the remainder (9 per cent) technically were original Commission proposals, but over
>   half came from the (European) Council or the Parliament.
>
> The Lisbon Treaty added a new, direct source of proposals: one million EU citizens can
> invite the Commission to submit a proposal. The Commission is not legally obliged to act
> on the initiative, but it would most certainly have to take it into account (see Box 6.7).
>
> **(Figures derived from Answer to Parliamentary Question E3775/2010)**

The Council (of ministers)

The Council of ministers was created as the EU's primary decision-making body.
The Treaties state that the Council shall consist of 'a representative of each member
state at ministerial level, who may commit the government of the member state in
question and cast its vote' and that it 'shall, jointly with the European Parliament,
exercise legislative and budgetary functions' and 'carry out policy making and
co-ordinating functions'.

It is thus both a legislative chamber of states (as half of the Union's bicameral legislative authority, together with the EP) and at the same time the body in which the governments of the member states come together to meet, to resolve issues of Union
policy or foreign policy and coordinate policies that are primarily a national responsibility, such as macroeconomic policy. It is in the Council that national interests, as seen
by the government of the day in each member state, are represented and articulated.

The Council is a complex system. The Treaties speak of only one Council, but it
meets in different configurations depending on what policy area is being discussed.
For example, when agriculture is discussed, agriculture ministers meet; when the

subject is the environment, it is environment ministers, and so on. There are alto-gether 10 different configurations of the Council, with the General Affairs Council (now largely Europe Ministers to relieve the burden on Foreign Ministers, so the latter can concentrate on foreign policy) holding a coordinating brief. The General Affairs Council is responsible for the dossiers that affect more than one of the Un-ion's policies, such as enlargement or the EU's budget and for preparing meetings of the European Council.

The Council is aided by a Secretariat of around 2,500 officials. It plays an impor-tant role in brokering deals and crafting compromises between member states. Even with the help of the Secretariat, the burden on EU Ministers has increased enor-mously. The agricultural, foreign, and economic ministers meet at least once a month, others from one to six times a year.

Given their core function—representing member states—it is easy to conclude that the Council and its preparatory bodies are purely intergovernmental. But, as constructivists would note (see Lewis 2003), regular ministerial meetings, informal contacts, and routine bargaining have provided the grounds for continual and close cooperation between executives from different member states. As a result, the Coun-cil has constructed a sort of collective identity that is more than an amalgamation of national views. That identity has helped push the Union forward.

Majority voting can be used in the Council in most areas of EU business. In fact, votes rarely take place (see Box 3.2), although more often now than before the 2004–7 enlargements. Council deliberations on legislation now take place in public: they are web-streamed or televised (there is no physical public gallery). This devel-opment is, however, recent. Previous to the Lisbon Treaty, the Council legislated behind closed doors, which made negotiations easier but left the Council vulnerable to the charge that it was the only legislative body in the democratic world that en-acted legislation without the public being able to see how members voted. The Council still meets behind closed doors on some non-legislative matters such as foreign policy and security discussions.

Vice President of the Commission/High Representative for Foreign & Security Policy

A recent and potentially major innovation is the merging of two previously separate posts: the Commissioner for External Relations and the Council's High Representa-tive for (the Common) Foreign and Security Policy (CFSP). The creation of the lat-ter post in the late 1990s reflected the reluctance of member states to extend the Commission's role in external representation. France and the UK in particular were averse to the idea of the Commission representing the Union beyond its existing remit in development, trade, and humanitarian aid. Thus, the top civil servant of the Council, its Secretary General, was designated High Representative for the CFSP. This division of labour, however, proved problematic and confusing. Non-EU countries were not always sure of whom to turn to in the first instance. In many situations, the Union had to be represented by both the High Representative and the External Relations Commissioner.

For these reasons, the Lisbon Treaty merged the two posts. Still called the High Representative—although also Vice President of the Commission—the appointee is chosen by the European Council with the agreement of the Commission President. The High Representative is charged with chairing meetings of the Council of Foreign Affairs Ministers. Moreover, the post-holder assumes authority for a new European External Action Service, intended as something like an EU 'foreign ministry' (EEAS; see Chapter 10).

Is the High Representative a Council cuckoo in the Commission nest or a Commission cuckoo in the Council nest? Some see it as a logical step towards bringing the tasks of the former Council High Representative fully into the Commission, ending the anomaly of foreign policy being different from other external policy sectors. Others see it as a smash and grab raid by the Council on the Commission's external representation role. The reality is an uneasy compromise, although one that potentially enables the Union's external relations to draw on both its traditional methods in a more unified way. The appointment of a sitting Commissioner, Catherine Ashton, as the first incumbent was not without significance. Interestingly, the post—in identical guise—was labelled the EU 'Minister of Foreign Affairs' in the Constitutional Treaty before that label was abandoned. Recycling the more anodyne title 'High Representative' for the post does not necessarily make it any less likely that its holder could become a high-profile and powerful figure representing the EU to the world. In any case, the High Representative is the most explicit case of seeking to combine the supranational and intergovernmental in one institutional post.

The Council Presidency

Except for meetings of Foreign Affairs Ministers, the Council is chaired by a minister from the member state holding the rotating 'Presidency of the Council'. Member states take it in turns to chair Council meetings for six months each. Although often referred to in the media as the 'Presidency of the Union', Presidencies are, in fact, simply the chair of just one EU institution. Assuming office as the Presidency does not confer any additional powers on the holder. Rather, the Presidency's job is to build consensus and move decision-making forward.

Holding the Presidency places the country concerned in the media spotlight and can give them added influence. For instance, the Presidency arranges meetings and can set the Council's agenda, determining which issues will be given priority. But holding the Presidency also has disadvantages. The time required of national officials is daunting, especially for smaller states. Much can go wrong in six months, whether or not the country holding the Presidency is responsible. Despite the media hype, the Presidency's scope for action is limited and its agenda is largely inherited, or often dictated by events.

BOX 3.2	How it really works: reaching decisions in the Council

Qualified majority voting (QMV) now applies to most areas of EU decision-making, and any national representative on the Council can call for a vote on any measure to which it applies. In practice, only a small number of decisions subject to QMV are actually agreed that way. Pushing for a formal vote too early or often creates resentment that disrupts the mood and effectiveness of the Council. Thus, whatever the formal rules say, decision-making in the Council—even one accommodating 27 states—usually proceeds on the understanding that consensus will be sought, but equally on the understanding that obstructionism or unreasonable opposition could be countered by a vote.

How is this consensus achieved? Imagine a contentious item on the Council's agenda (say, dealing with work and safety regulations). Perhaps a majority of states support the initiative but some are opposed or ambivalent. Before proceeding to a vote, several attempts will be made to achieve some sort of consensus. Bargaining is most intense at the level of Coreper. Phone calls or informal chats between national representatives prepare the ground for subsequent meetings where agreements can be struck. Informal agreements might also be reached at the meals that are very much a part of both Coreper and Council meetings. Ostensibly a time for break and refreshment, these lunches provide opportunities for a delicate probing of national positions. Similarly, a good Chair can make use of scheduled or requested breaks in the proceedings to explore possibilities for a settlement. These breaks may feature off-the-record discussions or 'confessionals' between the Chair and national representatives or amongst representatives themselves. Lubricating these discussions is the familiarity and personal relationships national representatives have built up over time. In the end, the objections of opposing states might be assuaged by a redrafting of certain clauses, a promise of later support for a favoured initiative, or the possibility of a derogation (postponement) of a policy's implementation for one or more reluctant states. The point is that the day-to-day practice in Coreper and the Council is characterized far more by the search for a consensus than by any straightforward mechanism of strategic voting.

Voting in the Council

The Treaties provide, in most policy areas, that a qualified majority (see Box 2.2) can approve a Commission proposal, whereas unanimity is required to amend it—a crucial feature of the 'Community method'. Some policy areas, however, require unanimity to approve any measure: it applies to sensitive matters such as tax harmonization, anti-discrimination legislation and, outside the field of legislation, foreign and security policy and constitutional questions such as the accession of new member states (see Chapter 8). A simple majority, with one vote per member state, is used rarely, primarily for procedural questions.

The chair of the Council decides whether and when to call for a vote, whatever decision rule applies (see Box 3.2). Even though consensus is always sought, and

TABLE 3.2   Voting in the Council of Ministers

Voting in an EU of 27 member states

Member state	Approximate population (millions) in 2010	Number of votes (until 2014*)	Number of citizens per vote (millions**)
Germany	82	29	2.8
France	65	29	2.2
UK	62	29	2.1
Italy	60	29	2.1
Spain	46	27	1.7
Poland	39	27	1.4
Romania	21	14	1.5
Netherlands	17	13	1.3
Greece	11	12	0.9
Portugal	11	12	0.9
Belgium	11	12	0.9
Czech Republic	10	12	0.8
Hungary	10	12	0.8
Sweden	9	10	0.9
Austria	8	10	0.8
Bulgaria	8	10	0.8
Denmark	5	7	0.7
Slovakia	5	7	0.7
Finland	5	7	0.7
Ireland	4	7	0.6
Lithuania	3	7	0.4
Latvia	2	4	0.5
Slovenia	2	4	0.5
Estonia	1	4	0.3
Cyprus	0.8	4	0.2
Luxembourg	0.5	4	0.1
Malta	0.4	3	0.1
TOTAL	498.7	345	

Cont. ➤

Cont.			
Qualified majority under Nice Treaty: 255 votes (around 74 per cent), including a majority of member states, as well as 62 per cent of the EU's population.	*Blocking minority under Nice Treaty:* 91 votes (around 27 per cent), or a majority of member states or 38 per cent of the EU's population.	*Qualified majority according to the Lisbon Treaty:* 55 per cent of member states comprising 65 per cent of the EU's population.	*Blocking minority under Lisbon Treaty:* over 45 per cent of member states or states representing over 35 per cent of the population

*Until 2014, a triple majority of states (51 per cent), population (62 per cent) and votes is required; after 2014, a double majority of states (55 per cent) and population (65 per cent) is needed.

**Rounded

Eurostat Demography Report 2010

usually achieved, formal votes are sometimes needed. Successive enlargements of the EU, adding mostly smaller or medium sized member states, led to a situation where—in theory—a qualified majority could be obtained by the representatives of a minority (or a small majority) of the EU's population. Larger member states felt they were becoming under-represented in the existing system, leading to pressures for reform.

Under the current (and complex) rules, a 'triple majority' is required: not just the requisite number of weighted votes, but also positive votes from a majority of Member states that represented at least 62 per cent of the Union's population. The Lisbon Treaty ushers in a simpler system, due to take effect in 2014. It will work on the basis of a 'double majority': 55 per cent of member states are required representing 65 per cent of the EU's population (see Table 3.2).

Coreper

Council decisions are preceded by extensive negotiation between national civil servants. Each EU member state has its own Permanent Representation ('Perm Rep') in Brussels, headed by a Permanent Representative who has ambassadorial status. The national officials who staff the Perm Reps sit on all manner of preparatory working groups within the Council system. Much policy substance is thrashed out at these levels, particularly by the Committee of Permanent Representatives, known by its French acronym Coreper. Composed of national Ambassadors to the EU and their staffs, Coreper's job is to prepare the work of the Council and try to reach consensus or suitable majorities ahead of Council meetings. Items on which agreement is reached at Coreper are placed on the Council's agenda as so-called 'A points' for formal approval: if no minister objects they are nodded through. Coreper is split (confusingly) into Coreper II, made up of the Permanent Ambassadors who deal primarily with the big political, institutional, and budgetary issues, and Coreper I led by Deputy Ambassadors who deal with most other issues. Some sensitive or especially busy policy areas—such as security, finance, and agriculture—have their own special preparatory committees, composed of senior officials from the member states.

To the uninitiated (and many of the initiated), Coreper and its various working parties are shadowy and complex. National ambassadors and senior civil servants preparing Council meetings are assisted by numerous (around 140) working groups and committees of national delegates who scrutinize Commission proposals, put forward amendments and hammer out deals in the run up to the Council meetings. The vast majority of Council decisions (around 70 per cent) are settled here, before ministers ever become involved (Hayes-Renshaw and Wallace 2006: 14). Some see Coreper as a real powerhouse: 'the men and women who run Europe'. For others, including Coreper's civil servants themselves, their role is merely that of helping ministers. A civil servant's quote from some years ago remains apt: 'If ministers want to let Coreper decide, that is a ministerial decision' (*Economist*, 6 August 1998).

European Council (of Heads of State or Government)

The European Council began in the 1970s as occasional informal fireside chats among Heads of Government (or, in the case of member states with executive Presidents, such as France, Heads of State). It became a regular get together, and known as the European Council, in the mid 1970s (although the term 'summit' is still frequently heard). For a long time, the European Council was seen simply as the pinnacle of the Council system, comprising Prime Ministers rather than sectoral ministers. However, its composition is formally different—the President of the Commission is a member of the European Council alongside the Heads of State or Government—and the very nature and dynamics of its meetings give it an unmistakably distinct character. The Lisbon Treaty formally made it a separate institution.

The European Council must meet at least four times a year, although six has been the norm in recent years. The Treaties state that the European Council 'shall provide the Union with the necessary impetus for its development and shall define [its] general political directions and priorities'. Even prior to its recognition in the Treaties, it became the major agenda setter of the Union. Initiatives such as direct elections to the European Parliament, monetary union, successive enlargements, strategy on climate change, and major treaty reforms have all been agreed or endorsed at European

Council level. Meeting at 'the summit' of each member state's hierarchy guarantees that its conclusions, even when not legally binding, are acted upon by the Council, the member states and, in practice, the European Commission.

The European Council's other broad function is more mundane problem resolution. Issues that cannot be resolved within Coreper or the Council are often resolved at this elevated political level, at times through informal persuasion, and other times through the forging of package deals that trade off agreement on one issue (say regional spending) in exchange for concessions on another (say agricultural reform). Serious deadlocks on the finances of the Union have often been resolved only through such deals in late night sittings. The Lisbon Treaty also recognizes what has become, over time, an important role of the European Council: to nominate the President of the Commission, the Governor and Board members of the European Central Bank and so on.

The Presidency of the European Council once rotated in tandem with that of the Council. With the Lisbon Treaty, it was agreed that Heads of State or Government would choose their own chairman for a $2^1/_2$ year (once renewable) period. The first such President, the former Belgium Prime Minister, Herman Van Rompuy, took office on 1 January 2010. A number of factors led to creation of a 'permanent' and full-time President. Previously, the six-month term of office meant a new President every second or third meeting, making continuity and consistency impossible. The preparation of European Council meetings, involving consultation of all Heads of Government, was, with successive enlargements of the Union, becoming increasingly onerous for any President or Prime Minister with their own national government to run. Also, the task of representing the EU externally at summit meetings on foreign policy issues, whilst at the same time representing their own country, was felt to be inappropriate.

Member states with an intergovernmentalist view of the EU saw the European Council President as a useful counterweight to the President of the Commission. Many French observers, given their domestic institutional system, see the President of the European Council as a sort of *Président* of Europe, with the Commission President demoted to the status of a French Prime Minister, devoted largely to internal affairs and even then deferring on major decisions to the President. That view is not shared by all. The first European Council President, Van Rompuy described himself as being less than a *Président* but more than a chairman: a facilitator, not a dictator.

The European Parliament

The EU is unique among international organizations in having a parliament: the European Parliament (EP) is the only directly-elected multinational parliament with significant powers in the world. The reasons for its unique status are twofold. Some saw the creation of a directly elected parliament as a means towards a more 'federal' system in which the Union would derive legitimacy directly from citizens instead of exclusively via national governments. Others simply saw the need to compensate the loss of national level parliamentary power, inherent in pooling competences at European level.

To its admirers, the Parliament is the voice of the people in European decision-making. To its critics, it is an expensive talking shop. Both of these portraits carry elements of truth. In contrast to most national parliaments, the EP cannot directly initiate legislation and its budgetary powers cover only spending, not taxation. The EP is dogged by image problems. Its housekeeping arrangements are clumsy and expensive: it is obliged by the member states to divide its activities between Brussels (three weeks out of four) and Strasbourg (for four days a month). The multiplicity of languages means that its debates lack the cut and thrust found in many national parliaments. There is no visible link between the outcome of the EP elections and the composition of the executive, which is what voters are used to at the national level. Turnout in European elections is lower than in most national elections and has been falling.

But the EP exercises its legislative powers forcefully compared to national parliaments, which rarely amend or reject government proposals. Because the EP is not controlled by the executive or any 'governing majority', it can use its independence to considerable effect. Every treaty change from 1970 onwards has strengthened the role of the Parliament. The Parliament is a legal and political equal to the Council in deciding almost all legislation as well as the budget and ratification of international treaties. It elects the President of the Commission and confirms (and can dismiss) the Commission as a whole.

The Lisbon Treaty caps the EP at 751 members with a minimum of six and a maximum of 96 seats per member state (roughly) according to their size. The members of the parliament (MEPs) sit in political groups, not in national blocks. Although there are over 150 national parties, they coalesce into seven groups, most of which correspond to familiar European political families: Liberals, Socialists, Christian Democrats, Greens and so on. Of course, national allegiances do not disappear. Nonetheless, EP political groups have become more cohesive over time. The EP lacks the strict whipping system found in national parliaments, but positions taken by the groups—and the negotiations between them—are what counts in determining majorities. And choices at stake when dealing with legislation are indeed typical political choices: higher environmental standards at greater cost to those regulated, or not? Higher standards of consumer protection or leave it to the market? On these subjects, there are nearly always different views within each member state, irrespective of the position taken by their ministers in the Council. These various views are represented in the Parliament, which contains members from opposition parties as well as governing parties in every member state. There is a considerably higher degree of pluralism in the Parliament than in the Council.

The leaders of each political group, along with the Parliament's President, constitute the Conference of Presidents, which sets the EP's agenda. But, like the US

Congress, the detailed and most important work of the Parliament is carried out in some 20 standing committees, mostly organized by policy area (such as transport, agriculture, or the environment) and some cross-cutting (such as budgets or women's rights). The committee system allows detailed scrutiny of proposals by members who are, or become, specialists.

The powers of the EP

The Parliament's powers fall under four main headings: legislative, budgetary, scrutiny, and appointments. The Parliament's legislative powers were originally very weak, having only the right to give an opinion on proposed legislation (see Box 3.3). After successive treaty changes the EP now co-decides nearly all EU legislation in what amounts to a bicameral legislature consisting of the Council and the Parliament. What is now, revealingly, called the Ordinary Legislative Procedure requires that both agree a text in identical terms before it can be passed into law. Similarly, international treaties or agreements are subject to the consent procedure: the Parliament has the right—in a yes or no vote—to approve or reject the agreement. When it comes to budgetary matters, the Lisbon Treaty provides also for a sort of co-decision.

BOX 3.3	How the European Parliament 'squeezes' power

The EP has tended to make the most of whatever powers it has had at any given moment. Even when it was merely consulted on legislation it developed techniques, such as the threat of delay, to make its influence felt. In budget negotiations the EP uses its power to sign off—or not—on the annual budget selectively but effectively.

Similarly, the EP has stretched its powers to oversee the Commission. Formally, the Parliament has only a collective vote of confidence in the Commission before it takes office. The EP has no right to hire or fire individual Commissioners. Yet, for example, in the parliamentary confirmation hearings of 2004 the EP objected to Italian Commissioner-designate Rocco Buttiglione's statements that homosexuality was 'a sin' and that women 'belonged in the home' (See Peterson 2012a:). These comments caused widespread consternation, especially as his portfolio was to include civil liberties. As it became clear that Parliament might vote to reject the entire Commission, President-elect Barroso formally withdrew the team on the eve of the vote and came back a few weeks later with a new College from which Buttiglione had been dropped. Note that the Parliament did not have *de jure* power to sack Buttiglione, but *de facto* they did just that.

Of course the EP's threats must seem real, and for that to happen it must stay united. Such unity is not easy to come by in such a large and diverse institution with over 700 members from a vast array of parties and backgrounds. Thus, despite its ability to 'squeeze' power, the Parliament does not always get its way.

The Parliament also exercises scrutiny of the Commission (and to a degree other institutions). Its oversight is exercised via its right to question (through written questions or orally at question time), to examine and debate statements or reports, and to hear and cross-examine Commissioners, ministers, and civil servants in its committees. The Parliament also approves the appointment of the Commission and, more spectacularly, can dismiss it (as a whole) through a vote of no confidence. The latter is considered to be a 'nuclear' option—a strategic, reserve power that requires an absolute majority of all MEPs and two-thirds majority of votes cast. As in most national parliaments, which do not make daily use of their right to dismiss the government, its very existence is sufficient to show that the Commission must take due account of Parliament. This power effectively was exercised only once, when it resulted in the fall of the Commission under the Presidency of Jacques Santer in 1999. Even then, the Commission resigned prior to the actual vote, once it was clear that the necessary majority would be obtained. One upshot of this episode was a treaty change to allow the President of the Commission to dismiss individual members of the Commission (which the EP cannot do). Thus, if the behaviour of a particular Commissioner gives rise to serious parliamentary misgivings (as Edith Cresson's did in the Santer Commission; see Peterson 2012a), the President of the Commission can take action before events move to the stage where the Parliament might dismiss the Commission as a whole. Besides the Commission, the Parliament also elects the European Ombudsman and is consulted on appointments to other EU posts (see Box 3.7).

In short, the European Parliament's powers have grown significantly since direct elections were first held in 1979. However, some still question its ability to bring legitimacy to EU decision-making. Its claim to represent the peoples of Europe is undermined by low and declining turnouts for its elections (43 per cent in the 2009 EP elections, and below 30 per cent in six of the new member states). The relative lack of citizen engagement, combined with the Parliament's image (accurate or not) as a 'gravy train' might well act as a brake on further increases in its powers. Ultimately, the Parliament's future role is tied up with larger questions of democracy and power in the EU (see Chapter 7).

European Court of Justice

At first glance, the European Court of Justice (ECJ) seems neither a particularly powerful nor controversial institution. It is located in an unremarkable building in Luxembourg, and is comprised of 27 judges (one from each member state) plus eight Advocate Generals who draft Opinions for the judges. It is supported by the Court of First Instance, a lower tribunal created in 1989 to ease the growing workload of the Court (it had dealt with nearly 17,000 cases by 2010). The ECJ's profile is generally low, apart from in European legal circles.

Put simply, the role of the ECJ is to ensure that, in the interpretation and application of the Treaties, the law is observed. The Court is thus powerful: it is the final arbiter in legal disputes between EU institutions or between EU institutions and member states. The Court ensures that the EU institutions do not go beyond the powers given to them. Conversely, it also ensures national compliance with the treaties and to the legislation that flows from them. The Maastricht Treaty even gave the ECJ the right to fine member states that breach EU law.

The Court is sometimes accused of having a pro-integration agenda, a reputation that derives mainly from its landmark decisions in the 1960s. In practice, the Court has to interpret the texts as they have been adopted. Significantly, its members are not appointed by EU institutions, but by member states. The ECJ therefore differs from the US Supreme Court, whose members are appointed by American federal institutions (see Box 3.4).

EU law is qualitatively different from international law in that individuals can seek remedy for breaches of the former through their domestic courts, which refer points of European law to the EU Court. The process allows national courts to ask the ECJ for a ruling on the European facet of a case before them. Such preliminary rulings are then used by the national courts in judging cases. This method has shaped national policies as diverse as the right to advertise abortion services across borders, roaming charges for mobile phones, and equal pay for equal work. If the Court has a pro-integration agenda, it is primarily to integrate national courts into an EU legal system.

Its critics sometimes claim that the Court has, in effect, become a policy-making body (see Weiler 1999: 217). Its defenders point out that it can only rule on matters referred to it, and then only apply texts adopted by legislators. Certainly, the Court's role in the 1960s was crucial in giving real substance to the EU legal system. Two landmark decisions stand out. In the 1963 *Van Gend en Loos* case, the Court established 'direct effect': the doctrine that EU citizens had a legal right to expect their governments to adhere to their European obligations. In 1964 (*Costa v ENEL*), the Court established the supremacy of EU law: if a domestic law contradicts an EU obligation, European law prevails.

Later, in the 1979 *Cassis de Dijon* case, the Court established the principle of mutual recognition: a product made or sold legally in one member state—in this case a French blackcurrant liqueur—cannot be barred in another member state if there is no threat to public health, public policy, or public safety. This principle proved fundamental to the single market because it established that national variations in standards could exist as long as trade was not unduly impeded.

These judgments took place in a period normally characterized as one of stagnation and 'Eurosclerosis', when political integration seemed paralysed. Scholars who take inspiration from neofunctionalist thinking often cite evidence from this period to undermine the intergovernmentalist claim that national interests alone dominate the rhythm of integration. But the Court's power is limited: it must rely on member states to carry out its rulings. The powers of the Court—and how they should be wielded—remain contested in EU politics.

BOX 3.4   **Compared to what? The ECJ and the US Supreme Court**

The European Court of Justice—like the EU more generally—is in many ways *sui generis*: an international body with no precise counterpart anywhere in Europe or beyond. But interesting parallels, as well as contrasts, can be drawn between the ECJ and the US Supreme Court.

The US Supreme Court exists to uphold the US Constitution, whereas the EU has no such constitution. Yet even here the difference may not be as stark as it appears. The ECJ must uphold the EU's Treaties. For some legal scholars, the cumulative impact of Court decisions that have interpreted the Treaties amount to a 'quiet revolution' that effectively has transformed the Treaties into a constitution insofar as they constitute the basic rule book of the EU (see Weiler 1999).

One difference is jurisdiction, or the power to hear and decide cases. The jurisdiction of the US Supreme Court is vast. It can hear all cases involving legal disputes between the US states. More important is its power to hear cases raising constitutional disputes invoked by any national treaty, federal law, state law or act. The ECJ's jurisdiction is far more confined. Its rulings on trade have had a fundamental impact on the single market and the EU more generally. But many matters of national law, and most non-trade disputes between states fall outside its remit. Moreover, unlike the US court, the ECJ cannot 'cherry pick' the cases it wants to hear. Finally, recruitment, appointment, and tenure differ. US Supreme Court judges are seated for life following an involved and often highly politicized appointment and confirmation process by the US President and Senate. Judges on the ECJ, by contrast, are appointed by the member state governments, with little publicity. They remain relatively unknown for their six-year renewable term.

Yet, the rulings of both the ECJ and Supreme Court take precedence over those of lower or national courts. These rulings *must* be enforced by lower courts. Like the US Supreme Court in its early decades, the ECJ's early decisions helped consolidate the authority of the Union's central institutions. But perhaps the most interesting similarities involve debates surrounding these courts' powers and political role. In the case of the US Supreme Court, concerns about its politicization and activism are well-known, especially in its rulings on abortion, racial equality, and campaign spending (see Martin 2010). In the EU too, concerns about the Court's procedure, its ability to push integration forward or limit it, and the expansion of its authority have propelled the Court into the heart of political debates about the future of the EU. Thus, whatever their differences, both courts raise fundamental questions about the proper limits of judicial activism and the role of courts in democratic societies more generally.

What is also contested is the relationship between the main institutional players— Commission, Parliament, Council, European Council and Court—which is constantly changing. Power shifts across and between institutions not only as a result of formal treaty changes, but also due to changes in practice, the assertiveness of the various actors, agreements between EU institutions, and Court judgments. For instance, the ability of the Council to impose its view has declined as the bargaining power of Parliament has increased. The European Council's growing power to set the EU

BOX 3.5   **How it really works: turf wars!**

Relations between EU institutions are both consensual and conflictual. Cooperation is unceasing because of the shared recognition that all institutions must compromise and work together to get a policy through or decision agreed. Even those final decisions that rest with one institution usually involve proposals from or consultation with another.

Yet inter-institutional rivalry is also fierce as each institution jealously guards its prerogatives (to initiate policy or control budgets). New institutionalist scholars such as Armstrong and Bulmer (1998) and Pollack (2009) have underlined the importance of this dynamic. Perceived attempts by one institution to encroach on another's 'turf' often elicit heated responses or fierce demonstrations of institutional loyalty. For example, in 2010, the Commission disliked the fact that the European Council had set up a Task Force, chaired by the European Council's President, to make proposals on the reform of economic governance procedures—something the Commission felt should be its job. Although represented on the Task Force, and broadly in agreement with its emerging recommendations, the Commission insisted on tabling them as its own legislative proposals to Parliament and Council only one week before their final approval by the Task Force.

---

agenda has usurped the Commission's traditional and legal right of initiative. The establishment of a full time President of the European *Council* challenges the primacy of the President of the *Commission*.

Both formal and informal institutional change has contributed to a blurring of powers among core institutions. This blurring of power does not mean that the formal rules do not matter. Rules and treaty provisions serve as the basis of authority from which the institutions can and do act. But the formal powers are starting points only: knowing how the institutions exploit, compete for, and ultimately share power is also crucial for grasping how the EU works (see Box 3.5).

Why Institutions Matter

Examining the institutions and how they work is essential to understanding EU policy and politics. First, it gives us a starting point from which to examine the Union's policy process. Second, it helps us to identify the diversity of actors involved and to understand how together they determine the shape and speed of integration. Finally, it reminds us that there are many interesting questions still to be answered about European integration. Is it heading towards a European federal state? Or a looser, more intergovernmental body? How democratic or efficient will it be? Who or what will determine the pace and shape of integration?

More particularly, the EU's institutions help illustrate the three central themes of this book: (1) the extent to which the EU is an experiment in motion; (2) the

importance of power sharing and consensus; and (3) the capacity of the EU structures to cope with the Union's expanding size and scope.

Experimentation and change

The EU's institutional system has evolved considerably since the establishment of
the European Coal and Steel Community in 1951. As we have seen, the institutions
have adapted over time to perform a variety of tasks. Some tasks are formally mandated by the founding treaties and subsequent changes to them. But others have
emerged as more informal experiments in cooperation. A variety of pressures has
combined to encourage a sort of task expansion and the reinvention of institutions
over time. In particular, gaps in the capacity of the EU to respond to events and crises
have resulted in an *ad hoc* expansion of the informal powers of the institutions. For
example, the need for common action on the environment meant that informal environmental agreements predated formal advances introduced by the Treaties. Sometimes member states agreed on the need to establish informal cooperation in new
areas, but were not initially ready to be legally bound by the treaties, as in the gradual
expansion of the powers of the EU institutions in the area of justice and home affairs
(see Chapter 9). Studying the institutional dynamics of the EU allows us not only to
understand the extent to which the EU is subject to experimentation and change,
but also to pose questions about where this process might be headed.

Power-sharing and consensus

Scholars of European integration have long and fiercely debated where power lies in
the EU. Do the EU's institutions drive the integration process forward? Or do national governments remain in control? The two sides of this debate have been taken
up by neo-functionalists and intergovernmentalists respectively. Both sides can cite
changes in formal EU rules to buttress their case.

For example, as the Parliament has gained powers and member states have accepted more proposals on the basis of QMV, it could be claimed that supranationalism is on the rise. On the other hand, as the European Council has come to dominate
high-level agenda setting, or as various countries have formally opted out of certain
policies (such as monetary union), it could be said that intergovernmentalism is
holding strong. But depicting integration as a pitched battle between EU institutions
and the member states misses the point. Competition is fierce, but so, too, is the
search for consensus. Enormous efforts go into forging agreements acceptable to all.

The overall trajectory of integration is thus a result of to-ing and fro-ing between
a rich variety of actors and external pressures. This image is quite neatly captured in
Wallace's description (2000) of EU governance as a pendulum, swinging sometimes
towards intergovernmental solutions and sometimes towards supranationalism, but
not always in equal measure. In this system, power is often a product of how well any

institution engages with other actors—lobbyists, experts, governments, and other international organizations—at different levels of governance. Focusing on the institutions and how they cooperate or compete with each other and other actors helps us to begin to make sense of the EU as a complex policy-making process.

Scope and capacity

The step-by-step extension of the scope of the EU's activities is one thing. Its capacity to deal with those subjects that fall within its remit and to cope with successive enlargements is another. Have the institutional structures, originally conceived for a Community of six member states, been sufficiently adapted to deal with the demands of an EU of 27 or more? (see Box 3.6) In most policy fields, the EU has

---

BOX 3.6	Enlargement's institutional impact

Enlargement has brought both opportunities and headaches to the EU's institutions. The impact has varied across institutions, with some adapting more smoothly than others. The European Parliament, despite real linguistic challenges (see Box 1.7) seems to have had the least difficulty absorbing new members (see Donnelly and Bigatto 2008). Decisions are based on majority votes and the EP has shown that it is still able to deal with difficult legislation even with more than 700 MEPs. Moreover, the quality of MEPs from the new countries generally has been high, with many having held important positions (including Presidents and Prime Ministers).

In the Commission, new and generally younger officials hold out the prospect of revitalizing and renewing the institution with fresh ideas and reform-minded Europeans. However, a Commission of 27 has resulted in a less cosy and, arguably, more **intergovernmental** body in a larger, less collegial Commission (see Peterson 2008). For the first time, the membership of the College—with one per member state—is now identical to that of the Council. Finding a sufficient number of responsible and interesting portfolios of relatively equal importance has proved difficult.

It is in the Council and the European Council that the challenges of enlargement have been most keenly felt. Since 2004, the Council has found it increasingly difficult to push through important decisions in areas, such as foreign policy and police cooperation, that require unanimity. National vetoes are not necessarily more common in an EU of 27 (see House of Lords 2006; Hagemann and De Clerck-Sachsse 2007). But Council meetings are more time-consuming and not always as productive. On important questions, all or most member states still want to present their positions and may insist on lengthy interventions. The result is less time for real discussion and compromise-seeking, which is the essence of what makes the Council and European Council function.

The impact of enlargement on the institutions reflects its wider impact on the EU. It has brought a mix of logistical headaches, challenges, doubts, and crises, but also the promise of fresh impulse, drive, and energy for a Union otherwise threatened by stagnation and inertia.

managed to avoid decision-making gridlock following each successive enlargement, though arguments continue as to whether enlargement has been at the cost of having to settle for lowest common denominator solutions. Certainly in areas that require unanimity within the Council, the EU now is vulnerable to slow, cumbersome decision-making and even total blockage at the instigation of one or another member state.

Strengthening European cooperation may appear to equate to empowering its institutions. Yet, policy cooperation has been extended in a variety of different ways that have expanded the scope of the EU without necessarily expanding institutions' powers. The careful exclusion of the ECJ and the weaker role played by the Commission and the EP in most aspects of foreign and security policy are examples. Finally, if there is one lesson to be learned from the study of EU institutions, it is their remarkable ability to adapt as new requirements are placed upon them. This chapter has tried to show that while the capacity of EU institutions may be limited, their ability to adapt often seems limitless.

Conclusion

The EU's institutional system is complex. But so, too, is the diverse polity it helps govern. We have attempted to cut through this complexity by focusing on the institutions' powers, and what they do with them. We have stressed the importance of both cooperation and rivalry between the institutions. Each institution may have its own agenda, but nearly all important decisions require some (and usually, quite a large) measure of consensus spanning the EU's institutions (see Peterson and Shackleton 2012). The institutions are as interdependent as the member states that make up the EU.

Moreover, EU institutions do not operate alone. Today they must deal with an ever broader range of actors, including an increasing number of member states (see Chapters 4 and 8), but also increasingly active groups of organized interests. Above all, understanding institutions helps us to explore broader questions of how and why the EU works the way it does.

As the EU takes on new tasks, the burden on its institutions will increase. The EU's growing role in areas such as migration, foreign and defence policy, food safety, and climate change means that other agencies and bodies (including international ones that transcend Europe itself) will join the institutional mix that helps govern EU politics (see Box 3.7). Further institutional reform may prove both necessary and inevitable to cope with the increasing size and policy scope of the EU. But given the challenge of obtaining unanimous support for institutional change, institutional reform—like so much else in the EU—is likely to be incremental and pragmatic rather than spectacular or far-sighted.

BOX 3.7	**Other institutions and bodies**

Several smaller institutions and bodies carry out a variety of representative, oversight, or managerial functions in the EU. By far the most significant of these specialized institutions is the **European Central Bank (ECB)**. Based in Frankfurt and modelled on the fiercely independent German Bundesbank, the ECB is charged with a fundamental task: formulating the EU's monetary policy, including ensuring monetary stability, setting interest rates, and issuing and managing the euro (see Chapter 5). The ECB is steered by an executive board (made up primarily of national central bank governors) and headed by a President who is chosen by member states, but who cannot formally be removed by them. The Bank's independence and power undoubtedly help ensure monetary stability but also have raised concerns about transparency and accountability. Its executive board is appointed by member states, and it must report to the EP several times a year. But its deliberations are not made public and it enjoys considerable independence from other institutions or member states themselves. While still a young institution, the Bank is certain to become a more important, but also controversial player in EU politics (see Hodson 2010).

Exercising an oversight function is the **Court of Auditors** whose 27 members are charged with scrutinizing the EU's budget and financial accounts. Acting as the 'financial conscience' of the EU, the Court has increased its stature and visibility in recent years as public concern over mismanagement and sometimes even fraud has mounted. Its annual and specialized reports consist mainly of dry financial management assessment, but they also have uncovered more spectacular and often serious financial misconduct (see Karakatsanis and Laffan 2012).

Several smaller bodies, not classified as institutions (therefore having fewer rights at the Court) carry out a primarily representative function (see Jeffrey and Rowe 2012). For instance the **European Economic and Social Committee (EESC)** represents various employer, trades union, and other social or public interests (such as farmers or consumers) in EU policy-making. Chosen by the national governments, these representatives serve in a part-time function advising the Commission and other institutions on relevant proposals. Their opinions can be well researched but are not usually influential. The **Committee of the Regions and Local Authorities** suffers from a similar lack of influence. Created by the Maastricht Treaty, the Committee must be consulted on proposals affecting regional interests (cohesion funding, urban planning) and can issue its own opinions and reports. However, it is internally divided and its membership debilitatingly diverse (powerful regional ministers from Germany and Belgium sit alongside representatives from English town parishes). It has yet to exert the influence its proponents originally envisioned, but perhaps its real role is as a channel of communication across several layers of governance.

The EU **Ombudsman** is empowered to receive complaints from any EU citizen or any natural or legal person residing in the member states concerning instances of maladministration in the activities of the Union institutions or bodies (other than the Court in its judicial capacity). The Ombudsman is chosen by the EP after each parliamentary election for the duration of its term of office.

DISCUSSION QUESTIONS

1. Which EU institution is most 'powerful' in your view and why?

2. Why has the balance of powers between the EU's institutions shifted over time?

3. Which institution could most accurately be described as the 'motor of integration'?

4. Is the relationship between the EU's institutions characterized more by cooperation or conflict?

FURTHER READING

For comprehensive analysis of all of the EU's institutions, see Peterson and Shackleton (2012a). Best *et al.* (2008) focus specifically on the effects enlargement on EU institutions. Helpful examinations of individual institutions include Kassim *et al.'s* (2012) analysis of the Commission; Hayes-Renshaw and Wallace's (2006) classic study of the Council of Ministers which also includes analysis of the European Council; Corbett *et al.'s* (2011) account of the workings of the Parliament; and Weiler's (1999) provocative and thoughtful essays on the Court and EU's legal identity.

Best, E., Christiansen, T., and Settembri P. (eds) (2008), *The Institutions of the Enlarged European Union: Continuity and Change* (Cheltenham and Northampton MA: Edward Elgar).

Corbett, R., Jacobs, F., and Shackleton, M. (2011), *The European Parliament*, 8th edn. (London: John Harper).

Hayes-Renshaw, F. and Wallace, H. (2006), *The Council of Ministers*, 2nd edn. (Basingstoke and New York: Palgrave).

Kassim, H., Peterson, J., Bauer, M., Dehousse, R., Hooghe, L., Thompson, A. and Connolly, S. (2012), *The European Commission of the 21st Century: Decline or Renewal?* (Oxford and New York: Oxford University Press).

Peterson, J. and Shackleton, M. (eds.) (2012), *The Institutions of the European Union*, 3rd edn. (Oxford and New York: Oxford University Press).

Weiler, J. H. H. (1999), *The Constitution of Europe* (Cambridge and New York: Cambridge University Press).

WEB LINKS

Most of the EU's institutions have their own website which can be accessed through the EU's official portal site, 'The European Union online' (http://www.europa.eu/). Below are the specific official websites of some of the institutions introduced in this chapter:

- European Commission: http://ec.europa.eu/index_en.htm
- Council of Ministers: http://ue.eu.int/
- European Parliament: http://www.europarl.europa.eu/
- European Court of Justice: http://curia.europa.eu/
- Court of Auditors: http://www.eca.europa.eu/
- Economic and Social Committee: http://eesc.europa.eu/

- Committee of the Regions: **http://www.cor.europa.eu/**
- European Central Bank: **http://www.ecb.int**

Anyone brave enough to consider working as an intern or *stagiaire* in one of the EU's institutions can find out more at **http://ec.europa.eu/stages/**. For recent updates on institutional developments, especially in relation to treaty reform, see **http://www.euractiv.com/**. The London-based University Association for Contemporary European Studies (UACES) (**http://www.uaces.org/**) announces regular workshops and lectures on the EU institutions held in the UK and (occasionally) on the European continent. For information on conferences and lectures held in the US, see the website of the US European Union Studies Association (EUSA) which can be found at **http://www.eustudies.org**.

Visit the Online Resource Centre that accompanies this book for additional material: **www.oxfordtextbooks.co.uk/orc/bomberg3e/**

CHAPTER 4

Member States

Brigid Laffan and Alexander Stubb

▌ Summary

This chapter focuses on the European Union's (EU's) most essential component: its member states. It examines six factors that determine how any state engages with the EU: date of entry, size, wealth, state structure, economic ideology, and integration preference. We then explore how member states behave in the Union's institutions and seek to influence the outcome of negotiations in Brussels. We focus throughout on the informal as well as formal activities of the member states. The final section explores the insights offered by theory in analysing the relationship between the EU and its member states.

Introduction

States are the essential building blocks of the EU. Without states there is no EU. All EU treaties are negotiated and ratified by the 'high contracting parties': that is, the governments of the member states. By joining the EU, the traditional nation-state is transformed into a member state. This transformation involves an enduring commitment to participate in political and legal processes that are beyond the state but embrace the state. Membership of the Union has significant effects on national systems of policy-making, on national institutions, and on national identity, sovereignty, and democracy. Put simply, once a state joins the Union, politics may begin at home but they no longer end there. National politics, polities, and policies become 'Europeanized' (see Box 4.1).

Member states shape the EU as much as the EU shapes its member states. The decision to join the Union is a decision to become locked into an additional layer of governance and a distinctive form of 'Euro-politics', which is neither wholly domestic nor international but shares attributes of both. This chapter explores this interactive dynamic. We tackle questions such as: what is the role of the member states in the EU system? What is it about the EU that has led the member states to invest so much in the collective project? How do member states engage with the EU? What factors determine how any member state behaves as an EU member?

BOX 4.1   **Key concepts and terms**

Acquis communautaire is a French phrase that denotes the sum total of the rights and obligations derived from the EU treaties, laws, and Court rulings. In principle, new member states joining the EU must accept the entire *acquis*.

Demandeur is the French term often used to refer to those demanding something (say regional or agricultural funds) from the EU.

Europeanization is the process whereby national systems (institutions, policies, governments, and even the polity itself) adapt to EU policies and integration more generally, while also themselves shaping the European Union.

Flexible integration (also called 'reinforced' or 'enhanced cooperation') denotes the possibility for some member states to pursue deeper integration without the participation of others. Examples include EMU and the **Schengen Agreement** in which some member states have decided not to participate fully. The Amsterdam and Nice Treaties institutionalized the concept of flexible integration through their clauses on enhanced cooperation.

Tours de table allow each national delegation in a Council of Ministers meeting to make an intervention on a given subject. In an EU of 27 member states *tours de table* have become less common. If every minister or national official intervened even for five minutes on each subject, the Council would not get any business done.

Six Determining Features

The 27 member states (as of 2012) bring to the Union their distinctive national histories, state traditions, constitutions, legal principles, political systems, and economic capacity. A variety of languages (there are 23 official working languages in the EU) and an extraordinary diversity of national and sub-national tastes and cultures accentuate the mosaic-like character of Europe. The enlargement of the Union (12 new states since 2004) has deepened its pre-existing diversity. Managing difference is thus a key challenge for the Union. To understand how the EU really works, we must seek to understand the multinational and multicultural character of the European Union and its institutions.

Classifying the member states—including how and why they joined and how they operate within the EU—is a good first step towards understanding the member states' relationship with the EU. Six factors are extremely important. No one factor determines the relationship between the EU and a member state, but together they provide a guide to understanding member states' engagement with the EU.

Entry date

It is useful to deploy the metaphor of an onion to characterize the expansion of the Union from its original 6 states to 9, 10, 12, 15, and finally to 27 or more states in the years ahead (see Figure 4.1). The core of the onion is formed by France, Germany, and the four other founding members. What is now the European Union was originally the creation of six states that were occupied or defeated in the Second World War. It is the creation especially of France, a country that needed to achieve a settlement with its neighbour and historical enemy, Germany. From the outset the key relationship in the European Union was between France and Germany. As explained in Chapter 2, the Franco-German alliance and the Paris–Bonn axis—now Paris–Berlin—have left enduring traces on the fabric of integration. The Elysée Treaty (1963) institutionalized very strong bilateral ties between these two countries. The intensity of interaction should not be taken as evidence of continuous agreement between France and Germany on major European issues. Rather, much of the interaction has worked to iron out conflicts between them.

Close personal relationships between German Chancellor Helmut Schmidt and French President Valery Giscard d'Estaing in the 1970s and Chancellor Helmut Kohl and President François Mitterrand in the 1980s and early 1990s were key to the most ambitious steps forward in European integration, including the creation of the European Monetary System (a precursor to EMU), the single market programme, and the euro. The Franco-German relationship was challenged by geopolitical change in Europe following the collapse of communism. German unification and the opening

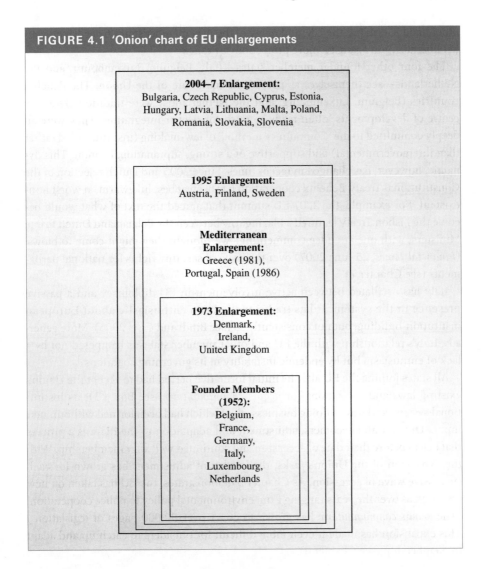

FIGURE 4.1 'Onion' chart of EU enlargements

2004–7 Enlargement:
Bulgaria, Czech Republic, Cyprus, Estonia,
Hungary, Latvia, Lithuania, Malta, Poland,
Romania, Slovakia, Slovenia

1995 Enlargement:
Austria, Finland, Sweden

**Mediterranean
Enlargement:**
Greece (1981),
Portugal, Spain (1986)

1973 Enlargement:
Denmark,
Ireland,
United Kingdom

**Founder Members
(1952):**
Belgium,
France,
Germany,
Italy,
Luxembourg,
Netherlands

up of the eastern half of the continent altered the bilateral balance of power, with Germany no longer a junior political partner to France. The change was symbolically captured by the relocation of the German capital to Berlin.

It is premature to talk of the demise of the Franco-German relationship; it remains important. But changing geopolitics and enlargement to the east have profoundly altered the context within which it is played out. To illustrate, France and the UK—not Germany—have been in the forefront of EU defence cooperation. Similarly, in negotiations on the financial framework for 2007–2013, France and the UK often joined forces against Germany, the biggest net contributor of the EU budget. On the other hand, Germany, the UK, and many of the new member states have driven market liberalization against a more protectionist France.

The four other founder member states—Italy, Belgium, Luxembourg, and the Netherlands—see themselves as part of the hard core of the Union. The Benelux countries (Belgium, Luxembourg, and the Netherlands) were traditionally at the centre of developments, often ready to push for deeper integration. They were all deeply committed to the 'Community method' of law-making (institution-led rather than intergovernmental) and supportive of a strong, supranational Union. This dynamic, however, has changed in recent times. Since 2005 and Dutch rejection of the Constitutional Treaty, Benelux cooperation has been at best lukewarm, at worst non-existent. For example, the 2007 EU summit that agreed the text of what would become the Lisbon Treaty featured a blazing row between the Belgian and Dutch Prime Ministers, with one attendee commenting: 'we thought they might come to blows' (*Financial Times*, 25 June 2007) over the issue of scrutiny rights for national parliaments (see Chapter 7).

Italy has oscillated between active involvement in EU diplomacy and a passive presence in the system. It has traditionally been enthusiastic about European institution-building, but not consistently so (see Bindi and Cisci 2005). More generally, Italy's relationship with the EU and other member states is hampered not by a lack of enthusiasm but by endemic instability in its governing coalitions.

All states joining the EU after its initial formative period had to accept the Union's existing laws and obligations (or *acquis communautaire*; see Box 4.1), its institutional system, and way of doing business, all of which had been formed without their input. Thus for all latecomers, adjustment and adaptation to the EU was a process that began before their date of accession and continued well after membership. With the expansion of the Union's tasks, the burden of adjustment has grown for each successive wave of accession. As Chapter 5 demonstrates, the EU has taken on new policy areas over the years ranging from environmental policy to police cooperation. (The *acquis communautaire* has grown to cover over 80,000 pages of legislation.) This expansion has made it even more difficult for outsiders to catch up and adapt to membership (see Chapter 8).

Size

As in all political systems, size matters in the EU. The distinction between large and small states is often evoked in political and media discussions about representation in the EU. At the cumbersome negotiations on the Treaty of Nice, which focused on the re-weighting of votes in the Council and the number of Commissioners each state could appoint, tensions between large and small states escalated. Nice settled little, and battles between large and small states marked negotiations surrounding the 2004 Constitutional Treaty and its eventual replacement (the Lisbon Treaty). But battles over voting weights are not only fought between large and small: in 2007, the President of Poland went as far as to argue that his country deserved more votes in the Council to compensate for the number of Poles murdered by the Nazis during the Second World War.

In any event, a more nuanced approach to understanding the impact of size is warranted. The EU really consists of four clusters of states—large, medium, small, and very small (see Table 4.1). The first cluster contains six large states: Germany, United Kingdom, France, Italy, Spain, and Poland. Together they make up about 70 per cent of the population of EU-27. (Even here we find dissent: Germany, France, and the UK are certainly seen as the 'big three', with Italy seen as less powerful, and some would dispute Spain's and Poland's categorization as large states.) The next cluster consists of medium-sized states: Romania, the Netherlands, Greece, Belgium, Portugal, the Czech Republic, and Hungary, whose populations range from 10 to 22 million inhabitants. The third cluster is one of small states: Sweden, Austria, Bulgaria,

TABLE 4.1   Clusters of member states and candidate countries by size

Current member states

(figure in brackets = approximate population in millions in 2010)

Large	Medium	Small	Very Small
Germany (82)	Romania (21)	Sweden (9)	Cyprus (0.8)
France (65)	Netherlands (17)	Austria (8)	Luxembourg (0.5)
UK (62)	Greece (11)	Bulgaria (8)	Malta (0.4)
Italy (60)	Belgium (11)	Denmark (5)	
Spain (46)	Portugal (11)	Finland (5)	
Poland (39)	Czech Republic (10)	Slovakia (5)	
	Hungary (10)	Ireland (4)	
		Lithuania (3)	
		Latvia (2)	
		Slovenia (2)	
		Estonia (1)	

Candidate countries

Turkey (71)		Croatia (4)	Montenegro (0.6)
		Macedonia (2)	Iceland (0.3)

Eurostat Demography Report 2010: http://epp.eurostat.ec.europa.eu/portal/page/portal/population/documents/Tab/report.pdf

Denmark, Finland, Slovakia, Ireland, Lithuania, Latvia, Slovenia, and Estonia, which all have populations of between 1 and 9 million. The fourth category, very small states, consists of Cyprus, Luxembourg, and Malta. Recent enlargements years have brought mainly an increase of medium, small, and very small states (Poland is the exception to the rule). Indeed one of the reasons Turkish membership of the EU is so contested is that its large population would have a profound impact on the size balances within the Union (see Chapter 8).

Size has implications for power and presence in the Union's political and economic system. The power of large states is not just expressed in voting power in the Council. It manifests itself in political, economic, and diplomatic influence (see Wallace 2005: 38ff). Large states can call on far more extensive and specialized administrative and technical resources in the policy process than small states, and their diplomatic presence is far stronger throughout the world. The German Chancellor, regardless of who holds the post, is usually the most powerful politician at European Council meetings. Small states, however, enjoy important advantages in EU negotiations. They tend to have fewer vital interests than larger states, their interests can be aggregated with much greater ease, and the potential for conflict and competing claims among different social groups is reduced. Luxembourg, for example, can concentrate all of its diplomatic energy on protecting its traditional industries, its liberal banking laws, and its presence in EU institutions.

Although size matters, it has little bearing on national approaches to substantive issues of EU policy that are formed by economic considerations, domestic interests, and the proposed nature of the change. Thus, small states are unlikely to band together against the large states in substantive policy discussions. Their interests, just like those of the larger states, diverge. Coalition patterns in the Council have always consisted of a mix of large and small states in any particular policy domain.

Small states do, however, have a common interest in maintaining the EU's institutional balance and they can deploy a variety of strategies to cope with the structural disadvantage they face (Panke 2010). For instance small EU states can band together to oppose proposals that privilege a small group of larger states. They are keen supporters of procedural 'rules of the game' which protect their level of representation in the system. The key point here is that the multilateral, institutionalized, and legal processes of the Union have created a relatively benign environment for small states.

In the past, the European Union successfully managed to expand its membership to include both large and small states without undermining the balance between them or causing undue tension. This balance began to shift in the 1990s. The 1995 enlargement and the prospect of further enlargement to the east and south heightened the salience of the small-state/large-state divide in the Union. The struggle for power—as reflected in number of Commissioners, votes in the Council, or seats in the European Parliament each member state receives—figured on the EU agenda for over a decade, from 1995 to 2009. Negotiating the relative power of member states has not been easy. Many would argue that the institutional debate has been the poisoned chalice of the EU over the past few years.

Wealth

The original European Economic Community had only one serious regional poverty problem: the Italian Mezzogiorno. As such, 'cohesion' (or regional development) was not an important concern. The first enlargement in 1973 to include the UK, Denmark, and Ireland increased the salience of regional disparities in the politics of the Union. The UK had significant regional problems, with declining industrial areas and low levels of economic development in areas such as Northern England, Scotland, Wales, and Northern Ireland. The Republic of Ireland had per capita incomes that were about 62 per cent of the EU average at the time. The Mediterranean enlargements in the 1980s to include Greece, Spain, and Portugal (all relatively poor states) accentuated the problem of economic divergence.

By the 1980s, the Union as an economic space consisted of a 'golden triangle' which ran from southern England, through France and Germany to northern Italy and southern, western, and northern peripheries. Although committed to harmonious economic development from the outset, the Union did not have to expand its budgetary commitment to poorer Europe until the single market programme in the mid-1980s. At that point, Europe's poorer states successfully linked the economic liberalization of the 1992 programme with an enhanced commitment to greater cohesion in the Union. This commitment manifested itself in a doubling of the financial resources devoted to less prosperous regions, especially those with a per capita income less than 75 per cent of the EU average (see Table 4.2). In addition, four member states whose overall gross domestic product (GDP) was low—Spain, Portugal, Greece, and Ireland—were granted extra aid (in the form of a Cohesion Fund) as a prize for agreeing to monetary union. Of the four states, Ireland was the first to lose its cohesion status.

With eastern enlargement in 2004 and 2007, the poverty gap between the member states grew considerably wider. Today GDP per capita in all new member states and candidate countries remains under the EU-27 average (see Table 4.2). Cyprus and Slovenia rank as the richest of the new members, while Romania and Bulgaria—the 2007 entrants—are the poorest. Most candidate countries are even poorer (see Chapter 8).

The promotion of economic and social cohesion will continue to resonate in the politics of integration well into the future. During the 2007–2013 financial framework period, cohesion policy accounts for around 35 per cent of the total EU budget (see Chapter 5). After eastern enlargement many of the former recipients of cohesion funds (including Spain and Ireland) were no longer eligible for many EU funds which were now funnelled towards the newer and poorer member states.

Economic divergence has a significant impact on how the EU works. First, it influences the pecking order in the Union. The poor countries are perceived as *demandeurs* in the Union, dependent on EU subsidies. Secondly, attitudes towards the size and distribution of the EU budget are influenced by contrasting views between net beneficiaries and net contributors. With the growth of the EU budget, a distinct 'net contributors club' has emerged in the Union, which is led by Germany but joined also by the United Kingdom, the Netherlands, Austria, Sweden, Finland, and Denmark.

TABLE 4.2 Member states' gross domestic product in 2010			
GDP per capita in Purchasing Power Standards (PPS)			
European Union average	100		
Luxembourg	271	Greece	93
Netherlands	130	Slovenia	87
Ireland	128	Czech Republic	80
Austria	122	Portugal	79
Sweden	120	Malta	78
Denmark	118	Slovakia	72
Belgium	116	Estonia	63
Germany	116	Hungary	63
UK	116	Poland	61
Finland	111	Lithuania	53
France	108	Latvia	49
Spain	104	Romania	45
Italy	102	Bulgaria	43 (2008)
Cyprus	98		
Candidate countries 2012			
Croatia	63		
Turkey	46		
Macedonia	34		

Eurostat 2010: Volume Indices of GDP per capita: http://epp.eurostat.ec.europa.eu/statistics_explained/index.php?title=File:Volume_indices_per_inhabitant,_2007–2009.PNG&filetimestamp=20110120133458

These states are committed to controlling increases in the EU budget and to limiting the budgetary costs of cohesion. As more states become 'net contributors', this club is set to grow. The poor countries as beneficiaries of financial transfers tend to argue for larger budgetary resources and additional instruments.

Thirdly, relative wealth influences attitudes towards EU regulation, notably in relation to environmental and social policy. The richer states have more stringent, developed systems of regulation that impose extra costs on their productive industries. They thus favour the spread of higher standards of regulation to peripheral Europe. By contrast, the poorer states, in their search for economic development, often want to avoid imposing the costs of onerous regulation on their industries. Overall, environmental and social standards have risen in Europe, particularly in peripheral Europe, but not to the extent desired by the wealthier states.

State structure

The internal constitutional structure of a member state has an impact on how it operates in the EU. The Union of 27 has three federal states—Germany, Austria, and Belgium. Others are unitary states or quasi-unitary. (The line is not always easy to draw. Unitary states can have subnational governments, self-governing regions, and autonomous communities. For example, Spain and the UK can be considered as *de facto* federations.) The subnational units in all three federal states have played a significant role in the constitutional development of the Union. The German Länder, in particular, insisted in the 1990s that they be given an enhanced say in German European policy. They have been advocates of sub-sidiarity (see Box 2.2) and the creation of the Committee of the Regions. In the 1992 Maastricht Treaty, they won the right to send Länder ministers and officials to represent Germany in the Council of Ministers when matters within their competence are discussed. Representatives of the German and Austrian Länder, representatives of the Belgian regions and cultural communities, as well as ministers in the Scottish government now sit at the Council table and can commit their national governments.

In addition to direct representation, there has been an explosion of regional and local offices in Brussels from the mid-1980s onwards. Increasingly, state and regional governments, local authorities, and cities feel the need for direct representation in Brussels. Their offices act as a conduit of information from the EU to the subnational level within the member states. They engage in tracking EU legislation, lobbying for grants, and seeking partners for European projects. Not unexpectedly, there can be tension between national governments and the offices that engage in paradiplomacy in the Brussels arena (see Chapter 6).

Economic ideology

Much of what the EU does is designed to create the conditions of enhanced economic integration through market-building. The manner in which this economic liberalization has developed has been greatly influenced by the dominant economic and social paradigms of the member states. Different visions of the proper balance between public and private power, or between the state and market have left their traces on how the EU works.

Although all six founding member states might be regarded as adhering to a continental or Christian democratic model of capitalism, there are important differences amongst them. For instance, France traditionally has supported far more interventionist public authorities than the German economic model would tolerate. But differences between France and Germany fade in comparison to differences between continental capitalism and the Anglo-Saxon tradition. The accession of the UK in 1973 and the radical deregulatory policies of successive Conservative governments brought the so-called Anglo-Saxon economic paradigm into the Union. The UK has been a supporter of deregulation and economic liberalization in the Union but not always of re-regulation at Union level, particularly in the social and environmental fields. The Anglo-Saxon tradition, however, has been somewhat balanced by the accession of the Nordic states with a social democratic tradition of economic governance and social provision, combined with a strong belief in market liberalization. The Anglo-Saxon economic model gained further ground with the 2004 and 2007 enlargements. The new Eastern states generally favour a more liberal economic agenda. They were instrumental in pushing for a more liberal services directive in 2006. However, as Goetz (2005) argues, the new member states brought a diverse set of interests to EU policy-making and intraregional cooperation between them is weak, making any notion of an 'eastern bloc' more myth than reality.

A battle of ideas continues in the Union, based on competing views about the right balance between state and market, the role of the EU in regulation, and questions of economic governance more generally. These differences were sharply exposed during the 2010 financial crisis when it became apparent that the public finances of a number of member states, notably Greece, Spain, Portugal, and Ireland were on an unsustainable trajectory. Following considerable disagreement, the 16 Euro member states (with Germany an primary paymaster) agreed to €500 billion of loan guarantees and emergency funding to address the Greek crisis. German Chancellor Angela Merkel made clear her preference that the treaties be changed to provide a legal underpinning for such a bail-out mechanism. In any event, there will undoubtedly be more stringent surveillance of the public finances of the euro members and more frequent health checks on their economies.

Integration preference

The terms pro- and anti-European, or 'good' European and awkward partner, are frequently bandied about to describe national attitudes towards the EU. The UK, Denmark, Poland, and the Czech Republic are usually portrayed as reluctant Europeans (see Table 4.3). Whilst not entirely false, such categorizations disguise several facts. First, attitudes towards European integration are moulded not just by nationality but (often more powerfully) by factors such as socio-economic class, age, or educational attainment. Secondly, in all states we find a significant split between the attitudes of those who might be called 'the top decision-makers' and the mass public. A very high proportion of elites accept that their state has benefited from EU membership, and that membership is in their state's national interest. These sentiments are not shared by the wider public in many states. For instance, the comparative Table 4.3 illustrates the particular impact of the economic crisis. Public opinion in most member states has shown a significant decline in those saying that membership of the European Union has been good for their states. The decline is particularly sharp in those states, Ireland, Spain, Greece, and Italy that are confronting a public finance crisis and in Germany, the member state that will be asked to come to the aid of those states. Most of the new member states are also characterized by a sharp decline. Of course, governments must take public opinion into account.

TABLE 4.3	Support for EU membership	
Member state	**% responding that EU membership is a 'good thing'***	
	2007	**2010 (% change)**
Netherlands	77	69 (-8)
Ireland	76	66 (-10)
Luxembourg	74	70 (-4)
Spain	73	59 (-14)
Belgium	70	64 (-6)
Poland	67	62 (-5)
Romania	67	55 (-12)
Denmark	66	66 (unchanged)
Estonia	66	59 (-7)
Germany	65	50 (-15)
Slovakia	64	59 (-5)
EU AVERAGE	57	49 (-8)
Slovenia	58	39 (-19)
Greece	55	44 (-11)
Portugal	55	43 (-12)
Bulgaria	55	47 (-8)
France	52	44 (-8)
Italy	51	48 (-3)
Malta	51	47 (-4)
Sweden	50	54 (+4)
Czech Republic	46	31 (-15)
Cyprus	44	33 (-11)
Finland	42	45 (+3)
UK	39	29 (-10)
Hungary	37	38 (+1)
Latvia	37	48 (+11)
Austria	36	36 (unchanged)

Question: 'Generally speaking, do you think that (YOUR COUNTRY)'s membership of the European Union is a good thing, a bad thing, or good and bad?'

NB: In the figure for Cyprus, only the interviews conducted in the part of the country controlled by the government of the Republic of Cyprus are recorded.

Eurobarometer Report 67: Public Opinion in the European Union (Nov 2007): **http://ec.europa.eu/ public_opinion/archives/eb/eb67/eb67_en.pdf**

Eurobarometer Report 73: Public Opinion in the European Union (Nov 2010): **http://ec.europa.eu/ public_opinion/archives/eb/eb73/eb73_vol1_en.pdf**

When coherent, public opinion sets the broad parameters of what is acceptable policy. But public opinion toward the EU—however reluctant—is only one of several factors shaping a government's position.

Some states certainly are more enthusiastic about certain developments (say, enlargement or greater transparency) than are others. But there is often an important difference between rhetoric and reality in EU negotiations. Some member states, including France and Germany, tend to use grandiose language in calling for deeper integration. However, around the negotiating table they are often the ones blocking an increase in qualified majority voting (QMV) on issues such as trade or justice and home affairs. The opposite can be true for states such as the UK. British ministers and officials are inclined to language that makes them seem reluctant about European integration. Yet, in negotiations on, for example, trade liberalization, they are often in the forefront of more or closer cooperation. In short, member states' attitudes towards integration are far more nuanced than is implied by the labels 'pro' or 'anti' Europe.

Different national preferences and attitudes are expressed most vividly during the Intergovernmental Conferences (IGCs) leading to treaty reform. These events traditionally have been managed by the states holding the Council presidency and finalized—amidst much media fanfare—at a European Council by the heads of state and government. In each IGC, member states need to decide what is negotiable and what is non-negotiable, or what they could trade in one area in return for concessions in another. The outcome has inevitably been a series of complex package deals (see Box 4.2).

An important feature of EU treaty change since the early 1990s has been the greater frequency with which states have been allowed to 'opt out' of certain policy developments. For example, Denmark has opted out of the euro, parts of the Schengen agreement on the free movement of people, and aspects of the Common Foreign and Security Policy. Similarly, the UK is not part of the euro, and neither it nor Ireland is a full participant in Schengen. Of the new member states, only Slovenia, Slovakia, Malta, Cyprus and Estonia are so far part of the Euro area.

When member states hold referendums on European treaties (of which there have been over 30), there is often a blurring of the boundaries between domestic politics and the future of the EU. The constitutional treaty was the subject of four referendums in 2005 and was defeated in two of those, held in France and the Netherlands. This round was followed by the defeat of the first referendum on the Lisbon Treaty in 2008 in Ireland. Three dramatic referendum defeats in as many years meant that the stakes in the second Irish referendum held in October 2009 were very high (see Box 4.3).

Taken together, the six factors introduced in this section tell us a great deal about how the EU works. Styles of economic governance and levels of wealth have a major influence on national approaches to European regulation, and on just how much regulation each state favours at EU level. A hostile or favourable public opinion will help to determine the integration preferences of particular states. How states represent themselves in EU business is partially determined by their state structure and domestic institutions. The point is that EU member states vary across several cross-cutting dimensions, and this mix is part of what makes the EU unique.

BOX 4.2	How it really works: intergovernmental conferences

The EU's Treaties state that the government of any member state, the European Parliament, or the Commission may submit proposals for the amendment of the Treaties. If the European Council, after consulting the EP and the Commission, decides (by a simple majority) that such a proposal has legs, it then must convene 'a Convention composed of representatives of national parliaments, the Heads of State or Government of the Member States, of the European Parliament and of the Commission' (unless the European Parliament decides that such a Convention is unnecessary because the extent of proposed changes are limited).

In any case, any proposed changes must be submitted to a 'conference of representatives of the governments', or what in EU-speak is called an **Intergovernmental Conference (IGC)**. An IGC is the means by which the EU changes its treaties or enlarges.

IGCs are often a long and tedious. In most cases, after months of discussions and seemingly endless *tours de table* (which allow the delegations to state and restate their national positions, see Box 4.1), the Council's General Secretariat and Presidency draft a proposed set of treaty amendments. Member states then suggest changes to the draft. Finally, a compromise is hammered out. Some issues can be solved by ministers. The most difficult questions are left to be resolved at the infamous all-night sessions of the European Council.

An IGC usually affects many different policy areas and has an impact on the entire administrations of member governments. A sound relationship between administrations in national capitals and their Permanent Representation in Brussels is crucial. In many instances, the actual IGC negotiators have positions that are closer to each other's than those between ministries at home. During negotiations it is usually not difficult to detect when a negotiator has been unable to get agreement for a proposal from their home administration. The code phrase is often: 'we are still studying the question back home'. An IGC may be avoided for minor Treaty changes that do not increase the competences of the EU. In such cases, the Lisbon Treaty's 'Simplified Revision Procedure' may be used. Minor amendments may be (unanimously) adopted by the European Council, although they still require ratification by national parliaments.

After some eight years of negotiations and ratifications in the run-up to the entry into force of the Lisbon Treaty in 2009, it was widely assumed that there was no appetite to change the Treaties again for a long time. However, two revisions were undertaken in 2010-2011. A short IGC was held (without a Convention) in 2010 adjusting the number of MEPs per member state. The European Council also used the Simplified Revision Procedure in 2011 to amend the treaty to permit the establishment of the permanent European Stability Mechanism to give loans to member states of the Eurozone with debt repayment difficulties.

BOX 4.3   The Lisbon Referenda in Ireland

The first Irish referendum on the Lisbon Treaty was held on 13 June 2008 and resulted in a decisive defeat for the proposition. In a turnout of just over half of the eligible electorate, 53.2 per cent voted 'No' and 46.4 per cent 'Yes'. Only 10 of the country's 43 constituencies voted in favour; opposition to the treaty was countrywide at this stage. Post-referendum opinion surveys highlighted the fact that a majority of women (56 per cent), young people in the 18–24 (65 per cent) and in the 25–39 (59 per cent) age brackets, manual workers (74 per cent) and those not working (56 per cent) had voted 'No'.

The scale of the rejection of the Lisbon Treaty in Ireland was a shock to the Irish government, the main opposition parties and Ireland's partners in the other member states. A sense of crisis in the Union was pervasive, not least because the vote marked the third rejection of a European treaty between 2005–8. Following the Irish 'No', the other member states and the EU spokespersons reiterated the importance of Lisbon to the Union. The then President of the European Council, Nicolas Sarkozy of France, was adamant that the treaty was not dead. Ireland was reminded that Lisbon had been worked on for many years and that it represented the available consensus.

The year following the Irish 'No' was punctuated with a flurry of activity, including research reports on why the Irish voted 'No', a parliamentary committee in Ireland seeking a way forward, and extensive diplomacy between Ireland, European institutions, and other member states. Ireland was given clarification on a number of issues in the treaty, and the principle of one commissioner per member state was re-established (so that Ireland would always appoint a commissioner). In response, the government signalled its willingness to hold a second referendum.

The second referendum was marked by intense mobilization. Support for the Treaty was drawn from the government parties, the two main opposition parties, the key economic interest organizations and several civil society groups. Ireland's Nobel Laureate came out in favour of the 'Yes' campaign and in the words of one of his poems encouraged the 'Yes' campaign 'Move lips, move minds and make new meanings flare'. Among those opposing the treaty were Sinn Féin (the only parliamentary party in the 'No' camp), anti-system parties (such as the Socialist Workers party) and protest movements such as People Before Profit and Libertas. For the duration of the campaign Ireland became a battleground between those forces in favour of integration and against. Campaigners for both sides flocked to Ireland and hit the streets.

Following a hard fought campaign, the Irish voted 'Yes' on 2 October 2009. When asked to think again about its verdict on the Lisbon Treaty the Irish electorate returned a very different result. With a turnout of 59 per cent, two-thirds of voters voted 'Yes' and one-third voted 'No'. This time, only two of the country's 45 electoral constituencies voted 'No'. The Lisbon Treaty was endorsed by a majority of men and women, all age groups and socio-economic classes.

Member States in Action

Member states are not the only players in town (see Chapters 3 and 6), but national governments retain a privileged position in the EU. What emerge as national interests from domestic systems of preference formation remain central to how the EU works. But member states are not unitary actors. Rather, each consists of a myriad of players who project their own preferences in the Brussels arena. National administrations, the wider public service, key interests (notably, business, trades unions, farming organizations, and other societal interests) all seek voice and representation in EU politics. A striking feature of European integration is the extent to which national actors have been drawn out of the domestic arena into the Brussels system of policy-making.

As Chapter 3 highlighted, the national and the European meet in a formal sense in the Council, the EU institution designed to give voice and representation to national preferences. On a midweek day, there are usually around twenty official meeting rooms in use in the Council building (named after the sixteenth-century Belgian philosopher, Justus Lipsius), apart from the month of August when the Brussels system goes on holiday. Formal meetings are supplemented by bilateral meetings on the margins of Council meetings, informal chats over espressos, and by media briefings. Thus the formal system of policy-making is augmented by considerable back-room dealing, arbitrage, and informal politics. In the evenings, national officials (from some member states more than others) frequent the many bars near the Rond Point Schuman, the junction in Brussels where several EU institutions are housed. The evening buses to Zaventem (Brussels airport) are often full of national officials making their way back to their capitals after a long day in Council working groups. Those within earshot can pick up good anecdotal evidence of how the EU actually works when member state officials pick over the details of EU proposals.

All member states have built up a cadre of EU specialists in their diplomatic services and domestic administrations who are the 'boundary managers' between the national and the European. Most are at home in the complex institutional and legal processes of the Union, have well-used copies of the EU treaties, may read *Agence Europe* (a daily bulletin on European affairs) every morning, know their field and the preferences of their negotiating partners. The EU is a system that privileges those with an intimate knowledge of how the Union's policy process works and how business is conducted in the Council, the EP, and the Commission.

National representatives in Brussels seek to exploit their political, academic, sectoral, and personal networks to the full. With more member states, a widening agenda, and advanced communications technology, there has been a discernible increase in horizontal interaction between the member states at all levels—prime-ministerial, ministerial, senior official, and desk officer. Specialists forge and maintain links with their counterparts in other member states on a continuous basis. Deliberations are no longer left primarily to meetings at working-group level in Brussels. Sophisticated networking is part and parcel of the Brussels game. Officials who have long experience of it build up extensive personal contacts and friendships in the system.

In addition to a cadre of Brussels insiders, many government officials in national capitals find that their work also has a European dimension. For most national officials, however, interaction with the EU is sporadic and driven by developments within a particular sector. A company law specialist may have intense interaction with the EU while a new directive is being negotiated, but may then have little involvement until the same directive is up for renegotiation.

The nature of EU membership demands that all member states must commit resources and personnel to the Union's policy process. Servicing Brussels—by committing time and resources to EU negotiations—has become more onerous with new areas of policy being added, such as justice and home affairs or defence. Once a policy field becomes institutionalized in the EU system, the member states have no choice but to service the relevant committees and Councils. An empty seat at the table undermines the credibility of the state and its commitment to the collective endeavour. Besides, the weakest negotiator is always the one who is absent from the negotiations.

Managing EU Business

All member states engage in internal negotiations and coordination, above all between different national ministries and ministers, in determining what their national position will be in any EU negotiation. The coordination system in most member states is organized hierarchically. National ministers and/or the head of government will usually act as the arbiter of last resort.

In addition, all member states have either a Minister or a State Secretary of European Affairs. The Ministry of Foreign Affairs plays an important role in all member states, and most central EU coordination takes place here. However, there are a number of member states, such as Finland, where the Prime Minister's Office takes the leading role. With the increasing prominence of EU policy in national administrations, more EU business is generally shifting to the offices of heads of government.

As discussed in Chapter 3, each member state also has a Permanent Representation in Brussels, a kind of EU embassy. In most cases it is the most important and biggest foreign representation the country maintains anywhere in the world. It is, for example, usually much bigger than an embassy in Washington DC or Moscow or a representation to the United Nations. Although the official role of the Permanent Representation of each member state varies, they all participate actively in several stages of the policy-making process. In certain member states they are the key player in the whole process.

Explaining Member States' Engagement

We have looked at the factors that determine the engagement of different states in the EU and at the member states in action. What additional purchase do we get from theory in analysing member states in the Union? The relationship between the EU and its member states has been one of the most enduring puzzles in the literature on European integration. From the outset, the impact of EU membership on statehood and on individual states has been hotly contested. At issue is whether the EU strengthens, transcends, or transforms its member states. Is the Union simply a creature of its member states? Are they still the masters of the Treaties? Or has the EU irrevocably transformed European nation-states? The relationship between the EU and its member states is a live political issue and not simply a point of contention amongst scholars. The theories and approaches introduced in Chapter 1 provide different lenses with which to analyse the member states in the Union.

Liberal intergovernmentalism provides a theoretical framework that enables us to trace the formation of domestic preferences in the member states and then to see how they are bargained in Brussels. It identifies the domestic sources of the underlying preferences and the subsequent process of interstate bargaining. The approach rightly concludes that the EU is an 'institution so firmly grounded in the core interests of national governments that it occupies a permanent position at the heart of the European political landscape' (Moravcsik 1998: 501). This approach is less helpful in tracing the impact of the EU on national preference formation or the cumulative impact of EU membership on its member states. Its focus on one-off bargains provides a snapshot of the Union at any one time rather than a film or 'moving picture' of how membership may generate deep processes of change (see Pierson 1996).

Contemporary theorists who view the EU through the lenses of multilevel (Hooghe and Marks 2003) or supranational governance (Sandholtz and Stone Sweet 1998) emphasize how the national and the European levels of governance have become fundamentally intertwined. Similarly, Bartolini (2005) links the dynamics of European integration to state formation, concluding that the EU represents the latest stage in the emergence and adaption of the European nation-state and state system. These approaches point to the influence of the supranational institutions—notably the Commission, Court, and Parliament—on the EU and its member states. The EU may be grounded in the core interests of the national governments, but the definition of core interest is influenced by membership of the EU and its continuous effects at the national level. Put another way, the EU has evolved into a political system in its own right that is more than the sum of its member states.

The new institutionalism offers at least two crucial insights concerning member states in the EU political system. First, its emphasis on change over time captures the give-and-take nature of EU negotiations and the manner in which norms and procedures are built up over time. Secondly, its concern with path dependency highlights the substantial resources that member states have invested in the Union (Meunier and McNamara 2007). The costs of exit are very high, so high that no state would seriously contemplate it. At best, member states have the choice of opting out of various policy regimes. Even then there are costs associated with having no seat at the table.

A policy network approach captures the fragmented and sectorized nature of the EU. It highlights the fact that the degree and nature of national adaptation differs from one policy area to another, and according to the different mix of players involved. Some policy fields, and the networks that preside over them, have been intensely Europeanized (agriculture) while others have not (transport). This approach helps us to gauge such variation and the varying involvement of different layers of government and public and private actors in different EU policy fields.

Finally, social constructivism helps us to analyse how national participants are socialized into the 'rules of the game' which characterize intergovernmental bargaining (Bulmer and Lequesne 2005a: 15). For constructivists, national interests are not predetermined but are shaped (or 'constructed') by interaction with EU actors and institutions (see Checkel 1999). In fact, the very identities of individual players in EU negotiations are viewed largely as being constructed within those negotiations,

---

BOX 4.4   How it really works: decision gridlock?

Taking decisions in a big group is never easy. When the EU almost doubled its membership from 2004–7 many feared that the EU would face permanent gridlock. How did things actually turn out? Studies show that from 2004–6, the amount of legislation decreased compared to the rate prior to the 'big bang' enlargement (Hagemann and DeClerck-Sachsse 2007; Heisenberg 2007). Yet at the same time the EU was able to hammer out compromises at approximately the same pace as before. And the average time from a Commission initiative to an approved legal act remained approximately the same for an EU of 27 as it was for an EU of 15 (Settembri 2007).

Enlargement has, however, changed the political dynamic of the EU institutions and the role of member states within them. All of the main institutions—the Commission, the European Council, the European Parliament, and the Council of Ministers—are less cosy than before. There are simply more players around the table. The dynamic of working groups, committees, and the actual Council meetings has also changed. In Council meetings member states no longer have the ability to express their view on all issues all the time. It would simply take too long. Member states raise issues when they have a serious problem.

Every enlargement is preceded by a debate about the EU's capacity to integrate or 'absorb' new member states. The debate is focused on whether the EU's institutions, budget, and policies can accommodate a larger membership. Those who want to slow down enlargement often argue that the EU is not ready to take on board new member states before it has revised its own institutions and working methods. Previous enlargements, however, seem to indicate that while the EU is never fully prepared to enlarge, it manages just the same.

and not fixed, leading constructivists to question whether national identities and interests are gradually being replaced by European ones.

Conclusion

It is impossible to understand how the EU works without understanding the member states and their central role in the establishment and operation of the EU. In turn, the EU has altered the political, constitutional, economic, and policy framework within which the member state governments govern. Each enlargement is different and each enlargement has changed the dynamics of the EU. Many were afraid that the EU's decision-making would grind to a halt with the latest enlargement. Generally, it seems that these fears were unfounded. As a matter of fact the pace of EU decision-making was not noticeably slower than before, despite (or perhaps because of?) its expansion to 27 member states (see Box 4.4), although it was widely agreed that it needed new rules to streamline decision-making to avoid paralysis in the longer term.

All EU member states, along with some states who aspire to join the EU, are part of a transnational political process that binds them together in a collective endeavour. Their individual engagement with the Union varies enormously depending on their history, location, size, relative wealth, domestic political systems, and attitudes towards the future of the Union. Yet, all member states are actively engaged on a day-to-day basis in Brussels. National ministers, civil servants, and interest groups participate in the Commission's advisory groups, the Council working groups, and meetings of the European Council. All member states engage in bilateral relations with each of their partners, with the Commission's services, and the Council Presidency in their efforts to influence the outcome of EU policy-making. In national capitals, officials and ministers must do their homework in preparation for the continuous cycle of EU meetings. Brussels is thus part and parcel of contemporary governance in Europe. The member states are essential to how the EU works, but in turn being a member of the EU makes a state something rather different from an 'ordinary' nation-state.

DISCUSSION QUESTIONS

1. What are the most important features determining an EU member state's attitudes towards integration?

2. Which is more powerful: the impact of the EU on its member states, or the impact of the member states on the EU?

3. How useful is theory in explaining the role of the member states in the EU?

4. How different are EU member states from 'ordinary' nation-states?

 FURTHER READING

The literature on the member states of the Union is very diffuse. There are a large number of country studies (see, for example, Closa and Heywood 2004, and Papadimitriou and Phinnemore 2007, Laffan and O'Mahony 2008), a more limited number of comparative works (including Wessels *et al.* 2003, Bulmer and Lequesne 2005b, and Henderson 2007), and a very extensive body of policy-related work that throws some light on the EU and its member states (see, for example, Falkner 2000 and Baun *et al.* 2006). For discussions of the relationship between statehood and integration, see Hoffmann (1966), Milward (1992), Moravcsik (1998) and Bartolini (2005). On national management of EU business and the impact of the EU on national institutions, see Rometsch and Wessels (1996) and Kassim *et al.* (2001).

Bartolini S., (2005), *Restructuring Europe: Centre Formation, System Building and Political Structuring between the Nation State and the European Union* (Oxford and New York: Oxford University Press).

Baun, M., Dürr, J., Marek, D., and Šaradín, P. (2006), 'The Europeanization of Czech Politics', *Journal of Common Market Studies*, 44/2: 249–80.

Bulmer, S. and Lequesne, C. (2005a), 'The EU and its Member States: An Overview', in S. Bulmer and C. Lequesne (eds.), *The Member States of the European Union* (Oxford and New York: Oxford University Press.

____ (2005b), *The Member States of the European Union* (Oxford and New York: Oxford University Press).

Closa, C. and Heywood, P. S. (2004), *Spain and the European Union* (Basingstoke and New York: Palgrave).

Falkner, G. (2000), 'How Pervasive are Euro-Politics? Effects of EU Membership on a New Member State', *Journal of Common Market Studies* 38/2: 223–50.

Goetz, K. H. (2005), 'The New Member States and the EU: Responding to Europe', in S. Bulmer and C. Lequesne (eds.) (2005), *The Member States of the European Union* (Oxford and New York: Oxford University Press).

Henderson, K. (2007), *The European Union's New Democracies* (London and New York: Routledge).

Hoffmann, S. (1966), 'Obstinate or Obsolete: The Fate of the Nation-state and the Case of Western Europe', *Daedalus* 95/3: 862–915 (reprinted in S. Hoffmann (1995), *The*

European Sisyphus: Essays on Europe 1964–1994 (Boulder CO and Oxford: West-view Press)).

Kassim, H., Peters, B. G., and Wright, V. (eds.) (2001), *The National Co-ordination of EU Policy: The European Level* (Oxford and New York: Oxford University Press).

Laffan B. and O'Mahony J. (2008), *Ireland in the European Union* (Basingstoke and New York : Palgrave).

Milward, A. (1992), *The European Rescue of the Nation-state* (London and Berkeley: Routledge and University of California Press).

Moravcsik, A. (1998), *The Choice for Europe: Social Purpose and State Power from Messina to Maastricht* (Ithaca NY and London: Cornell University Press and UCL Press).

Naurin, D. and Wallace, H. (2008), *Unveiling the Council of the European Union: Games Governments Play in Brussels,* (Basingstoke and New York : Palgrave).

Papadimitriou, D. and Phinnemore, D. (2007), *Romania and the European Union* (London and New York: Routledge).

Rometsch, D., and Wessels, W. (1996), *The European Union and Member States: Towards Institutional Fusion?* (Manchester and New York: Manchester University Press).

Wessels, W., Maurer, A., and Mittag, J. (eds.) (2003), *Fifteen Into One? The European Union and its Member States* (Manchester and New York: Manchester University Press).

WEB LINKS

The Institute for European Politics' (Berlin) website features an enormously useful 'EU 25–27 watch' which offers a round-up of current thinking on EU policies and issues in all the member states: **http://www.iep-berlin.de/index.php?id = publikationen&L = 1**.

The best place to search for websites of the member and candidate states' national administrations is **http://www.europa.eu/abc/european_countries/index_en.htm**.

Other useful links can also be found on the homepage of the European Commission **http://ec.europa.eu/index_en.htm**.

Visit the Online Resource Centre that accompanies this book for additional material: **www.oxfordtextbooks.co.uk/orc/bomberg3e/**

PART III

Policies and Policy-making

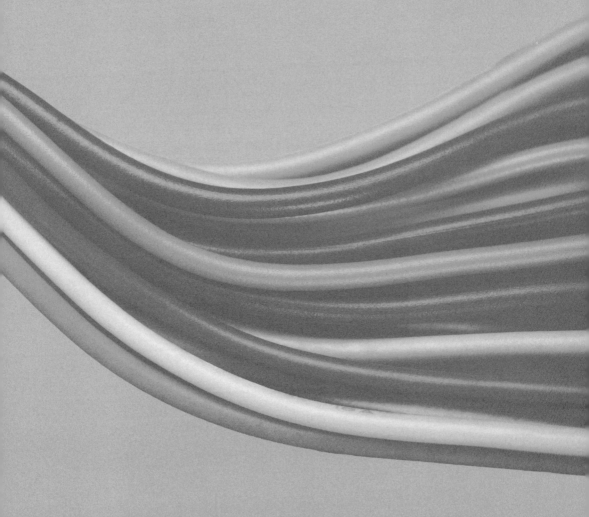

CHAPTER 5

Key Policies

Alberta Sbragia and Francesco Stolfi

▌ Summary

European Union policies affect the lives of millions of people in Europe and beyond. The variety of actors involved, the wide policy remit of the EU, and constant policy change make this area of study challenging but fascinating. This chapter describes some of the most important areas of policy-making in the European Union, focusing primarily on economic and related policies. We begin by explaining how EU policy-making differs from national policy-making, and then describe the most important policies aimed at building the internal market and limiting its potentially negative impact on individuals, society, and the environment. We highlight the varied and contested nature of EU policies and also how they matter.

Introduction

The European Union sets policies in so many areas that it is difficult to think about national policy-making in Europe in isolation from Brussels. While the euro—the common currency used by seventeen of the EU's 27 member states—is perhaps the most visible manifestation of European integration, a diverse set of public policies (see Box 5.1) affecting the everyday lives of Europeans are shaped by the decisions taken at the EU level. Agriculture, environmental and consumer protection, international trade, and the movement of goods, services, labour, and capital across borders are all regulated by decisions taken in Brussels.

Yet the role of the EU should not be overestimated; it is not a 'superstate' exercising control over all areas of policy. It should be thought of as a 'selective' policy-maker whose power varies significantly across different areas. Most of the policies for which it is responsible are related to markets (see Box 5.1): some build and extend markets, some protect consumers or producers from market forces, some try to cushion the impact of market forces. Market integration is central to the process of European integration (Majone 2009: 129).

The differentiated role of the EU across policy areas is not unusual if we compare it to federal systems where power is shared between the national and subnational level (see Box 5.1). In such systems the national level may not be allowed to legislate in certain areas, leaving policy discretion to the constituent units. Canadians, Australians, and Americans, for example, take for granted that many decisions affecting their lives will be taken at the state or provincial levels rather than nationally. In the European Union, citizens are becoming accustomed to such a system of differentiated policy responsibilities. Just as Washington lets each state decide whether to allow the death penalty within its borders, the European Union does not legislate on Ireland's abortion policy, Sweden's alcohol control policy, or Spain's policy on bullfighting. Citizens of a federal polity accept that at least some unequal treatment comes with living in a federation. In a similar vein, it matters a great deal—and will continue to matter—where one lives within the European Union.

However, the impact of the European Union is such that the member states of the EU are, in many ways, much more alike now than they were 50 years ago. In certain policy areas, especially those related to economic activity, member state governments as well as private firms either have had to engage in new activities (such as environmental protection) or alternatively change their traditional practices. And of course the introduction of the euro in seventeen member states has not only changed the landscape of monetary affairs but also made European citizen constantly aware of that changed landscape in their everyday life.

The world of money and business has been changed by EU policies in very fundamental ways, but so have many related areas. Environmental protection, gender equality in the workplace, and occupational health and safety have all moved the EU

BOX 5.1   **Key concepts and terms**

Benchmarking is the use of comparisons with other states or organizations (for instance on issues such as pension reform and employment practices) with the aim of improving performance by learning from the experience of others.

A **directive** is the most common form of EU legislation. It stipulates the ends to be achieved (say, limiting the emissions of a harmful pollutant) but allows each member state to choose the form and method for achieving that end. It can be contrasted with a regulation which is directly binding in its entirety on all member states.

The **Eurozone** refers to the countries that are part of the Economic and Monetary Union (EMU). EMU was launched in 1999 (with notes and coins entering into circulation in 2002) with eleven members (Austria, Belgium, France, Germany, Finland, Ireland, Italy, Luxembourg, the Netherlands, Portugal, and Spain). Greece joined in 2001, Slovenia in 2007, Cyprus and Malta in 2008, Slovakia in 2009 and Estonia in 2011. All remaining new EU member states are expected to join once their economies are ready. The UK, Sweden, and Denmark have thus far chosen not to join.

Federalism is a constitutional arrangement in which the power to make decisions and execute policy is divided between national and subnational levels of government. In a federal system both national and subnational units wield a measure of final authority in their own spheres and neither level can alter or abolish the other.

A **market** is a system of exchange bringing together buyers and sellers of goods and services. In most markets, money is used as means of exchange. Markets are regulated by price fluctuations that reflect the balance of supply and demand. To function properly, markets require the existence of law, regulation, and property rights. Virtually all markets are subject to some sort of regulation.

Non-tariff barriers refer to regulations, such as national standards or requirements (for instance health requirements) that increase the cost of imports and thus have the equivalent effect of tariffs. Often these regulations do not only serve bona fide social purposes (such as the protection of the environment or consumer health), but also protect national producers from foreign competition.

Public policy is a course of action (decisions, actions, rules, laws, and so on) or inaction taken by government in regard to some public problem or issue.

---

towards a system in which many of the negative consequences of market activity are addressed in Brussels rather than in national capitals. This expansion in the EU's remit is the result not of some well-orchestrated plan but rather the product of constant problem solving, bargaining, and experimentation which mark the EU as a unique policy-making system (see Chapter 1). The 2010-11 crisis that engulfed the euro and fiscal governance is a case of EU problem-solving under pressure: decisions made by European institutions and member states will probably have lasting consequences on the shape and nature of European integration.

This chapter introduces some of the key policies of the European Union. Since economic integration is at the core of what the EU does, we focus on economic and related policies (security and related polices are discussed in Chapters 9 and 10). The inclusiveness of these economic policies—how open they are to a large set of actors—varies, but a constant across policies is the preference for consensus rather than conflict. Furthermore, the chapter shows how the remit of the European Union has dramatically increased over time, but also how its capacity has remained limited in many policy areas when compared to that of a 'traditional' nation-state.

Key Features of EU Policies

Differences between national and EU policies

Policies in the European Union differ in some important ways from policies decided at the national level by member state governments. At their most basic level, policies are different because the European Union and its member states are structured and financed very differently. These varying financial structures lead to three wider differences between national and EU policies:

- with a few exceptions, EU policies typically involve the spending of very little money, whereas national policy typically involves spending a good deal of it;
- the distance between those who formulate policy and those who actually execute it in practice is far greater in the EU than it is in most of the national systems which make up the Union;
- the EU is active in a narrower range of policies than are national governments.

Thus, knowing about national policies is not a particularly good template for understanding EU policies. Let us examine each of these differences in more detail.

Money

One way to understand the European Union's relative poverty in the area of public finance is to compare its budget with the budgets of central governments in its member states. As Table 5.1 illustrates, even though the central governments of France, Germany, and the United Kingdom are each responsible for only a fraction of the EU's total population, each of those central governments spends a great deal more than does Brussels. Another useful comparison is with the federal government's budget in the United States. The European Union has a larger population than does

TABLE 5.1	Compared to what? EU and national budgets compared			
EU Budget (2010)	Germany Federal Budget (2009)	France Central Budget (2009)	UK Central Budget (2009)	US Federal Budget (2008)
€ 127 billion	€ 1145 billion	€ 1068 billion	€ 809 billion	€ 4006 billion*

*US dollars converted to euros at average exchange rate for 2009.
For the EU, see Commission 2010a. For the national budgets, OECD 2010.

the United States, but the budget of the US federal government is roughly thirty times as large as the EU's budget.

The Union therefore relies on the power of law (as embodied in legislation and court decisions) rather than money to carry out most of its policies. The lack of money shapes what the content of policies can be. The Union can afford only a small number of policy areas that cost a great deal, whereas national systems typically have a large number of expensive policy areas, including those which fall under the rubric of the welfare state. The Union, given its current fiscal structure, could not, for example, finance health care for EU citizens or provide old age pensions or finance systems of public education. Overwhelmingly, the EU regulates economic activity; that is, it subjects it to rules and standards. However, and in spite of the relatively small size of the EU budget, the approval of the revenues and expenditures of the European Union can become contentious (see Box 5.2).

Legislation versus execution

In most national systems, the national government makes policy decisions and then has numerous ways of ensuring that those policies are actually executed 'on the ground'. Although that link is far from perfect in actual practice, it is far tighter in most national systems than it is when EU policy is involved. Policy decided in Brussels faces several unique hurdles before it can be successfully executed on the ground.

The first step is known as 'transposition.' That is, framework laws (known as directives, see Box 5.1) adopted by the Council of Ministers need to be 'transposed' into national legal codes before they can be executed by the member state's public administration or formally shape the behaviour of private actors in significant ways. The Commission monitors that transposition is timely and correctly implements the European legislation. Member states that fail on these accounts can be taken before the European Court of Justice. Although transposition has become increasingly timely, differences still exist among the member states. In 2008, for instance, the best performing member states (Cyprus, Estonia, Luxembourg, and Slovenia) accounted for

BOX 5.2	How it really works: budget bargaining

Unlike national governments, the EU cannot run a deficit; its revenues limit the amounts it can spend. Various economic formulae are used to help determine the EU's overall budget *revenue* (derived primarily from custom duties, value added tax, and national contributions) and budget *allocation* (who gets what?). As in the past, Germany remains the 'paymaster of Europe'. It is by far the largest net contributor to the European coffers, followed by France and Italy. On the expenditure side, two documents are important: the yearly budget, which sets the overall expenditure level and how it is to be divided between the various policy areas, and the multiyear 'financial perspective' which sets broad spending patterns for seven-year periods.

Formulae aside, the EU's budget is a result of politics as much as mathematics. Reaching a decision over the financial perspective can be a highly contentious and a decidedly intergovernmental affair. Although the absolute amounts involved are not large—the overall EU budget equals only around 1 per cent of the member states' GDP—no government wants to appear weak in the eyes of its voters during the negotiations with other member states. Moreover, and especially in the case of the CAP, the amounts involved can mean a great deal to strong domestic constituencies.

It is thus not surprising that the intergovernmental negotiations for the last financial perspective in December 2005 almost collapsed. UK Prime Minister Tony Blair tried to hold on to the rebate that Margaret Thatcher had negotiated for Britain's contributions in the 1980s, while French President Jacques Chirac defended the CAP, some of whose main beneficiaries are French farmers. A late-night agreement was finally reached only when Blair agreed to give up part of the rebate, and Chirac accepted the CAP would begin to be reviewed in 2008. The Commission wants the next financial perspective (2014–2021) to shift more resources towards job creation, climate change policy, and foreign affairs at the expense of cohesion and agricultural policies. Since the latter constitute nearly 80 per cent of the EU budget, current beneficiaries will strongly oppose it during the negotiations over the financial perspective.

8.5 per cent of the new infringement cases started by the Commission, while the worst performing states (Bulgaria, Italy, Romania, and Spain) accounted for 23 per cent of the total (Commission 2009b). Interestingly, at least in this area the division between older and newer member states does not seem to apply. Sometimes, moreover, the implementation of EU law might be overzealous rather than too lax (see Box 5.4).

In sum, Union policies do not become 'policy' at the national level uniformly across the EU's member states. For example, a directive transposed in Finland shortly after its adoption in Brussels may not be transposed in France or Greece until several years after the Finnish action. These differences suggest that Brussels formulates and adopts policy but its actual impact will be shaped by national systems of governance. National governments play a central role in the EU's policy process because they hold a monopoly of power in the actual execution of most policies adopted in Brussels. The EU has minimal administrative presence within the member states. The Commission, for example, has almost no capacity to monitor the execution of EU law. It must instead rely on complaints from citizens, firms, and non-governmental organizations. Even then, it can only try to persuade national governments to improve execution.

The difficulties surrounding execution and monitoring mean that policies that affect a dispersed set of actors are less likely to be executed uniformly than are those policies that affect a few. For example, environmental policy, which attempts to shape the behaviour of huge numbers of both public and private actors, is executed with a tremendous degree of variability across the Union. In general, the transposition of EU directives into national law is often shaped in important ways by individual national ministers and administrative actors (Steunenberg and Rhinard 2010). By contrast, the Commission's decisions about mergers and acquisitions are implemented uniformly. The number of firms affected by any single Commission decision is very small and a non-complying firm would be very visible.

Jurisdiction

A third difference between EU and national policies concerns policy competencies (see Box 5.3). While certainly broader than other international organizations, the EU's policy remit is narrower than that of national governments. Health care, urban regeneration, family assistance, old age pensions, public health, child care, poverty alleviation, abortion, prison administration, and education, for example, are not matters for EU legislation because the Union has not been given competence in those areas by the member states. Other areas remain under national control because of the decision-making rules that apply to them. In the areas of taxation and energy, for example, the decision-making rule is one of unanimity (although pressures for a common EU energy policy are increasingly powerful). Since the member states have been unable to agree on any single policy, those policy areas effectively remain under national control.

Recently, various 'soft' measures such as benchmarking (see Box 5.1) or the open method of coordination (OMC) of national policies have been used to encourage national governments to address issues such as their pension burden. But in general the welfare state and the direct provision of social services is primarily under national control, with the notable exception of welfare related to agriculture (see below).

Most policies that have a moral or cultural dimension also remain under national control. The Irish do not permit abortion, for example, and the EU does not have the power to tell the Irish either to change their abortion law or to keep it. The Swedish and Finnish alcohol control system has been under strain due to the ability of individual revellers to bring liquor in from other EU countries. But alcohol control policy in both Sweden and Finland is under national control.

However, and in spite of the circumscribed jurisdiction of the European Union, it is important to note that the EU can and often does have important *indirect* effects beyond the immediate scope of its competencies. For instance, energy policy (energy taxation especially) is still under national control because EU policy-making requires unanimity in that area. However, the energy market is being liberalized as

---

BOX 5.3   **The policy competencies of the EU**

Policy competence refers to the legal authority to act in particular policy areas. The Lisbon Treaty divided policy areas into three categories depending on the degree of EU competence: (1) exclusive competence; (2) shared competence between the EU and the member states: and (3) competence to support, coordinate, and supplement the actions of the member states.

1. The EU has *exclusive* competence in few, but important, policy areas: external trade in goods and services, monetary policy (for the Eurozone), customs, and conservation of marine resources.

2. *Shared* competences are most plentiful. They include agriculture and fisheries, justice, environmental policy, consumer protection, mergers and acquisitions, research, development aid, transport policy, energy, visas, asylum, and immigration.

3. Finally, in some policy areas the member states remain the main players, even if the EU is involved in some general coordination or is engaged in a few specific projects. Education, culture, sport, employment, public health, and research policies fall into this domain.

The Lisbon Treaty increased the degree of EU competence, most notably in trade : the EU now has exclusive competence on foreign direct investment and trade in goods and services, including intellectual property rights. The EU's competence also widened in the areas of energy and public health, and, to lesser degree, civil protection, tourism, and administrative cooperation

In some policy areas it is difficult to place policies in one of these categories because the line between shared competencies and member state competencies is blurred.

In foreign and security policies, for instance, it is often unclear how much weight the EU has because the member states in the final analysis must allocate the resources necessary to execute the EU's foreign and security policy.

---

the EU requires national governments to allow (selected) consumers a choice of electricity suppliers. Similarly the commitment of the EU to meet the Kyoto Protocol requirements to combat global climate change stimulated the creation of a European market where industrial producers can trade carbon emissions permits, with the purpose of limiting overall emissions.

To take another example, education at both pre-university and university level are under national control, but the EU has been a prime mover in encouraging university students to study in another member state. These Commission programmes on student mobility—primarily the ERASMUS programme—have led to major changes in universities' administrative structures and have encouraged universities to work toward much greater cross-national standardization in degree programmes (such as the length of time required to receive a first degree). The lack of formal competence at the EU level does not mean that Brussels lacks influence in shaping the terms of debate within a policy area. The programmes that Brussels adopts, while not legally binding in the way that legislation is, are very important in providing incentives to national and subnational governments to carry out certain activities.

The primacy of economic integration

The EU's unique history and development has privileged some areas as important for the Union while leaving others aside. As Chapter 2 explained, in the 1950s European states chose to defend each other within a transatlantic rather than a European organization (NATO includes Canada and the US). Policy areas concerning defense as well as foreign policy and security, therefore, were not central to the integration process and have become subject to it only recently.

By contrast, economic cooperation was viewed as a politically acceptable way of increasing integration while laying the groundwork for political cooperation at a future date. Consequently, policy areas related to economics have been privileged from the very beginning. The 1957 Treaty of Rome, by calling for a customs union and a common market (now referred to as a single or internal market), steered the process of European integration toward the liberalization of cross-border trade, a unitary trade policy vis-à-vis non-members, and the free movement of capital, goods, services, and labour. The centrality of that effort to European integration symbolizes the importance that economic integration has within the European Union.

'Market-building' Policies

The focus on liberalization and creation of a **single market** highlights the EU's concern with 'market building' and what is sometimes termed 'negative integration'. Building markets involves both *removing* barriers to trade and carrying out regulatory reform. So negative integration involves *eliminating* things, including various tariff and non-tariff barriers (see Box 5.1) to trade. It also includes reform of economic regulations that may stifle trade, and ensuring that competition among firms is encouraged. The goal is to facilitate cross-border economic transactions with the expectation that the resulting greater efficiency will lead to higher levels of prosperity for the citizens of Europe. This same aim is pursued globally within the World Trade Organization (WTO).

The political economy of the member states has been profoundly affected by the privileging of economic policies at the EU level (Sbragia 2001). In this arena, policies adopted in Brussels usually 'pre-empt' national policies and the EU is said to have 'exclusive competence'. Monetary policy falls under this category, although it only applies to the members of the Eurozone (see Box 5.1).

In general, the kind of 'negative integration' that characterizes the EU is far more penetrating than that found at the global (World Trade Organization) level or in other regional arrangements such as the North American Free Trade Agreement (NAFTA). The EU's ambitions in market building are serious and their scope very wide (Egan 2010). The core foundation of the single market involves the 'four freedoms'—freedom in the movement of capital, goods, services, and people. However, a single market such as that envisaged by the founders of the Community does not occur simply by removing obstacles to trade. A whole host of interventions must be put into place to ensure that the hoped-for market will operate smoothly and efficiently. In the last decade enlargement has introduced new competition dynamics as firms from the new member states competed with old member state firms on the latter's domestic market (Lindstrom 2010).

The construction of the European market has led to such widespread regulation from Brussels that Giandomenico Majone (1999) has termed the EU a 'regulatory state'. Whereas a welfare state engages in redistribution and spends a great deal of money in providing social welfare (such as social security), a regulatory state exercises its influence primarily by passing legislation that regulates the behaviour of actors in the economy. The development of a far-reaching regulatory regime in Brussels also has led to frequent complaints from those affected by such regulation—who typically blame 'Eurocrats' even when the blame should be placed elsewhere (see Booker 1996; Box 5.4).

BOX 5.4	How it really works: 'goldplating' and EU policy

Sometimes the member states implement EU legislation in a far more stringent manner than was ever intended. In the UK the sometimes overzealous interpretation of EU legislation on the part of the British bureaucracy has attracted much popular attention, even receiving its own moniker: 'goldplating'. The extent to which seemingly anodyne EU directives can be transformed into nightmare regulations is illustrated below with some examples from the UK.

CIVIL SERVANTS WORKING OVERTIME

One often-cited illustration of British civil servants 'over-defining' EU directives is found in amendments to the Working Time Directive (2003/88/EC). Transposition of that directive into Swedish law took just two sheets of paper; for England and Wales, the same piece of legislation was published in a booklet with more than 60 pages of often rigidly defined rules and regulations (see *Financial Times*, 3/4 January 2004: 3).

'PULL THE OTHER ONE'

In December 2010 the British *Daily Mail* derided as 'EU inspired diktat' the UK Pyrotechnics Articles (Safety) Regulations, which threatens retailers with six months in jail or a £5,000 fine if they sell Christmas crackers—a dinner party favour that 'pops'—to under-sixteens (*The Daily Mail*, 9 December 2010). In fact, the Act was a result of UK civil servants goldplating an EU directive that limited the sale of fireworks to those over 12 years of age. The raising of age from 12 to 16, and the interpretation of Christmas crackers as 'class 1 fireworks' was a UK, not EU, invention.

Competition policy

One of the most important market-building powers given to the EU—the Commission specifically—is that of competition policy. The Commission operates as an independent institution in this policy area, and the Council of Ministers is not usually involved in these policy decisions. In essence, competition policy—known as anti-trust policy in the United States—is about encouraging competition among firms and battling monopolistic or oligopolistic practices or those that privilege national producers over those in other EU member states. The requirements can be tough for any member state, but competition policy poses particular challenges for the new member states from Central and Eastern Europe. Moving from economies that were largely under public control to ones in which the market is dominant has been difficult, and the rigour of the EU's competition policy has made that transition in some respects even more onerous.

The Commission has the authority to rule on many mergers and acquisitions, fight cartels, and rule on the appropriateness of many forms of state aid given by national or regional authorities to firms. In this policy area, the Commission is an international actor as well as an EU actor. For example given the level of foreign direct investment in Europe by American firms, the Commission has the power to sanction the strategies of American firms with extensive operations in Europe even if they have been approved by American anti-trust authorities. Just to mention a couple of high-profile cases, the Commission vetoed the proposed merger between General Electric and Honeywell, fined Microsoft a total of 780 million euros for anti-competitive behaviour in 2006, and in November 2010 initiated a formal investigation into Google's method of ranking websites.

Trade associations and firms as well as member state authorities and ministers (and at times prime ministers and presidents) lobby, especially informally, vis-à-vis specific competition cases. However, the Commission needs to engage in far less negotiation than is required in other policy domains and has turned a deaf ear to lobbying by very important national politicians. In this area, the Directorate-General for Competition and the Commissioner for Competition are the central actors.

Commercial (trade) policy

The key goal of the Treaty of Rome was to create a common market across national borders. The objective required liberalizing many national markets (that is, allowing imports to compete with domestically-produced goods) which had been heavily protected for many decades. Over time, the national economies of the member states have become far more interdependent. In 2009 trade within the EU accounted for 66 per cent of the overall exports of the member states and 64 per cent of their imports (IMF 2010). However, trade with countries outside the EU is still very important for many member states.

The application of a single external tariff (which is applied to non-EU producers) in the late 1960s led to the decision that the European Economic Community (as the EU was then known) would need to speak 'with one voice' in negotiations involving international trade policy. The Treaty of Rome gave the EEC competence in international trade negotiations involving trade in goods, and that power was considerably strengthened by the Lisbon Treaty. The Commission has traditionally acted as the sole negotiator, and Lisbon allows the Commission to negotiate trade in goods, services, intellectual property rights, and foreign direct investment (negotiations in the latter area seek to maximize access for European investors in trading partners' markets). However, the competence to decide the EU's position in international trade negotiations was given to 'the member states operating through the European institutions', not to the Commission acting on its own. Therefore, although the Commission is the negotiator, the member states play a key role in shaping the negotiating mandate which the Commission pursues. In practice, the relationship between the member states (or at least selected ones) and the Commission is often conflictual as both argue for maximum institutional power in setting the terms of the negotiations.

Economic and Monetary Union (EMU)

At the 1992 Maastricht summit EU member states decided to create an Economic and Monetary Union, with a common currency and centralized responsibility for monetary policy. For the first time since the Roman Empire, Western Europe was to have a common currency. It was thought that a common currency would help keep a unified Germany tied to the project of European integration, increase economic efficiency in the EU and thereby raise the standard of living, and develop a sense of 'European' identity. A common currency requires a single central bank in charge of monetary policy, and the European Central Bank was created to run monetary policy with the goal of price stability (anti-inflation) as its top priority.

Part of the bargain that underpinned the decision to move to a single currency by 1999 was an agreement that states wishing to adopt the euro must meet certain requirements (informally known as the Maastricht criteria) with regard to levels of inflation and interest rates, as well as the size of the government deficit and debt. The decision was taken by the heads of state and government, but the preparation that underpinned it was carried out by finance ministers and a relatively small group of national civil servants and central bank staff. Private businesses such as banks were not intimately involved, and the policy process was relatively closed.

The decision to move towards a single currency had profound implications for the member states, as the budget deficit requirements forced the restructuring of public finances in several states adopting the Euro (the so-called Eurozone countries). In the Italian case, the restructuring was so profound that the country's ministerial organization and budgetary process were radically transformed in part to meet the requirements of participation in the euro project (Stolfi 2008). In some cases, the desire to join the EMU was so strong that countries—Greece for instance—resorted to questionable budgetary tricks in order to qualify. The original members of the EMU were Germany, France, Luxembourg, Belgium, the Netherlands, Spain, Portugal, Austria, Italy, Finland, and Ireland. Greece joined in 2001, while the United Kingdom, Sweden, and Denmark have chosen to remain outside the EMU at least for the time being. All new member states of the EU are expected eventually to join the EMU. However, so far only a minority has done so: Slovenia (2007), Cyprus (2008), Malta (2008), Slovakia (2009), and Estonia (2011). Lithuania applied to join in 2006, but its application was rejected by the ECB.

Countries using the euro no longer have an independent monetary policy. The European Central Bank (ECB), headquartered in Frankfurt, makes decisions about monetary policy that apply to all member states using the euro. National governments or central banks therefore can no longer control the level of interest rates, a control which previously gave them some leverage over the direction of the economy. The ECB is mandated to privilege price stability and thereby avoid inflation, but it has been criticized by some (especially the French government) who would rather it adopt lower interest rates so as to stimulate the Eurozone economy and thereby (hopefully) create more employment. The Bank, however, has argued that job creation requires the adoption of a more flexible labour market and more liberalization of markets in general. It has not tailored its interest rate policy to the wishes of the member states, nor to societal actors. The ECB has become an important, and very independent, actor in the field of economic policy-making although the 2010–11 Eurozone crisis led to a closer relationship with national governments.

Even after the creation of the EMU, the stringent fiscal requirements remained. EMU members agreed to respect a Stability and Growth Pact (SGP), which included financial penalties for the countries that violated it. Following the adoption of the euro in 1999 (bank notes and coins became available on 1 January 2002), several member states found their macroeconomic policies under scrutiny as they struggled to meet the budget deficit requirements of EMU membership. By 2003 four countries, including the three largest economies of the Eurozone (Germany, France, and Italy), were in breach of the fiscal requirements set by the Pact. Reasons for the breach varied, and some were more serious than others. But a subsequent decision to relax and then modify the Pact raised serious questions about its effectiveness in the face of member state intransigence.

Economic emergencies continued to test the EU. During the 2010 financial crisis, it became clear that Greece required an aid package large enough to reassure the markets while not antagonizing the German taxpayers (who would carry much of the burden for any bail-out). Further, Greeks themselves were asked to accept painful financial measures. In an attempt to offset future crises the European Council agreed in May 2010 to a stabilization fund worth €500 billion to be loaned to countries in a financial emergency. Furthermore, the ECB announced that it would in future intervene in the Eurozone bond market when it was not functioning properly.

(The decision effectively reversed the ECB policy of not financing the debt of Euro-zone governments.) Finally, in December 2010 the European Council agreed to a change in the Lisbon Treaty that created a permanent European Stability Mechanism, which is expected to enter into force in January 2013. EMU continues to be one of the most challenging, rapidly changing policy areas of the EU.

'Market-correcting' and -'Cushioning' Policies

Although policies related to building markets have been a central feature of the Union's policy activity, the Union has also been very active in policies which might be viewed as 'market correcting' or 'cushioning'. Market correcting policies, such as the Common Agricultural Policy and cohesion policy, attempt to compensate for the cost to particular groups imposed by the building of market or to limit inequality. Market cushioning policies, such as environmental and social regulation, attempt to limit the potentially harmful effects of the market on human beings and the environment.

Common Agricultural Policy

Perhaps the best-known policy designed to offset market forces is the Common Agricultural Policy (CAP), for which the European Union has almost exclusive competence. Although welfare state policies have been peripheral to the EU's policy agenda, the CAP, with its system of agricultural support and subsides, is an exception to that rule. As Rieger (2005: 182) argues, '[t]he key to understanding this policy domain is to see the CAP as an integral part of the west European welfare state'. The CAP is also unique in the amount of money it receives from the EU budget (see Figure 5.1), the degree of power the Union exercises, and the amount of contestation it causes. Although the CAP created a market for agricultural goods within the EU, its market correcting properties have been the most controversial outside the Union because third parties have found their agricultural goods subject to high tariffs when exported to the EU. In July 2006 the Doha Round of WTO negotiations failed precisely over a dispute on agricultural tariffs between the United States and the EU.

The CAP stirs up plenty of internal debate as well. The benefits of the CAP are distributed very unequally across member states. Although new member states depend much more on agriculture than do older members, the largest recipients are still all older members (see Table 5.2). However, some redistribution of agricultural funds from the older to the new member states has already occurred: from 2007 the funds for farmers in the old member states have begun to decline in order to make room for greater allocations for the farmers in the new member states.

More generally, pressure from enlargement has spurred some CAP reform including a shift from supporting production, which in the past had often led to

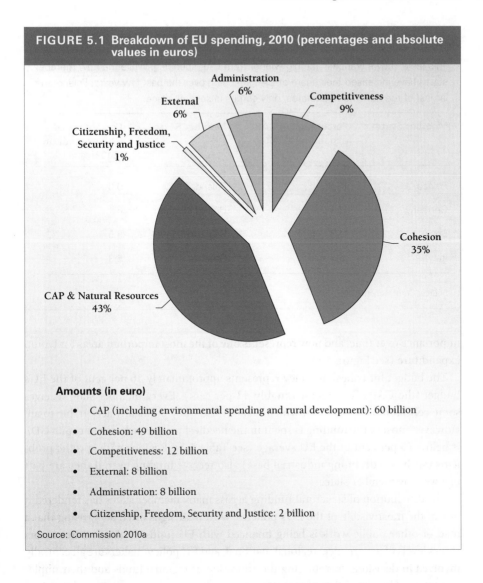

FIGURE 5.1 Breakdown of EU spending, 2010 (percentages and absolute values in euros)

Administration
6%

External
6%

Citizenship, Freedom,
Security and Justice
1%

Competitiveness
9%

Cohesion
35%

CAP & Natural Resources
43%

Amounts (in euro)

- CAP (including environmental spending and rural development): 60 billion

- Cohesion: 49 billion

- Competitiveness: 12 billion

- External: 8 billion

- Administration: 8 billion

- Citizenship, Freedom, Security and Justice: 2 billion

Source: Commission 2010a

overproduction and waste, to supporting rural development and rural environ-ment (Grant 2010). Further reform (optimistically labelled 'Health Check of the CAP') was agreed in 2008. Even so, CAP remains a politically fraught policy area in which the interests of member states, European institutions, farmers, and other stakeholders continually collide (Daugbjerg and Swinbank 2007).

Cohesion policy

Cohesion policy was introduced to reduce inequality among regions and compen-sate poor countries for the costs of economic integration. It became part of the EU's policy mix after the first enlargement (UK, Denmark, and Ireland), has increased in

TABLE 5.2	CAP spending breakdown		

This table shows France is the big winner from CAP spending. While the new member states have increased their share of CAP spending over the past few years, Poland, the largest of the new member states, only comes in seventh place.

Member State	Percentage of CAP expenditure (2009)	Member State	Percentage of CAP expenditure (2009)
France	13.3	Poland	9.0
Germany	11.4	United Kingdom	6.1
Spain	11.3	Belgium	5.5
Italy	9.1	Greece	5.3

Source: Commission 2010b

importance over time, and now represents one of the most important areas for Union expenditure (see Figure 5.1).

The budget for cohesion policy represents approximately 36 per cent of the EU's budget (the CAP accounts for roughly 43 per cent). Every member state receives some cohesion policy monies, which makes this policy politically acceptable to all. However, most of the funding is spent in the neediest regions, where per capita GDP is below 75 per cent of the EU average (see Table 5.3). Regions with specific problems (such as a declining industrial base) also receive funding even if they are part of a wealthy member state.

The distribution of structural funding across many member states has rendered it one of the most visible of the EU's policies, with road signs often advertising that a road or other public work is being financed with EU funds. It also features actors across levels of governance: regional, national, and EU policy-makers are all centrally involved in decisions surrounding the allocation of regional funds and their implementation. The interaction of actors from several levels of governance, and the sharing of power between them gives rise to the notion of the EU as a system of multilevel governance (Bache 2008) (see Chapter 1). Because regions in all member states have benefited from some form of regional spending, cohesion policy has escaped some of the intense controversy surrounding CAP. However, enlargement has made it more controversial, pitting net contributors against new recipients, or 'old' versus 'new' member states. Because the new member states are significantly poorer than the old ones, the poorest regions of Europe are now all concentrated in the new member states (see Table 5.3), and this has clear implications for the distribution of European funds. In fact, the tensions arising from enlargement and the financial crisis that began in 2008 might give new impetus to the drive to renationalize cohesion policy

TABLE 5.3	The 10 poorest regions in GDP (euros per inhabitant)	
The poorest regions of the European Union are all in the new member states		
Rank	Region and country	Euros
1	Nord-Est (RO)	5430
2	Severozapaden (BG)	6023
3	Yuzhen tsentralen (BG)	6026
4	Severen tsentralen (BG)	6205
5	Sud-Vest Oltenia (RO)	6293
6	Sud – Muntenia (RO)	6527
7	Severoiztochen (BG)	6874
8	Sud-Est (RO)	6921
9	Yugoiztochen (BG)	7405
10	Lubelskie (PL)	7839

Source: Eurostat 2010

by reducing the role of EU institutions (especially the Commission) and subnational governments, and increasing the control of national governments (Allen 2010).

Environmental and social regulation

Although the CAP and cohesion policy are probably the best-known of the EU's policy areas outside of the single market, other policy areas have been initiated as relatively marginal and become far more important over time. Such policy areas can be grouped under the rubric of 'social regulation' and they are designed to cushion the impact of the market on society. Occupational health and safety legislation is one such area in which the EU acted rather early. Another important type of social regulation is that concerned with the protection of the environment. In environmental policy (especially in the area of pollution control) the EU became active after a customs union had been created, but before many of its member states had become environmentally conscious. Environmental policy was initially put on the agenda both because of international salience and because it would affect trade in goods such as automobiles. Over time, the focus was enlarged into areas that are not market-related, such as the protection of environmentally sensitive habitats.

In many areas of environmental policy (primarily those outside of pollution control), national governments are free to supplement EU legislation. Some do. In general, the Scandinavian member states, along with Austria, the Netherlands, and Germany are the most active in supplementing EU legislation with their own. But most member states choose not to act unilaterally, thereby leaving the EU as the *de facto* primary actor in this area. An example is the so-called REACH regulation for the 'Registration, Evaluation and Authorization of Chemicals' which brings roughly 30,000 chemical products under the EU's regulatory jurisdiction. Another example of the EU's central role is found in climate change policy, now an encompassing, core area of EU activity. Indeed Jordan *et al.* (2010: 258) demonstrate how the EU's climate policy has become 'an organizing focus for virtually all of its policies'. In this area as in others, however, some of the poorer new member states, led by Poland, have negotiated special concessions sparing them from the full burden of reducing carbon emissions (Lenschow 2010; Buchan 2010).

Consumer protection represents another area of social regulation. A series of food scares and concern over genetically modified organisms (GMOs) have propelled this issue up the EU's agenda and resulted in the establishment of a Food Safety Agency. It has also caused conflict with the United States, which is the largest producer of GMOs, and which accuses the EU of using unscientific concerns as a way to shield European agriculture from foreign competition. Social regulatory policies that are related directly to the single market (such as regulations on product safety) pre-empt national policies, whereas in other areas (such as hygiene standards) the EU stipulates minimum standards that national governments can exceed if they so wish.

The EU has also been active in the area of gender equality. National pension systems have had to be restructured to treat men and women equally. More generally, the EU has been a significant actor in the move toward equal pay (both in terms of income and benefits) in the workplace (Caporaso 2001). Most recently, the EU passed laws against sexual harassment. While some member states already had tough laws, Spain, Portugal, Greece, and Italy had no laws which held employers responsible for harassment within the workplace, and Germany defined sexual harassment more narrowly than did the EU legislation. Member states can adopt stricter definitions of harassment, but now the EU legislation provides a 'floor' for any national legislative activity in that area.

Comparing EU Policy Types

How can we make sense of all these policies? To start, note each category of policy presented above has certain characteristics that distinguish it from others. While the categories are clearly not watertight, they do differ in significant ways along a number of dimensions highlighted in Table 5.4. First, those policies that fall under 'market-building' stimulate market forces and encourage regulatory reform. Because of their emphasis on competition, such policies tend in practice to favour (although not require) privatization and the withdrawal of the state from those areas in which it has protected national producers. Many of the policies in this

Type	Level of EU competence	Key features	Primary actors	Examples
Market-building	Nearly all exclusive; covering an extensive range of economic policies	Emphasis on liberalization and increasing economic efficiency; strong role for supranational institutions	Business actors; EU institutions; national finance officials; central bankers	Internal market policies (such as telecommunications or air transport); EMU
Market-correcting	Mostly shared, sometimes exclusive but only in limited areas	Controversial; has redistributive implications;	Farm lobbies, national officials; Commission	CAP; cohesion policy; fisheries
Market-cushioning	Shared with member states	Significant implementation problems	Supranational institutions; sectoral ministers; public interest groups	Environmental protection; occupational health and safety; gender equality in the workplace

TABLE 5.4   Policy types in the EU

category are regulatory. In general, they also tend to be made by the Community method in which the EU's supranational institutions are normally most active, the Union's competence tends to be most comprehensive, and national policy activity is largely pre-empted (see Chapter 6).

The creation of markets is also marked by a variety of political dynamics and a range of political actors. The different theoretical approaches introduced in Chapter 1 shed light on these different dynamics. A few policy areas, such as energy and pharmaceuticals, feature what Peterson and Bomberg (1999: 81) conclude is 'a relatively stable and cohesive policy network'. That is, policies are shaped by a tight and insular group of actors. Traditionally, the area of monetary policy has also been quite insulated from actors outside the central banking community. The financial crisis of 2008–2011, however, introduced a set of new actors—such as officials from the International Monetary Fund—and opened up what was previously insulated policy-making dynamic. Moreover, most other areas related to economic activity do not exhibit such single-mindedness among the key actors. Most policies are made in what are often fragmented and internally divided networks.

'Market correcting' policies differ from market-building in that they tend to protect producers from market forces. Most are redistributive—from consumers to farmers, and from rich regions to poor regions. Because they are so overtly redistributive rather than regulatory, they tend to be very difficult to change as the impact of any change is quite transparent. For this reason, market-correcting policies tend to be dominated by intergovernmental bargaining rather than by the EU institutions. Liberal intergovernmentalists show how major decisions in these areas are dominated by national governments, responding to strong societal actors (say, agricultural lobbies), but national ministers ultimately decide when other considerations will trump the demands of those lobbies.

'Market-cushioning' policies try to minimize the harm economic activities impose on nature and humans. These policies tend to be regulatory in nature, impose demands on private actors, and fall under the shared competence of the EU because both Brussels and national capitals typically co-govern in these areas. The role of institutions in propelling these areas forward, often with strong support from a variety of representatives of civil society, provides fertile ground for the new institutionalists' claim that 'institutions matter'.

Conclusion

If institutions and member states are the skeleton of the EU, policies are its flesh. It is through its policies that the EU affects people's lives, within and beyond its own borders. The Italian retailer who can sell non-durum wheat pasta against the opposition of the Italian authorities or the British holidaymaker who may pay less for his mobile phone calls when holidaying in Spain both feel the influence of the European Union in their daily lives. So does the American shareholder who sees the price of her Microsoft stocks affected by the competition policy decisions of the European Commission or the Indian farmer adversely affected by the high tariffs the EU imposes on agricultural products.

What makes studying EU policies enormously challenging—as well as fascinating— is that each policy has its own features and trajectory, as this chapter has illustrated. But amidst all that variation, common themes also emerge. In particular, policies and policy-making in the EU reflect the three major themes of this volume: experimentation as a driving force of European integration, the astonishing array of actors and the power-sharing and consensus-building amongst them; and the contrast between the scope and the capacity of the EU.

Thus, for instance, the creation of the EMU was in part the result of dramatic experimentation. One of the main reasons for moving to a common currency was that the old status quo, with exchange rate agreements that had proved prone to collapse, was no longer tenable. Yet monetary union as the way forward was an untested course. As the former chief economist of the ECB has argued, European governments met the challenge by consciously choosing to take a risk and take 'the big leap into monetary union' (*Financial Times*, 27 October 2006). The Eurozone crisis of 2010–11 dramatically illustrated that such a leap was indeed dangerous—and faced an uncertain outcome.

Different policy areas also show different levels of inclusiveness and power-sharing. In some areas, such as competition policy and monetary policy, power is concentrated amongst a limited set of actors. In many others, however, a larger set of actors is involved. Both environmental and cohesion policy exemplify the involvement of a large number of actors at different levels of governance—including EU institutions, national governments, and private stakeholders—and the preference for consensus-building. But consensus-building in Brussels comes at a price: decisions made by the EU, no matter how well thought-out, seem to many Europeans to be made too far away from their control. That citizen control is still largely exercised through the democratic process in each member state rather than through citizen participation in European decision-making. Although the Lisbon Treaty has tried to address this concern, many Europeans still feel disconnected from the way decisions are made in the EU.

Finally, the policy capacity of the EU remains well short of any nation-state, relying as it does on a very limited budget and on the national implementation of European legislation. At the same time, we have seen how the pressure of economic integration has led to the continuing expansion of the scope of the EU's policy remit, from policies directly related to market-building, to market-correcting and then market-cushioning policies. The current Eurozone crisis might advance this pattern: if the Eurozone survives, European economic governance may well emerge much changed and more integrated than previously.

DISCUSSION QUESTIONS

1. Why has the EU privileged economic policies over social welfare policies?

2. Why is the EU budget so much smaller than that of its major member states?

3. What implications does a single monetary policy have for the development of other types of policies within the EU?

4. What obstacles to the execution of EU policies exist that do not exist at the national level?

5. The CAP (Common Agricultural Policy) is often criticized on efficiency grounds. What environmental or social considerations can be brought to bear to support the CAP?

6. Why has the implementation of the Stability and Growth Pact been so difficult?

FURTHER READING

For an in-depth analysis of the EU's major policy areas, including those discussed in this chapter, see Wallace *et al.* (2010). For an introduction to the development of the Common Agricultural Policy written by an insider, see Garzon (2006). Readers can follow the evolution of cohesion policy, including how it has been affected by enlargement, with Leonardi (2005) and Baun and Marek (2008). A comprehensive overview of environmental policy is provided by Knill and Liefferink (2007), and an excellent collection on climate change is found in Jordan *et al.* (2010). A provocative interpretation of the process of economic integration as a consistent strategy to achieve broader integration goals is provided by Jabko (2006). A very clear explanation of the economics of EMU is found in De Grauwe (2009) while Quaglia (2007) discusses the impact of EMU on central bank governance. An overview of the current state of the single market is provided by Howarth and Sadeh (2010), and the changing role of trade policy is analysed by McGuire and Lindeque (2010). The question of the (lack of) implementation of EU legislation by the Member States is addressed by Falkner *et al.* (2008).

Baun, M. and Marek, D. (2008), *EU Cohesion Policy after Enlargement* (Basingstoke and New York: Palgrave Macmillan).

De Grauwe, P. (2009), *Economics of Monetary Union*, 8th edn. (Oxford and New York: Oxford University Press).

Falkner, G., Treib, O., and Holzleithner, E. (2008), *Compliance in the Enlarged European Union* (Aldershot: Ashgate).

Garzon, I. (2006) *Reforming the Common Agricultural Policy: History of a Paradigm Change* (Basingstoke and New York: Palgrave Macmillan).

Howarth, D. and Sadeh, T. (2010) 'The Ever Incomplete Single Market: Differentiation and the Evolving Frontier of Integration', J*ournal of European Public Policy*, 17(7): 922–35.

Jabko, N. (2006), *Playing the Market* (Ithaca NY: Cornell University Press).

Jordan, A. Huitema, D., van Asselt, H., Rayner, T., and Berkhout, F. (2010), *Climate Change Policy in the European Union: Confronting the Dilemmas of Mitigation and Adaptation?* (Cambridge and New York: Cambridge University Press).

Knill, C. and Liefferink, D. (2007), *Environmental Politics in the European Union* (Manchester and New York: Manchester University Press).

Leonardi, R. (2005), *Cohesion Policy in the European Union: The Building of Europe* (Basingstoke and New York: Palgrave Macmillan).

McGuire, S. M. and Lindeque, J. P. (2010), 'The Diminishing Returns to Trade Policy in the European Union', *Journal of Common Market Studies* 48(5): 1329–49.

Quaglia, L. (2007), *Central Banking Governance in the European Union: A Comparative Analysis* (London and New York: Routledge).

Wallace, H., Pollack, M., and Young, A. (2010), *Policy-Making in the European Union*, 6th edn. (Oxford and New York: Oxford University Press).

 WEB LINKS

To locate EU publications covering policy, try the EU portal EUR-Lex at **http://eur-lex. europa.eu/**. It is bibliographical in nature, but contains links to many full-text documents. For a summary overview of EU law in 32 different areas, search this site: **http://europa. eu/legislation_summaries/index_en.htm**.

For full text, non-EU documents see the websites 'European Integration Online Papers' at **http://www.eiop.or.at/eiop/** and 'European Research Papers Archive' at **http://**

www.eiop.or.at/erpa/erpaframe.html. Leading think tanks that offer up-to-date commentary on and analysis of EU policies include the Centre for European Policy Studies (**http://www.ceps.eu/**), the European Policy Centre (**http://www.epc.eu/**), and Centre for European Reform (**http://www.cer.org.uk/**).

 Visit the Online Resource Centre that accompanies this book for additional material: **www.oxfordtextbooks.co.uk/orc/bomberg3e/**

CHAPTER 6

How Policies Are Made

Rory Watson and Richard Corbett

▌ Summary

The major stages of the EU formal policy-making process are clearly set out in the Treaty on European Union, as amended by Lisbon. It confirms that the Council and the EP act as equals when approving legislation in almost all policy areas. However, the treaty is silent on the earliest stage of the process—the actual genesis of proposals that emerge from the European Commission. Nor does it say anything about the informal political give-and-take that occurs or the growing range of interest representatives that seek to influence decision-making. This chapter presents a comprehensive picture by examining both formal and informal features of the policy-making process.

Introduction

Policy-making in the EU is complex, with a rich variety of different procedures and actors (see Box 6.1). To most ordinary European citizens, the system appears arcane, rigid, and incomprehensible. But the formal procedures set down in the EU's Treaties allow for informal input from a vast range of voices and interests. Representatives of European civil society—firms, trades unions, local governments, non-governmental organizations, and others—make their views heard by the Commission when it drafts legislation. Equally, they lobby national governments and MEPs when they examine, amend, and adopt it. We will look at how policies are made, how interest representatives (or 'lobbyists') have grown in number, and how the EU institutions, initially wary of this input, are learning to accommodate it.

The Basics

Why do so many Europeans find the EU distant and alien? As Herman Van Rompuy (2011), the President of the European Council has explained:

In many ways it is natural and unavoidable that European citizens are wary of European institutions. They are more distant from people than are national and local institutions.

BOX 6.1	Key concepts and terms

Civil society refers to the broad collection of associations and groups (including private firms, trades unions, community groups, and non-governmental organizations) active between the level of the individual and the state. These groups generally operate independently of direct government control.

Lobbying is an attempt to influence policy-makers to adopt a course of action advantageous, or not detrimental, to a particular group or interest. A lobbyist is a person employed by a group, firm, organization, region, or country to carry out lobbying. Lobbyists in Brussels are increasingly referred to as interest representatives.

A **rapporteur** is the Member of the European Parliament responsible for preparing a report of one of the Parliament's committees.

Transparency refers to the process of making EU documents and decision-making processes more open and accessible to the public.

'Venue shopping' refers to the activities of an interest group searching or 'shopping' for a decision setting most favourable or receptive to their policy claims.

The institutional structure is more complex and less familiar. Many of the treaty amendments over the last two decades have sought to allay such suspicions and reassure citizens through a whole range of instruments and procedural safeguards. Admittedly, some innovations have made the structure even more complex. However, the same is true for political life in, for instance, Washington. Complexity is a feature of almost any system of government ... except for dictatorships!

In reality, the process for approving the vast majority of EU legislation mirrors many national systems. In London, for instance, it is the civil service and the government that draft and table legislation. In Brussels, that task is performed by the Commission. In the UK, the text is then examined, amended, and (usually) approved by both the Houses of Commons and Lords. In the EU, that legislative role is given to the Council and the Parliament. If the proposal is relatively straightforward and these two co-legislators can agree on its contents, then the text may be approved after just one reading in each institution. If agreement between the two is harder to reach, then two or even three readings may be required.

As with national procedures, the devil is in the detail (see Box 6.2). For EU legislation, the majority required in the Council can vary from one subject to another. Most legislation follows what is now (post-Lisbon) called the 'ordinary legislative procedure', under which co-decision applies. But there are exceptions, such as when the Parliament is merely consulted or else simply has to give its consent in a single yes/no vote. In many cases, Commission proposals are also sent to two advisory bodies: the European Economic and Social Committee (EESC) and the Committee of the Regions (CoR). They only have a consultative role, but ensure that the views of their constituents (economic and social actors in the first, and regional and local governments in the second) can be fed into the system. Draft legislation is also sent to national parliaments. They have eight weeks to determine if a text respects the principle of subsidiarity. They may also use this time to influence the position taken by their national government or raise their concerns with the Commission (see Chapter 7).

BOX 6.2   Types of legislative act

There are three main types of legislative acts:

- **Regulations** are binding and directly applicable in all member states.
- **Directives** are binding on member states, but leave them free to determine how to achieve the objectives set out in the text and decide (for example) whether domestic legislation is needed.
- **Decisions** only bind the specific individuals or firms to which they are addressed.

While a wide variety of institutions are involved, the substantive legislative work is carried out in the Council and Parliament.

Parliament

Parliament sends proposals to its specialized parliamentary committees. Draft legislation affecting banking, for instance, goes to the economic and monetary affairs committee. The committee appoints a *rapporteur*. This decision is important since this MEP produces the first draft of the committee's views on the proposed legislation, and subsequently presents the committee's final opinion to Parliament and to the outside world. The appointment is a decision reached among the different EP political groups.

The EP committee gradually assembles its opinion on the proposal. This process inevitably involves political trade-offs, not between national positions as in the Council, but between different political groups. The two most important—the centre-right Christian Democrats (EPP) and the Socialists—more often than not find themselves on different sides of the argument. They can try to negotiate a compromise or they can look for reinforcements to secure the necessary majority. The centre-right's natural allies tend to be on the right, while the Socialists' are on the left (especially the Greens). Frequently, it is the Liberals—the Parliament's third largest group—that swings the balance. For example, on economic issues the Liberals tend to veer more towards the right and on social and justice matters to the left. But EPP-Socialist compromises—often taking the views of Liberals and others on board too—remain common, both because of the generally consensual nature of the Union and since trying to accommodate allies further to the left or right can be problematic.

The final stage of the committee procedure gives every MEP the opportunity to table amendments. Much effort is spent trying to construct cross-group political alliances to back amendments. After voting on the amendments, the committee's version of the proposed legislation moves to the full Parliament for a debate and vote on the text.

Between adoption in committee and the final vote in plenary, each political group will deliberate on the matter. At this stage, wider political considerations come into play. One is the extent to which the political groups might review their committee position. Those who were in a minority in the committee may consider how far they are willing to move in order to try to reach a compromise with the majority. Those who were in the majority may consider whether they are willing to water down their position to secure a larger majority in the Parliament ahead of negotiations with the Council.

It is not unusual for MEPs to come under pressure from their own governments to vote in a particular way—pressure that can lead to conflicting loyalties: does an MEP vote with their political group or along national lines? Often, they have more in common with their group, on the particular issue or on the wider European value of legislation, than they have in common with their national governments, especially (but not only) if their political party is in opposition at home.

To reconcile such conflicting imperatives, MEPs often draft composite amendments intended to garner the widest possible political support when the draft legislation is voted on by the EP as a whole. At the same time, before the Parliament's plenary votes on a proposal, efforts are often made to try and reconcile the possibly different views between the Parliament and the Council. For instance, key MEPs, including the *rapporteur*, may have discreet discussions with national government representatives in the Council to try and establish common ground and shorten the legislative process. If they succeed, it is possible for a proposal to be formally adopted in around 12 months. This pace compares well with many national systems given the number of actors involved.

Council

In parallel, the Council has also been working on the same text. The proposal goes to one of the many specialized working groups that contain a civil servant from each member state's relevant government department. They will meet regularly over many months, carefully scrutinizing the text, and assessing its implications for their own government's policy. Some of the issues debated will be highly political, others more technical. Typically, for example, a proposal for energy efficiency legislation will see debate range from its impact on the environment to how it will affect economic activity.

Members of Council working groups will also have in their minds the broader principles of subsidiarity and proportionality. Should specific issues be tackled at a European level or could some be left to be determined nationally? Is it proportionate to the issue it is looking to address, or does it go further than is necessary? Should the EU be involved at all? Public health is a clear example. Responsibility for its organization and delivery rests clearly with national authorities, but increasingly European action is needed on cross border questions, such as organ donation or epidemics.

Once the working group has achieved as much consensus as it can, the proposal moves to a higher political level in the Council: Coreper. Now, it is the turn of national ambassadors, or their deputies, to try and iron out the difficulties that remain. National ambassadors are appointed, not elected. But Coreper is the highest level of officials to review proposed decisions before they are passed to politicians in the Council. By the time Coreper considers any proposal, most outstanding problems will be well known and member states will trust some of their best legal and civil service minds to try to hammer out potential solutions.

However, some proposals will be so politically sensitive—the impact of new environmental standards on a country's coal production, for instance—that they will be passed further up the political ladder to ministers, or even prime ministers. Here member state representatives may strike wider deals: they might, for instance, delay implementation of the proposed measures for all or some member states ('derogations', in EU-speak). Or a member state may reluctantly agree something in one area in exchange for more favourable treatment in another.

Before it finally approves draft legislation, the Council will consider the version which has been voted on by the Parliament. If it accepts it, then the act is adopted. Increasingly, there is pressure in both the Council and Parliament to approve legislation at this stage—after just one reading in each institution—in order to speed up policy-making. Extensive informal negotiations between them are usually required. The Council President, the relevant Commissioner and the EP's committee chair and *rapporteur* play pivotal roles in these talks that have become known as 'trialogues'.

If give and take does not produce agreement, the conciliation process is formally triggered. A conciliation committee is established, which consists of members of the Council and key MEPs (normally including the *rapporteur*, representatives of party groups, and a vice-president), and the relevant Commissioner. The participants now know the issues—and each other—well. All will feel the pressure to find compromises. If they fail, the draft legislation falls. Neither side wishes to be held responsible for killing a proposal if there is general agreement that the measures envisaged are necessary. If a conciliation committee succeeds in agreeing a joint text, the Parliament and the Council formally can adopt it (or not). Clear deadlines exist for each stage of the legislative process once the first reading has taken place so as to keep up the momentum.

One important difference between the deliberations in the Council's working groups and the Parliament's specialized committees is that the former meet behind closed doors while EP committees are open to the public, including journalists. As a result, media interest in the MEPs' deliberation is heightened. On particularly sensitive subjects, the EP's committee room can be packed and outside observers have to stand. The discomfort is not just physical. By not being seated, they do not have access to headphones to tune in to the interpreters translating the speakers' original language into one they understand. The problem is now alleviated by the frequent web streaming of committee meetings, with choice of language.

In general, the parliamentary process is far more transparent than the Council's, even though many Council ministerial meetings are now also web streamed. Some believe this move has brought greater transparency; others that it has simply meant the more sensitive issues are discussed over lunch (which is not broadcast). It is not unusual for 'lunch' to last four to five hours, not because of the gastronomy on offer, but because ministers have needed that much time to put together discreetly some form of agreement.

How the EU Legislates

The process that we have described above is the most widely used form of EU policy-making: the adoption of legislation through the ordinary legislative procedure. However, other procedures also exist (see Box 6.3), as does policy-making in

---

BOX 6.3   **The EU's mosaic of procedures**

Besides the ordinary legislative procedure, the EU employs a variety of other methods of legislating, including:

- The **consent procedure**: for international agreements entered into by the Union, which are normally negotiated by the Commission (or the High Representative) on the basis of a mandate given by the Council. Normally, the consent of the EP is needed on a straight yes/no vote without amendments. The consent procedure is also used for some internal decisions of a quasi-constitutional nature, such as the electoral system for European elections.

- The **consultation procedure**: there are still some cases where the European Parliament is merely consulted, and the final decision on legislation rests with the Council, usually requiring unanimity. One example is the harmonization of indirect taxation.

- The **budget procedure**: this procedure is similar to the ordinary legislative procedure, but normally with only one reading each in Parliament and Council.

- **Enhanced cooperation:** allows a group of member states to act together if agreement cannot be reached at the level of the 27. At least nine member states must be ready to participate and demonstrate to the Commission that they are able to meet all the necessary conditions of a proposed agreement. In the Council, only those members partaking in enhanced cooperation may vote on the proposal, although all can take part in the discussion. Parliament's consent is also required and all MEPs may vote, even those from countries that are not participating. Other member states may join the policy area being covered by enhanced cooperation at a later date.

- **Delegated powers**: just as national legislation often empowers the government to adopt secondary legislation in the form of statutory instruments (UK) or decrees (several continental countries), so European legislation frequently gives the Commission the right to adopt implementing measures, or to adapt legislation to technical progress.

---

non-legislative fields (such as foreign and security policy). In all cases, however, certain key features characterize the EU's legislative process.

First, as a general rule, all procedures require some form of inter-institutional consensus, even if the role(s) of specific institutions varies. To illustrate, when the Commission negotiates international agreements, the Council usually follows the detailed negotiations closely. So does the Parliament. Even though the EP is unable to amend the final agreement, it typically debates the matter prior to the start of negotiations and sometimes adopts a resolution setting out its views. It expects the relevant parliamentary committee to be briefed by the Commission in the course of negotiations and sometimes (notably for major multilateral conferences such as on climate change) sends a delegation of MEPs. Final approval (or rejection) by the Parliament also follows a committee stage similar to that under the ordinary legislative procedure.

The crafting of compromises is another feature of every EU legislative procedure. Take the budget: both the Council and EP must negotiate a (massive) compromise, and the relevant parliamentary committee plays a key role. And the annual budgets must comply with a multiannual (usually seven-year) financial framework proposed by the Commission, adopted by the Council (by unanimity), with the consent of Parliament.

Enlargement obviously makes the crafting of compromises increasingly difficult. That challenge has led to experimentation with **enhanced cooperation** (see Box 6.3), which makes it possible for sub-sets of all member states formally to strike cooperation agreements drawing on the Union's institutional resources. The concept was first introduced in the 1997 Amsterdam Treaty and has subsequently been refined. In practice, it has been largely used as a threat to encourage reluctant member states to sort out their difficulties and join the majority. Hesitation in using this option stemmed partly from concern that it could result in a complex political and legal situation if different groups of countries were doing different things in different areas. Even so, in 2010 it was used twice. On the first occasion, 14 countries agreed to move ahead with legislation on cross-border divorces. On the second, 25 member states ended years of deadlock by triggering the procedure to adopt a European patent.

A final feature, which intergovernmentalist theorists would highlight, is the continued assertion of national control. Even when powers are formally delegated to the Commission, the member states retain control mechanisms including via the controversial 'comitology' system. It obliges the Commission to work with committees of national representatives at civil servant level, which sometimes have the power to delay or block a Commission decision. The awkward term 'comitology' was coined to describe this process and its number and variety of committees.

Critics believe the comitology system, which evolved over decades, is a secret form of law-making which gives undue influence to civil servants. The EP in particular has complained that it does not contain sufficient democratic checks. Its defenders reply that it is necessary to keep the technical content of legislation up to date without having to embark on a lengthy, full-blown legislative procedure.

Deciding, not legislating

The EU also has a variety of ways in which it makes decisions without legislating. For instance, decisions under the **Common Foreign and Security Policy** (see Chapter 9) are taken by unanimity in the Council, without necessarily requiring a Commission proposal. Proposals may be initiated by the High Representative, who is Vice President of the Commission, or individual member states. As the decisions are (usually) not legislative, the agreement of the Parliament is not required. But it must be kept informed and regularly consulted on key foreign policy choices. It holds debates on foreign policy matters with the High Representative, and MEPs may table parliamentary questions.

Moreover, coordination of national positions can take place through the Council on matters of essentially national competence, but where coordination is desired. It can even take a binding form, such as the Stability and Growth Pact, under which member states undertake not to run excessive budgetary deficits or pile up excessive debts. If they do, they can ultimately be fined by a Council decision. Such (politically-charged) decisions are prepared by the Commission, but it only makes a 'recommendation' to the Council, not a proposal. In practice, no member state has even been fined under the terms of the Pact (see Chapter 5).

Other types of coordination can be looser and non-binding. For instance, member states use an 'open method of coordination' to compare and benchmark their national performances in different economic and social fields. In these cases, peer pressure, not fines, are the only constraint on national policy. The same method has been used to beef up the 'battle groups' that are a feature of the European Security and Defence Policy (see Chapter 9). And in response to the crisis in the Eurozone, member states (of the Eurozone in particular) agreed in 2011 on deeper cooperation on national policies affecting competitiveness, with further progress in this area to be assessed by their peers annually.

A final type of decision-making takes place amongst heads of state and government on the **European Council**. It does not normally participate in day-to-day procedures. Rather, the European Council is the EU's strategic body, charged under the treaty with defining its 'general political directions and priorities'. In practice, it also deals with major crises and internal deadlocks. Bringing together the most powerful political figure in each of the member states and the President of the Commission, and now having its own influential full-time President, The European Council's political clout is enormous. Its meetings are the focus of far more media attention than the day-to-day activities of any Union institution (see Box 6.4).

Preparing Commission Proposals

To trigger most of the EU's procedures, a Commission proposal for a draft legislative act is needed. These do not come out of the blue. Although the Commission alone has the right to draw up the first draft, the initial impetus can come from many different directions (see Box 3.1). Furthermore, the Commission usually flags up its intentions at the earliest possible stage. Widespread consultation is positively encouraged before any prospective policy sees the light of day. The intent is to give outside parties an opportunity to make their views heard, particularly at very early stages of the legislative process. Moreover, the Commission itself is resource poor— it needs to rely on others to gather different views, perspectives, and information on early proposals.

BOX 6.4	The media in Brussels

The role of the media in Brussels has grown in scale and importance. With just over 800 journalists accredited to the EU institutions, the Brussels-based media is, along with Washington, one of the two largest international press corps in the world. It contains full-time correspondents, freelance journalists, and (increasingly) online services from around 70 countries, including all EU member states, potential future members such as Croatia and Turkey, as well as countries further afield. The most numerous are German, reflecting the strongly regionalized press in the country.

The media shape policy by presenting news in a particular way (for a detailed illustration, see Lefebure and Lagneau 2001). With few exceptions (such as, perhaps, the *Financial Times* or the Brussels-based publications *European Voice*, *Europolitics* and *Agence Europe*), they invariably view EU developments through a national prism. As a social constructivist would remind us (see Table 1.1), these national prisms can lead to the presentation of the same facts in very different ways. Take as examples these different headlines after the June 2006 European summit which considered the future of the EU's Constitutional Treaty. 'New proposals regarding the European Constitution by 2008' (Austria, *Kurier*). 'The constitution has been put on the back burner' (Belgium, *Dernière Heure*). 'No EU-treaty before 2010' (Danish media). 'The 25 want to renegotiate the Constitution' (France, *Le Monde*). 'EU Constitution must survive' (Germany, *Frankfurter Allgemeine Zeitung*). 'Constitution a corpse' (UK, *Times*). Parts of the British press have a reputation for presenting anything to do with the EU in a negative light, or even inventing stories.

As in national politics, policy-makers cultivate contacts with the media, looking to present their case to a wider audience. It is not uncommon for a particular proposal to be leaked to a favoured newspaper before details are officially in the public domain. The tactic is used both by supporters of a proposal, in an attempt to influence the debate by presenting details in the most sympathetic light, and by critics looking to build up a groundswell of opposition. Hence, the media do not only report, analyse, and comment. In the EU as elsewhere, the distinction between commenting on events and trying to influence them is blurred.

It is now common practice for the Commission to publish an annual work programme for the year to come. It lists broad priorities, and initiatives the Commission intends to take during the year. For example, in 2011 these ranged from specific action in the financial services sector and the promotion of energy efficiency to the creation of a legal framework to protect individuals' personal data. The Commission's work programme for 2011 also listed existing legislation that it intended to simplify to make it less administratively burdensome and a score of proposals that had become obsolete and that it wished to withdraw.

When the Commission is considering a significant legislative proposal, the Directorate-General (DG) in charge of the policy area will take the lead in the drafting process. It will consult other Commission departments if their interests in a proposal overlap. An energy green paper, for instance, would also attract particular input from DGs dealing not just with energy, but also with industry, transport, consumers, and the environment.

Consultation is not simply an internal Commission exercise. Outside opinions will also be canvassed: representatives of civil society, national and subnational governments and parliaments and academics will all have an opportunity to contribute to this initial stage. The result will be a consultative Green Paper setting out the issue to be addressed, and triggering a formal consultation process. The number of responses will vary depending on the sector or issue involved, but typically around a hundred are received.

The consultation stage fulfils many functions. It can throw up issues the Commission may not have considered. It can show the depth of support or opposition for a particular course of action and the wisdom or otherwise of taking it. Both the Commission's legitimacy and the quality of the legislation can benefit from as wide a group of interests as possible sharing ownership of the policy being prepared. As well as inviting outside actors to feed their views into the Commission's internal drafting procedures, Commission officials are also proactive on the most sensitive legislative proposals. They commission studies, attend seminars and public events— 'to open our eyes and ears', as one puts it—and create specialist panels.

After consultation, the relevant DG will then draft an initial version of the proposed legislation. Every Commission DG will have an opportunity to comment in what is called inter-service consultation. Particularly controversial proposals often provoke strong arguments not just between officials in the different DGs, but between their Commissioners. These debates are usually fundamentally political (see Box 6.5). Would an environmental protection measure harm economic growth? Would energy efficiency plans harm industry? Would mandatory limits on working hours limit the rights of employers, and employees, to determine how many hours can be worked? Or would they guarantee individuals' health and safety and improve their work/life balance?

At the end of the day, the Commissioner in charge of the particular policy area, his or her colleagues, and increasingly the President, will have to make a political judgement. They may want an ambitious long-term solution to the issue they are trying to address (say, measures to address climate change or unemployment), but realize that the consultation process has revealed this kind of solution will have little chance of being approved by the Council and the Parliament. Instead, they might decide on a more pragmatic approach, which could create a legislative foundation from which further momentum could be gained in the future.

Interest Representation and Lobbying

During the policy-making process, all decisions are formally taken by official actors: the college of Commissioners when agreeing on draft legislation, government ministers in the Council, and MEPs in the Parliament when it is adopted . But during this

BOX 6.5	**How it really works: the REACH Regulation on Chemicals**

The REACH Regulation (Registration, Evaluation, Authorisation and Restriction of Chemicals) took over three years to be approved. The Commission introduced its proposal in 2003 and it was adopted by Parliament and Council in December 2006. This unusually long period reflected bitter divisions between those for and against the legislation, and allowed interest representatives to make full use of their various lobbying techniques.

The legislation was controversial even before the Commission presented its proposal. Drafting had started two years earlier in 2001 and had immediately provoked a powerful reaction from both sides of the debate. Those in favour of controls on the use of chemicals required by the legislation pointed to a significant potential reduction of occupational cancer cases per year, and savings in health costs alone of €50 billion over 30 years. In contrast, the chemical industry forecast a cost of many billions due to lost revenue, an undermining of its international competitiveness, and major job losses.

Given the controversy, the Commission took the unusual step of organizing an internet consultation in mid-2003. The response was dramatic, with many non-EU governments, notably the US, China, and Japan, making their concerns known. Although environmental and consumer protection groups—and even bodies such as the Women's Institute—from inside and outside the EU argued for a strong proposal, the version that emerged in the autumn of 2003 was weaker than expected.

Co-decision rules allow the Parliament to give its view first, and it decided to wait until after the European elections of 2004. The pause gave organized interests further time to prepare their arguments. At that point, the Commission took another unusual step: it set up a high-level group composed of two Commissioners, three MEPs, the Council Presidency, plus representatives of industry and environmental organizations. The group met over nine months in 2004–5 and produced three business case studies to try to assess the impact of the proposal. These studies suggested that the proposals were workable but that there would be significant costs for small furnis and the newer member states.

It became apparent that the opponents of the proposals were not of one mind, varying across different parts of the chemical sector, with a more flexible approach from the French, British, and Italian industries but a harder line from German companies. This tough stance was reflected in the position of most German MEPs who favoured, for example, setting a high threshold below which a chemical would not need to be tested. Parliament sought to bring together opposing interests. After a vote in the EP Environment Committee in autumn 2005, a technical working group met not just with MEPs but also with experts from industry, the scientific community, and the Commission. This group offered a key opportunity for interests to put forward their point of view.

The effort paid off. A compromise was reached on parts of the proposal. After extensive back-and-forth negotiations between the Council and EP, an agreement was reached that was acceptable to a majority. The resulting final legislation adopted in late 2006 proved weaker than some had hoped, but stronger than many in the chemical industry would have liked at the outset. In other words, REACH was a compromise, the main contours of which were thrashed out in the Parliament, reflecting effective lobbying on both sides of the issue.

lengthy process, which may take between 18 to 36 months and, sometimes even longer, many other voices make themselves heard. Representatives of various interests may put their message across publicly or they might work quietly behind the scenes to ensure policy-makers take their concerns on board. All EU institutions, but especially the Commission and the Parliament, have had to respond to the growth of this extra dimension to policy-making.

These interest representatives come in many shapes and sizes. Initially, the collective term for such a disparate group was 'lobbyist', as its members lobbied official policy-makers. However, to some people the term appeared pejorative (see Box 6.6). Its practitioners preferred to describe themselves as consultants or working in public affairs. Now the Commission uses the term 'interest representatives', indicating a degree of acceptance and respectability.

The increase in the number of interest representatives reflects the deepening and widening of the EU itself. Initially, the focus of these actors was on coal, steel and agriculture—the EU's first common policies. Later, the push towards the single market in the 1980s and 1990s saw numerous trade associations and individual companies scrambling to set up in Brussels. The late 1980s brought an increase in the presence of regional governments. In parallel with the extension of the EU's remit, its expansion from six to 27 member states has multiplied the number of organized interests represented in the European capital.

It is difficult to provide a precise figure for the total number of people working for these different groups. They range in size from one or two people, to large offices with scores of staff. In early 2011, the European Commission's public register (see below) contained 3,562 entries for interest representatives. However, these entries were not individuals, but organizations. A rough guess is that well over 15,000 individuals represent organized interests in Brussels.

Types of actor

Lobbyists (or interest representatives) provide a wealth of information to EU policy-makers. They contribute a diverse range of views to the legislative process in every policy area in which the EU is involved. They also raise questions about whose interests are being served in EU decisions.

The largest category consists of **private economic and business interests** that come together to represent their points of view in pan-European trade federations or associations. They cover a staggering variety of business interests, ranging from the mighty (European Chemical Industry Council) to the tiny (European Lift Components Association); from the broad (Alliance for a Competitive European Industry) to the specific (Association of European Candle Manufacturers). Associations with powerful members such as automobile manufacturers, pharmaceutical companies, or food industries are extremely well resourced.

| BOX 6.6 | Compared to what? Lobbying in Brussels and Washington |

Brussels and Washington appear to have much in common as political capitals. Both are relatively small cities: Washington ranks as only the twenty-fourth largest city in the US, while Brussels' population is much smaller than those of either London or Paris. Brussels and Washington are federal-style capitals and centres of considerable power. Decisions taken in both affect the lives of millions of citizens geographically removed from where policy is made. Newcomers often express surprise at how much Brussels and Washington feel like 'villages': the number of policy entrepreneurs seems rather small, everybody appears to know everybody, and nothing remains a secret for very long.

However, any lobbyist who approaches lobbying in Brussels in the same way as in Washington is likely to fail. In Washington successful lobbying campaigns can be highly aggressive and public. They are often more concerned with defeating a bill than achieving some sort of consensus. In contrast, lobbying in Brussels tends to be far more discreet, low-key, consensus-seeking, and informal (Coen 2004). The Scottish government's Brussels office, for instance, organizes music and film evenings as a way to break down formal barriers, present itself to different audiences, and extend its network of influence. Successful lobbying in Brussels must be sensitive to over a score of different national (and subnational) cultures, and those who neglect that diversity do so at their cost (see Woll 2006). A big advantage comes from being able to speak multiple languages: English and French as a minimum, but also German, Spanish, and even Dutch, since it is Belgium's majority language. As party political funding is organized differently than in the US, political campaign contributions are very rarely used to try to affect EU policy outcomes, in stark contrast to traditional practice in Washington.

Perhaps the biggest difference is in the value attached to reliable expertise and information. The EU's institutions are resource-poor compared to their closest equivalents in Washington. For example, the Parliament has nothing remotely similar to the respected and well-funded (US) Congressional Research Service. Brussels is home to relatively few think tanks, which generate policy ideas and debates, while Washington boasts a large and diverse collection, better funded and more closely linked to major political parties (or factions within them). With fewer providers of expertise, and public institutions that are more desperate to acquire it, the power which comes from being able to gather, process, and disseminate reliable information opens more doors in Brussels than in most political capitals.

Among the groups that enjoy the best access are those that represent pan-European interests. In the economic field, these tend to be umbrella associations such as the main confederation of European business, BusinessEurope, the European Trade Union Confederation (ETUC); and the Committee of Agricultural Organizations (COPA). Many multinational companies, such as Microsoft and IBM, also have representational offices in Brussels.

A second category contains a multitude of European **non-profit organizations** representing a wide range of public interests. Among the most active are environmental, public health, human rights, and animal welfare NGOs such as Greenpeace, the World Wide Fund for Nature (WWF), the Euorpean Environmental Bureau, the European Consumers Organization (BEUC), the European Public Health Alliance, Human Rights Watch, or the International Fund for Animal Welfare. Environmental groups have built up particularly extensive contacts inside the different institutions. With the help of certain 'greener' governments and MEPs, they have influenced tangibly the Commission's sustainable development and climate change policies.

A rather different kind of non-profit interest is represented by various Brussels think tanks, such as the European Policy Centre, the Centre for European Policy Studies, and several others. These bodies bring together officials, academics, interest groups, and the media to analyse topical aspects of EU policy. A final category includes **governmental organizations and representatives**. This group includes representatives of the different levels of regional government in the EU, non-EU countries, and over 100 international organizations.

Organized Interests at Work

Interest representatives try to make their voices heard in different ways at different stages of policy-making. Once draft legislation leaves the Commission, interest representatives' focus moves in two directions. One is national as they look to present their case to governments in an attempt to influence the position they will take in the Council. The other direction is towards the European Parliament. Most MEPs are prepared to listen to a wide range of outside views when carrying out their work. Interest representatives will seek out sympathetic MEPs and frequently draft amendments, which members will table in their name. One estimate suggests that up to 75–80 per cent of amendments tabled in the most active parliamentary committees emanate from outside Parliament (Judge and Earnshaw 2002). Most MEPs believe that this professional understanding of the issues at stake helps them to draft better legislation, provided they take the final decision. Parliamentary committees or political groups now regularly hold hearings, inviting acknowledged experts to present their insights. However, some MEPs also complain that interest representatives can be overzealous, pestering MEPs unnecessarily and, in the process, damaging their case.

European institutions' response

Questions of ethics and propriety always surround lobbying. The Parliament was the first institution to address its relationship with interest representatives. That relationship had grown more intense as the Parliament's own power increased. The development was neatly summed up by one long-serving MEP who said, only partly in jest: 'In 1979, we were begging people to come and see us. Now we are trying to keep them away.'

To 'keep them away'—or at least monitor their activities—the Parliament established a register in 1996 containing the names and personal details of individual lobbyists. Anyone seeking a regular visitor's pass needed to fill out a form containing their details, and undertake to respect a code of conduct (failing which the pass is withdrawn). The information is contained in a register, which holds around 3,400 names and may be consulted on the Parliament's website. It also introduced rules for MEPs in their dealings with outside interests (such as banning the receipt of gifts).

The Commission initially took a different approach. In the 1990s, it encouraged organized interests to introduce self-regulation and voluntary codes of conduct. But, in response to concerns about a continued lack of transparency, the Commission introduced a 'Transparency Register' in 2007, which it asked all interest representatives to sign. The register recognized the **legitimacy** of lobbying, but also the need for clarity about the interests being represented. It now contains a wealth of detail. For instance, public affairs consultancies have to list policy areas of interest to them, name their clients and give their annual turnover. The Register now includes a complaint mechanism that sets out the procedure in cases of non-compliance by its signatories.

In early 2011, the Parliament and the Commission agreed, after almost a year of negotiations, to join forces on this issue. Now both use the Transparency Register. This cooperation ensures that two of the EU's most heavily lobbied institutions apply the same criteria, procedures and rules in their dealings with interest representatives. It offers a one-stop shop for non-legislative actors wishing to indicate their intention to input into EU policy-making, while making publicly available details of who they are.

Conclusion

Policy-making in the EU presents a paradox. On one hand, many of its core procedures are open, pluralistic, consensual and transparent. On the other hand, there is very little public knowledge of EU institutions and procedures which, for most citizens, remain distant and only occasionally feature on their radar screen. As a result, processes that are not necessarily (much) more elaborate than equivalent national procedures often appear to outsiders to be frightfully complex.

EU procedures have also evolved tremendously over the last few decades. Of course, no procedure could be hallowed by centuries of tradition as might be found in some member states. But what is striking about the EU is that virtually no procedure has remained unchanged for more than two decades. That fluidity is likely to remain. As the Union has grown both in size and importance, the number of actors seeking to influence encourage, block, or simply report on its policies, has grown immensely.

BOX 6.7   Citizens' Initiative

The Lisbon Treaty introduced the 'Citizens' Initiative', with the aim of giving ordinary citizens a greater say in EU initiatives. If a petition gathers at least one million signatures from EU citizens in 'a significant number of member states' (now fixed at one quarter), the Commission is invited to table a proposal to address the issue raised.

This attempt to introduce direct democracy into EU decision-making had not been formally used by the time this edition was published. Legislation needed to determine all the practicalities of putting the principle into practice will only come into force in early 2012. It had been used informally on over 20 occasions, but in the absence of the necessary implementing legislation, no further action was taken.

The very first informal petition to attract over one million signatures was a call to have just one seat (not two: Brussels and Strasbourg) for the European Parliament. Others included a request for work-free Sundays, effective rights for the disabled, and a moratorium on genetically modified foods. The subject of Citizens' Initiatives must be in an area where the EU has competence. So, there is no possibility of the device being used to try to, say, legalize euthanasia or abolish university tuition fees.

How this initiative will work out in practice is unclear. In particular, the Commission is not bound to bring forward a proposal even if the million signatures are secured and the subject is one where the EU has competence. Nor is it prohibited from taking up suggestions from a single individual.

We have highlighted the rich variety of actors and interests involved in shaping policy-making. Representatives of different member states, political viewpoints, sectoral interests, social partners, regions and localities, non-EU countries, and public interest NGOs of all kinds all jostle for influence. There are ample opportunities for different interests to make their voice heard. As at the national level, however, there are also concerns that some interests—especially the best-financed interests—exert undue influence compared to other public interests with fewer resources (Warner 2007; Bernhagen and Mitchell 2009).

Yet, the EU also provides an alternative arena where groups that are not gaining access at the national level—say, environmental or women's groups—have a second chance to be heard. The EU's complex and multilevel character can make access difficult (see Aspinwall and Greenwood 1998) but it can also provide groups with opportunities for **venue shopping**—that is, pushing issues towards the level, institution, or venue with the greatest receptivity to their own point of view (see Box 6.1; Baumgartner 2007: 484). By this view, the EU thus enhances the quality of European democracy (see Box 6.7 and Chapter 7).

The bottom line of where the final decision is taken in EU policy-making is in the hands of elected representatives: those elected directly by citizens in the European Parliament or via their member state in the Council or European Council. As in every national system, their decisions will be influenced by outside pressures and arguments. But they remain the ones ultimately accountable to the electorates.

DISCUSSION QUESTIONS

1. Why does the EU need so many—and so many complicated—decision-making procedures?

2. What is 'enhanced cooperation'? Why is it seen to be needed in an EU of 27 member states (plus)?

3. Does the increasing involvement of outside interests in the EU's decision-making process make for better policy?

4. Is democracy strengthened or undermined by the presence of non-elected interest groups in the EU decision-making process?

FURTHER READING

The definitive guide to policy-making in the EU remains Wallace *et al.* (2010). Richardson (2005) is also useful. There is also a very wide literature on lobbying in the European Union that can be divided into general texts, specific case studies or analyses, and practical guides and reference works. The most recent general text is Coen and Richardson (2009), but Greenwood (2003) also provides a useful, detailed examination of different interest groups. A special issue of the *Journal of European Public Policy* (2007) is devoted specifically to lobbying. Goergen (2006) offers a very comprehensive practical guide to lobbying, and the regularly updated publication, the stakeholder.eu directory (2011), compiled by the former MEP Frank Schwalba Hoth, offers an overview of the wide range of actors involved. On the European Parliament, including its political groups, see Corbett *et al.* (2011, Chapter 10) and Judge and Earnshaw (2002).

Coen, D. and Richardson, J. (2009), *Lobbying in the European Union: Institutions, Actors and Issues* (Oxford and New York: Oxford University Press).

Corbett, R., Jacobs, F., and Shackleton, M. (2011), *The European Parliament*, 8th edn. (London: John Harper).

Goergen, P. (2006), *Lobbying in Brussels: A Practical Guide to the European Union for Cities, Regions, Networks and Enterprises* (Brussels, D&P Services).

Greenwood, J. (2003), *Representing Interests in the European Union* (Basingstoke and New York: Palgrave).

Journal of European Public Policy (2007), Special issue on 'Empirical and Theoretical Studies in EU Lobbying', 14/3.

Judge, D. and Earnshaw, D. (2002), 'No Simple Dichotomies: Lobbyists and the European Parliament', *Journal of Legislative Studies*, 8/4: 61–79.

Richardson, J. (2005), *European Union: Power and Policy-Making*, 3rd edn. (London and New York: Routledge).

Stakeholder.eu: the Directory for Brussels (2011) (Berlin: Lexxion).

Wallace, H., Pollack, M. A., and Young, A. R. (eds.) (2010), *Policy-Making in the European Union*, 6th edn. (Oxford and New York: Oxford University Press).

WEB LINKS

- The Commission has established a directory of non-profit pan-European organizations. This electronic database, known as 'The Register of Interest Representatives', now holds details of nearly 1,000 European bodies grouped by category—for instance trades unions, professional federations, profit-making bodies, and religious interests. The site provides basic data on each organization and lists representatives with which the Commission has formal and structured consultations. It can be found at: **https://webgate.ec.europa.eu/transparency/regrin/welcome.do?locale=en#en**.

- The websites of the major umbrella organizations mentioned in this chapter (Business-Europe, ETUC, COPA) can also all be accessed via the Register of Interest Representatives site.

- For the public register of expert groups advising the Commission, see **http://ec.europa.eu/transparency/regexpert/**; for details of recipients of EU grants, see **http://www.ec.europa.eu/grants/beneficiaries_en.htm** and for beneficiaries of EU public contracts, see **http://www.ec.europa.eu./public_contracts/beneficiaries_en.htm**.

- This 'world newspapers' site provides links to newspapers from all over the world, including pan-European newspapers and links: **http://www.world-newspapers.com/europe.html**

- Some of the organized interests discussed in this chapter are also represented through formal institutions. See the websites of the Committee of the Regions (**http://www.eesc.europa.eu/**) and the Economic and Social Committee (**http://www.esc.europa.eu/**).

- The website of stakeholder.eu is: **http://www.stakeholder.eu/**

- Finally, the websites of some of the think tanks mentioned include the Centre for European Policy Studies (**http://www.ceps.eu/**); the European Policy Centre (**http://www.theepc.be/**); the Centre for European Reform (**http://www.cer.org.uk**); and the Trans European Policy Studies Association (**http://www.tepsa.be**).

Visit the Online Resource Centre that accompanies this book for additional material: **www.oxfordtextbooks.co.uk/orc/bomberg3e/**

CHAPTER 7

Democracy in the European Union

Richard Corbett

▎ Summary

With so many decisions taken at EU level, what are the implications for democracy? All EU member states are (indeed, have to be) democratic. But when they take collective decisions through European institutions, the individual choices available to national democracies are naturally constrained. To what extent do democratic procedures at the European level compensate for this narrowing of choices at national level? Is there a 'democratic deficit'? How, anyway, do we measure 'democracy'? National democratic systems are diverse, but do have some common features: can we evaluate the EU using them as a yardstick?

Democracy Beyond the State?

Economic, environmental, and other forms of interdependence mean that a growing number of problems cannot be adequately dealt with by national authorities alone. Many require concerted international action at various levels. But traditional methods of international cooperation are slow, cumbersome, and frequently opaque. They involve negotiations among officials and, later, ministers representing their countries. In most cases, nothing can be agreed without consensus—thus creating a bias towards weak, lowest common denominator agreements. When an agreement is reached, it is submitted, if at all, as a *fait accompli* to national parliaments on a take-it-or-leave-it basis. The quality of democracy on such issues is low. Such are the working methods of the World Trade Organization (WTO), the International Monetary Fund (IMF), the World Bank, the United Nations (UN, including on climate change), NATO, and regular summits such as the Groups of 8 or 20 (G8 and G20) and countless other structures.

The European Union (EU) purports to be different. It is not (always) in hock to the lowest common denominator. There is an elected Parliament, directly representing citizens and bringing into the process representatives of both governing and opposition parties in each country. Decisions on legislation are taken in public. It has an independent executive, the European Commission, headed by Commissioners who are politically accountable to the elected Parliament. It has a common Court to ensure uniform interpretation of what has been agreed. It has safeguards to ensure that it respects fundamental rights. It has more developed mechanisms than any other international organization for informing, and sometimes involving, national parliaments. So, can we say that 'the EU not only forms a Union of sovereign democratic states, but also constitutes a democracy of its own' (Hoeksma 2010)? Can democracy work at all on an international basis?

Some argue that democracy can only work when there is a demos, that is, a common feeling of belonging to the same community (see Moravcsik 2002). A demos usually involves speaking the same language, tuning into the same media and having a shared past and similar expectations about behaviour and values. Others argue that this view of democracy is tribalist and point out that if speaking a common language is a requirement, then Switzerland, India, Canada, South Africa, and many others can never be categorized as democratic. Debates around 'demos' and decision-making will continue, but most agree that, as some decisions *are* taken at European level, it should be in as transparent, accountable, and democratic a way as possible.

The EU's basic rule book is set out in the treaties. They lay down its field of competences, the powers of its institutions, how to elect or appoint people to those institutions, and the details of its decision-making procedures. Some scholars argue that the treaties can be described as a *de facto* constitution (see Weiler 1999; Box 11.1). But, an attempt to rewrite those treaties and formally label them as a 'constitution' failed in part because of reticence in some countries to the idea of the EU being a state-like federation. Opinions diverge as to what the nature of the EU should be and how far its democratic accountability should flow through democratically chosen governments in each county or through the directly elected Parliament, or through both. The EU has a dual democratic legitimacy, represented by its bicameral legislature: the Council representing the governments of the member states, whose democratic legitimacy is conferred on the national level, and the European Parliament, directly elected by citizens. It is not a question of whether national governments *or* the European Parliament best represent EU citizens: both sustain the EU's claim to be democratic.

Caveats, however, apply. First, the EU does not operate by simple majoritarian rule. The adoption of legislation by a qualified majority vote in the Council may indeed achieve more than the lowest common denominator consensus that applies in traditional international organizations. But it still requires a hefty majority: as we saw in Chapter 3, a qualified majority must comprise at least 62 per cent (and soon 65 per cent) of the represented population in the Council. One or more member states may be outvoted and still be obliged to respect the terms of a decision they opposed. And in the Parliament, MEPs do not represent citizens equally, as the ratio of member to population is considerably lower in the smaller member states. This point was highlighted by the German Constitutional Court in its 2009 ruling on the Lisbon Treaty in which it held that, for that very reason, the EP could not be compared to a parliament representing a single people. Second, democratic choice of the executive is not visible in the way that citizens are used to in a national context (see Hix 2008). Neither by direct election nor through parliamentary elections does the electorate determine the political composition of the executive—or at best, it does so only in a roundabout way. Do these caveats render the EU undemocratic? Is there a democratic deficit in the EU? (See Box 7.1.)

To shed more light on this discussion, we evaluate the democratic credentials of the EU by asking whether it matches some key features common to many modern democratic systems:

1. representation: is legislation adopted by representative assemblies?
2. are powers separated?
3. is the executive democratically accountable?
4. are fundamental rights guaranteed? and
5. do competing political parties offer voters genuine choice?

Legislating through Representative Assemblies

Under the Union's 'ordinary legislative procedure, proposals need to be approved by directly elected representatives in the Parliament and indirectly elected representatives in the Council. The budget is similarly subject to the approval of both, as are almost all international agreements entered into by the Union. This dual requirement involves a scale of parliamentary scrutiny not found elsewhere beyond the level of

BOX 7.1	Key concepts and terms

Bicameralism: from Latin *bi*, two + *camera*, chamber. The principle that a legislature should comprise two chambers, usually chosen by different methods or electoral systems.

Democratic deficit: was a term initially used to denote the loss of democratic account-ability inherent in national parliaments transferring their right to legislate to ministers meeting in the Council. It was considered that this transfer of power should be compen-sated for by giving the EP the right to approve or reject EU legislation. Now that the EP has such powers (in most policy areas), the term has taken on a less precise meaning, often linked to the distance between EU institutions and voters.

European Convention on Human Rights: (ECHR) formally the *Convention for the Protection of Human Rights and Fundamental Freedoms* is an international treaty drafted in 1950 by the then newly formed **Council of Europe**. All (the now 47) Council of Europe member states are party to the Convention. Any person who feels his or her rights, as defined in the Charter, have been violated by a state can appeal to the **European Court of Human Rights** (which is completely separate from the EU's own Court of Justice). Judgments finding violations are binding on the state(s) concerned.

Charter of Fundamental Rights of the European Union: the EU has its own Charter of Rights that binds the EU institutions and EU law. Adopted initially as a political declara-tion by the EU institutions in 2000, it was given treaty status by the Treaty of Lisbon. It includes, but goes beyond, the rights contained in the ECHR.

the nation state. And, as we saw in Chapter 3, the EP is not a rubber stamp, subservi-ent to the executive through a governing majority party or a coalition. It has been described as one of the most powerful legislatures in the world. We also saw that it has not always been thus. Originally, the EP was merely a consultative body, with final decisions being taken behind closed doors in the Council. After the first direct elections in 1979, it took three decades and successive revisions of the treaty to change this state of affairs. Public perceptions have lagged behind, and the Parlia-ment is still seen by many as a toothless tiger.

The EP is also sometimes held to be inadequate in another respect. It is not just the approval of legislation, but the right to initiate it which is held to be an important democratic criterion. After all, people are elected to parliaments having made prom-ises to their voters: at least some of those promises require initiating legislation, or repealing it. But in the EU, there is a gap insofar as the EP cannot (except in a few specific cases) itself table proposals for adoption.

Yet this difference must be nuanced. Parliament and Council both have the right to request the Commission to put forward a legislative proposal. If it does not, both have ways and means to make life difficult for the Commission. Conversely, in national parliaments, which in most (but by no means all) cases do enjoy a right of legislative initiative, it is almost invariably the government which initiates proposals. It is in the give-and-take of debate and discussion between the legislature and the executive that ideas and initiatives emerge. This dynamic is not so different in the EU context.

How representative are the Parliament and the Council?

Where the *Parliament* is concerned, the question of representation is often linked to electoral turnout. Turnout in the most recent EP elections has been around 43 per cent, or about the same as for mid-term US Congress elections (that is, when there is no Presidential election). By one view, it is normal that turnout is lower than for national parliamentary elections in European countries—less is at stake. But turnout for EP elections has also fallen—by around 20 percentage points over a 30-year period. This decline (accentuated by the accession of new member states, several of whom have a low turnout in all elections) is no greater than the decline in turnout in national parliamentary elections in several countries. Declining participation is a challenge for democracy at all levels, not peculiar to the European level, even if the latter does have special features (see also Box 7.2).

BOX 7.2	Compared to what? Referenda in EU member states

An alternative to representative democracy is direct democracy: the organizing of referenda to settle issues. National traditions diverge enormously, with referenda being (almost) unknown in most member states, or at least reserved only for constitutional changes. There is no provision under the treaties to allow for EU-wide referenda, even on 'constitutional' changes to the EU system. Occasional proposals to introduce them come up against the opposition of countries that do not have referenda as part of their national traditions. Even if member states did agree, the question remains of by what majority decisions should be taken: just a simple majority of those voting, or a majority (or more) of states as well?

Some member states have organized national referenda on European issues. Most countries acceding to the EU did so, with only Norway deciding not to join. Some have had referenda on treaty changes: two frequently (Ireland and Denmark, because of national constitutional requirements) and four (France, Luxembourg, the Netherlands, and Spain) occasionally. The UK coalition government in 2010 introduced legislation to require a national referendum for any future treaty change that transfers powers or competences from the UK to the EU.

Debate on the merits of referenda on treaties reached a crescendo during the ratification stage of the Constitutional Treaty in 2005. Most member states considered that it required detailed scrutiny and a vote by their national parliament. Four member states held national referenda: two approving it (Spain and Luxembourg) and two rejecting it (France and Netherlands). Although the grand total of the votes in the four countries showed a majority in favour—and every parliamentary vote approved it—the need for every single member state to ratify individually caused the Constitutional Treaty to fall.

Even on a low turnout, European elections do result in all the main strands of public opinion being represented in the EP. A transnational parliament highlights that most policy choices at European level have political, not national, dividing lines, with the different sides of an argument present in every member state. MEPs come from parties of the left and of the right and even some parties who are opposed to the very existence of the EU. Because EP elections frequently fall mid-term in national political cycles, they often result in a larger share of the seats going to opposition parties and smaller parties than would be the case in most national elections. EP elections thus can perhaps be dismissed as little more than a protest vote, but the results matter: they elect a wide variety of parties and thus have the effect of balancing the Council, whose members come exclusively from governing parties. The Parliament thus enhances pluralism and ensures that the EU decisions are not taken exclusively by ministers, diplomats and bureaucrats.

In the *Council*, member states' representatives (ministers) cast a number of votes related to their size, unlike in many federal systems where the chamber of states often gives equal representation to states of quite different sizes. This proportionality can be seen as making the Council more representative of citizens. Yet, the fact that Council representatives must cast all their votes on behalf of their member state as a bloc could be viewed as distorting the representation of the people. However it is viewed, the weighted bloc vote is a feature that Council shares with the German Bundesrat, with which it also shares a number of other structural similarities (see Table 7.1).

TABLE 7.1	Compared to what? The Council and the German Bundesrat	
	Council	**Bundesrat**
Composition	Ministers from member state governments. Preparatory meetings by Permanent Representatives (Ambassadors) of member states in Brussels	Ministers from State (*Länder*) governments. Preparatory meetings by Permanent Representatives of States in Berlin
Voting	Each member state's vote weighted by size and cast as a bloc	Each State's (*Land*) vote weighted by size and cast as a bloc
Majorities required	Usually, threshold higher than simple majority (qualified majority or unanimity)	To disagree with Bundestag, threshold usually higher than simple majority (absolute majority)
Reconciliation with elected chamber	Conciliation Committee with EP	Conciliation Committee with Bundestag

As we saw in Chapter 3, what had originally been the key aspect of this weighted bloc vote, namely a fixed number of votes, will disappear in 2014/17. The new system will feature a double majority based on one vote per state on the one hand, and a vote weighted by population (still cast as a bloc) on the other. Thus, the two traditional representation aspects found in bicameral federal systems—equality of states in one chamber and equality of citizens in the other—will both be found in a single chamber in the EU: the Council. Meanwhile, representation in the Parliament will 'over-represent' smaller states.

Nonetheless, the Parliament and Council between them can test the acceptability of proposals from the point of view of both a majority of component states and the majority of the component population, with states represented as such in one chamber, and citizens in the other. They perform these functions in the context of a consensual system where high thresholds are needed, notably in the Council, to adopt any legislation, budget or policy. All in all, the EU system involves a greater number of representative channels than can be found anywhere else in the world above the level of the nation state.

Involving national parliaments

Also unique are the Union's provisions for helping *national parliaments* scrutinize the participation of their government in EU institutions. In certain cases, national parliaments may intervene directly themselves independently of their national government. The Lisbon Treaty lists a number of ways in which national parliaments 'contribute actively to the good functioning of the Union'.

One notable innovation in the Lisbon Treaty is a Protocol 'on the Application of the Principles of Subsidiarity and Proportionality'. It contains a new procedure allowing national parliaments to send, within eight weeks of receiving a legislative proposal, a reasoned opinion to the EU institutions stating why they consider that the draft does not comply with the principle of subsidiarity (that is, it goes beyond the remit of the EU). If such reasoned opinions come from enough national parliaments (roughly one-third), then the draft must be reviewed by the Commission, which must then justify its decision to maintain, amend, or withdraw its proposal. Employing a football analogy, this procedure is known as the 'Yellow card'. Alternatively, if such reasoned opinions come from more than half of EU parliaments, then a special vote must take place in the Council and in the EP, either of which can immediately kill off the proposal (by a simple majority in the EP or by a majority of 55 per cent of the members of the Council). This special vote is known as the 'Orange card procedure', as it was proposed by the Dutch (whose football team wears orange) and is not quite a red card. These procedures are an important safeguard to prevent over-centralization of powers, even if it is unlikely that they will be frequently needed. In the first year of operation of the procedures, no proposal came anywhere near receiving the number of reasoned opinions needed to trigger even a yellow card.

But the very existence of these procedures is likely to mean that more parliaments will pay close attention to the shaping of European policy in their country—and on the substance, rather than just checking subsidiarity. More may start holding committee hearings of their country's minister before Council meetings, as is already standard practice in the Nordic countries, or send comments on the substance of proposals directly to the Commission (there are currently some 200 such submissions per year). Also, parliaments confer among themselves, exchanging documents through an electronic exchange system, or meeting together at committee level.

National parliaments are also involved in the process of future Treaty change. Any intergovernmental conference to revise the Treaty must (unless the EP decides otherwise) be preceded by a Convention composed of members of national parliaments, the EP, the Commission, and a representative of each government. And of course, in most member states, national parliaments must ultimately ratify such treaty changes.

The Treaty provisions involving national parliaments are thus quite numerous. In truth, most national parliaments have little time to devote to the nitty-gritty detail of EU issues. Unlike the EP, most are in a classic government/opposition structure where governing majorities mean that there is, in practice, little scope to amend government texts or reverse their policies. National parliaments also have less time, expertise, and staff to devote to European matters than does the EP, which works full time on EU affairs. National parliamentary procedures, practices, and timetables all diverge. Nonetheless, national parliaments are able to scrutinize and sometimes take part in EU decision-taking to a degree that simply does not exist in other international organizations. In sum, the involvement in the adoption of legislation of both a dedicated parliament, elected at its level, and of national parliaments, means that the EU's credentials measured against this particular yardstick of democracy are substantial.

Separation of Powers

Most democracies operate a separation of powers, although the separation of the legislative, executive, and judicial functions is not always clear. Indeed, many speak of a 'sharing' of powers across institutions, with checks and balances, rather than a separation of powers (Neustadt 1991). In particular, the executive and the legislative functions have tended to merge in most European democratic systems, (although they remain more distinct in presidential systems, notably in the Americas).

Some European countries blur this distinction completely. The UK and Ireland, for instance, actually require members of the government to be simultaneously members of the legislature (even if this sometimes just means appointment to the House of Lords or Senate). By contrast, in France, a parliamentarian who becomes a minister must resign his/her seat for the duration of his/her ministerial mandate. Either way, it is the norm in most European countries for the executive to have a majority in Parliament which, through the party system and other mechanisms, is usually compliant to the wishes of the executive. The separation between these two branches thus becomes less than clear. Only the judicial function remains clearly separate.

In the EU, the separation between the executive and the legislature is in some ways more distinct. Commissioners may not simultaneously be MEPs. In the EP there is no compliant governing majority for the executive. Thus, in adopting legislation, a majority has to be built anew for each item through explanation, persuasion, and negotiation. The EP's role is thus more proactive than that of most national parliaments in Europe.

The Council (of ministers) is the institution that muddies the waters. It is, of course, a co-legislature with the EP. However, it is also empowered to act as an executive in specific cases. When acting on macroeconomic policy or foreign affairs, it is fulfilling an executive rather than a legislative function, albeit one that consists largely of coordinating national executives rather than constituting a European one.

The European Council (of heads of state and government) does not directly act as an executive nor as a legislature (indeed it is precluded from exercising a formal legislative role by the treaty). Yet it influences both. Formally, it is the strategic body, charged with defining the 'the general political directions and priorities' of the Union. Informally, as a meeting of the most powerful political figures of the member states and the Union, it is often called upon to settle thorny political questions that can be of an executive, legislative, or constitutional nature. It also nominates or appoints a number of key posts in the Union. Its own President has a representational role in addition to his main task of preparing and building consensus. The European Council could be considered as a sort of collective 'head of state' of the Union. Its significant political role is similar to that of heads of state in national semi-presidential systems.

As for the judicial function, the European Court of Justice (ECJ) is composed of judges 'chosen from persons whose independence is beyond doubt'. They must take an oath to 'perform their duties impartially and conscientiously'. The deliberations of the Court are secret, so individual judges cannot be pressurized about judgments. We never know how any judge voted on any case unless they reveal how they voted in their memoirs.

Interestingly, the Court's members are appointed neither by the EU's executive nor by its legislature. Instead, they are appointed by the member states. The Court thus differs from the US Supreme Court, whose justices are appointed by the federal authorities (President and Senate), not by the states. The only common European element in the appointment procedure of the members of the ECJ was introduced in the Lisbon Treaty. Appointees are now scrutinized by a panel chosen by the Council and consisting of seven former judges of the Court (or of national supreme courts) or eminent lawyers.

The appointment of individual judges therefore depends more on the government of the member state from which they originate than on the European executive or legislature. If there is any political consideration in their appointment, it is at the member state level and diffuse: each national government is involved in the nomination of only one judge. Another method used in many democracies to lessen political pressure on judges is to appoint them for a lengthy term of office, or even for life, as in the US Supreme Court. Judges in the ECJ are appointed for a (renewable) six-year term of office.

The Court has exercised an important independent function, ensuring that the institutions respect the law, though it can only do so when a matter is referred to it. The independence of the judiciary is clear. It has both struck down acts of the Union's political institutions and ruled against member states when they have failed to apply European law. Overall, the Union system is characterized by a separation or sharing of powers that is at least as distinct as is the case in most of its member states.

Executive Accountability

The relationship between the outcome of European parliamentary elections and the composition of the executive is not as visible as it is in most European national parliamentary elections. But, the view that the Commission is 'unelected', unlike national governments who are, is simplistic. The UK government, for example, is not elected by the people: it is appointed by the head of state (an unelected one at that), but crucially it must enjoy the confidence of the directly elected House of Commons. Similarly, the European Commission must enjoy the confidence of the European Parliament. The EP always had the right to dismiss the Commission. It recently acquired the right to approve the appointment of the Commission, and indeed to elect its President. In fact the EP took such votes even before such procedures were laid down formally in the treaties (see Table 7.2). The grilling that candidate Commissioners receive from EP committees at their confirmation hearings prior to their confirmation is unknown for ministers in most European countries.

Despite this scrutiny, few citizens would consider the Commission to have an elected mandate. They might if the college of Commissioners were composed to reflect a majority party or, more likely, a majority coalition, in the EP. Yet a Commission thus composed is unlikely to emerge in the short to medium term: most governments want to nominate as the Commissioner from their country a member of their own political 'family'. What *has* begun to change is that the vote on the President of the Commission is becoming more political and linked to the outcome of elections. That vote is increasingly important as the President's pre-eminence within the Commission grows.

The change to the Treaties brought in by Lisbon refers to the 'election' of the President of the Commission by the Parliament. This vote is, as before, on a proposal of the European Council but the latter must now 'take into account the results of the European elections' in making its nomination. This provision potentially makes the nomination

TABLE 7.2	Election of Commission President by the European Parliament	
	Incoming Commission Presidents	**Parliamentary Votes**
July 1992	Jacques Delors (third term)	278 votes for, 9 against
July 1994	Jacques Santer	260 votes for, 238 against (23 abstentions)
May 1999	Romano Prodi (for unfilled portion of Santer term)	392 in favour, 72 against, (41 abstentions)
September 1999	Romano Prodi (full 2000–5 term)	426 in favour to 134 against (32 abstentions)
July 2004	Jose Manuel Barroso (first term)	431 in favour to 251 against (44 abstentions)
September 2009	Jose Manuel Barroso (second term)	382 in favour to 219 against (117 abstentions)

similar to that of a head of state choosing a candidate Prime Minister who is capable of enjoying a parliamentary majority (see Box 7.3).

Eventually, European political parties may start nominating their candidates for Commission President ahead of the European election campaign. Even before Lisbon, the European People's Party (centre-right) was very clear that, in the event of it having the largest number of seats in the EP, it would expect the nominee for Commission President to come from its ranks. The Greens actually nominated Daniel Cohn-Bendit as their candidate, in the unlikely event that they would obtain a parliamentary majority. In 2009, the Party of European Socialists decided that it would designate a candidate ahead of the 2014 European elections. There appears to be momentum in this direction of tighter links between European parties and the choice of the Commission President.

In practice, it is always unlikely that any single party will win a majority of seats in the EP. Some bargaining and coalition forming will remain the most likely scenario of the future. But this kind of negotiation also occurs in most member states. The spectacularly direct link between the outcome of a parliamentary election and the designation of a prime minister seen (usually) in the UK is the exception rather than the norm. But the outcome even in, say, the Netherlands is that the public sees

BOX 7.3	Compared to what? How are heads of executives chosen?

Commission President: elected by EP by an absolute majority on a proposal of the European Council, which must take account of the results of European Parliamentary elections.

German Chancellor: elected by the Bundestag by an absolute majority on a proposal of the Federal President.

UK Prime Minister: appointed by the Queen in light of advice as to who can secure a parliamentary majority in the lower chamber (House of Commons), but with no formal vote in parliament.

US President: chosen by an electoral college, whose members are elected in each state, normally as a function of which presidential candidate they support.

French Prime Minister: chosen by the directly elected President, without requiring a vote by parliament. However, the lower chamber (*Assemblée*) may dismiss the government by an absolute majority.

Swiss government: college of seven (with annual rotation of President among them), elected by the two chambers of the parliament (and comprising members of all major parties).

Swedish Prime Minister: nominated by Speaker of the parliament and serves unless opposed by an absolute majority of (single chamber) parliament.

Italian Prime Minister: nominated by President. His cabinet then requires approval by both chambers of the parliament (simple majority).

that the executive—usually consisting of a coalition of parties—that emerges is connected to an election and reflects its pattern of votes.

If this outcome becomes established at the EU level over the next few years, it will happen only as regards the *head* of the EU's day-to-day executive: the Commission President. Does this 'halfway house' mean the Union is not comparable to a national democracy and can never be? Not necessarily. Take the case of Switzerland, which for over half a century has been governed by a coalition of the four largest parties, with an annually rotating President. Is such a collegiate system undemocratic? Does the lack of a direct relationship between the outcome of the parliamentary elections and the governing coalition render elections meaningless? Most Swiss would seriously object to their country being described as undemocratic. Yet the composition of the European Commission too is always (in political terms) a coalition of at least the three main political parties in Europe (the second Barroso Commission contained

13 Christian Democrats, 6 Socialists and 8 Liberals). The Commission would appear to be edging towards a hybrid of Swiss-style collegiality in its overall composition with a more majoritarian approach to designating its leader.

If so, it is part of a long-term trend. Prior to the 1994, Commissioners were simply designated by the Member States to serve a four-year period without further ado. The Maastricht Treaty changed the term of office to five years to coincide with the cycle of European Parliamentary elections, and provided for a vote of confidence by Parliament on the Commission as a whole. From 1999, the Amsterdam Treaty required a decisive Parliamentary vote on the designation of the President. The Lisbon Treaty characterized this vote as an election—further implying that the parliamentary majority is what will be decisive.

What of the President of the European Council? From January 2010 this post became a full-time and longer-term position, and thus vital for the dynamics of the European Council. But its wider systemic implications remained to be seen. Certainly, it can be a confusing post for the public to understand. The press already uses the term 'President of Europe' in some cases (and in some countries) for the President of the European Council while in other cases (and other countries) the label refers to the President of the Commission. The difference between the two Presidents will not always be clear to average Europeans. Nor indeed for third countries: both Presidents represent the Union at external summit meetings.

But above all, the two Presidents have quite different forms of democratic legitimacy. The source of legitimacy of the Commission President (elected by the EP and linked to majorities resulting from the its elections) is likely to be more visible than that of the President of the European Council (elected by the heads of state or government of the member states). Suggestions that one or both should be directly elected are unlikely to get very far and would in any case likely cause further problems in the relationship between the two. Even with the best will in the world, some degree of uncertainty about these respective 'presidential' roles is likely to continue for many years to come. The possibility of merging them, as has been done at the level of the High Representative, may return to the agenda, but it is unclear that it would ever gain a consensus.

Finally, to the extent that the Council has an executive role, to whom is it accountable? Collectively, to no one—though most decisions require EP approval. But individually each of its members is accountable through a national government to a national parliament. Given the Council's main 'executive' tasks are essentially about coordinating national policies (foreign policy, defence, macroeconomic coordination), that member state-based accountability may be considered appropriate. In any event, the Council must also justify itself in EP debates and answer parliamentary questions.

To sum up, accountability of the executive is present in the EU even if it is complex. For the main executive body (the Commission), a system close to what is found in most national contexts—that is, accountability to a Parliament—has been established. However, the system is not well known to citizens and the link between the results of parliamentary elections and the composition of the executive is not very visible. As regards executive functions exercised elsewhere, they are either in an institution that is deliberately independent (the Central Bank), or else through institutions (Council and European Council) whose members are accountable individually to separate parliaments.

Respecting Fundamental Rights

Democracy is frequently defined as rule by the majority. But in modern times, it is increasingly seen as going hand-in-hand with respect for minorities and for the rights of individuals. Governments and even elected parliaments can be challenged in the courts should they fail to respect fundamental rights.

This feature can also be found in the EU. Initially it was exercised via case law: the ECJ acknowledged that the Union had to respect the fundamental rights that are common to the constitutional traditions of the member states. The Court recognized that all member states had signed the ECHR (the European Convention on Human Rights of the Council of Europe) and that it should be a source of law for its own deliberations. The Maastricht Treaty after 1992 entrenched this case law in the Treaty itself.

With the Lisbon Treaty, the Union obtained its own Charter of Rights (see Box 7.1), intended both to make those rights already contained in the ECHR visibly applicable to the Union but also to complement them with other rights. The Charter was framed in such a way as to be binding in the field of EU law. In other words, it binds the EU institutions, and member states when applying European law. It means that decisions or acts of the Union can be struck down by the Court should they fail to respect the rights contained in the Charter.

Furthermore, the Lisbon Treaty provided for the Union itself to accede to the ECHR. The result will give plaintiffs the right to appeal to the European Court of Human Rights should they fail to gain satisfaction from the ECJ, much in the same way as in member states an appeal can be made against the final judgment of a national court. In other words, the EU's legal system will be subject to the same external yardstick as member states' legal systems. Thus, in relation to the formal criterion of respecting fundamental rights, the EU system and procedures measure up well.

Political Parties

Besides the constitutional requirements for democracy to function effectively, a functioning system of political parties is a practical need. As we have seen, the EP provides a pluralistic forum, with over 150 national political parties converging into seven political groupings. But to offer choice to the electorate in elections, and to channel and aggregate policy demands into workable programmes, party structures beyond Parliament are needed. One of the main points of debate about democracy in the EU is about whether pan-European democracy is impossible in the absence of pan-European parties (see Lindberg *et al.* 2008). In the European context, such parties have evolved as federations of national parties, but they are looser groupings than are parties in most national European contexts (see Box 7.4).

The recognition and the development of these parties has been incremental. The Treaty of Maastricht introduced a new article referring to the importance of European political parties. Later, they were granted legal personality and—crucially—access to funding, provided certain conditions are met, such as being represented in a sufficient number of member states (at least one quarter) and respecting the principles of the EU (such as liberty, human rights, and so on), although they do

---

BOX 7.4   European political parties

European political parties are cross-national and reach beyond the EU. They are linked to but distinct from the political groups in the European Parliament. Three existed before the first direct elections to the EP:

- the Party of European Socialists (PES), comprising parties affiliated to the Socialist International;
- the European People's Party (EPP), comprising Christian Democrats and other centre-right or conservative parties; and
- the European Liberal, Democratic and Reformist Party (ELDR), comprising a variety of liberal and allied parties.

Two more emerged between 1979 and 2004 (and MEPs from these two parties currently sit in the same Group in the Parliament):

- the European Green Party
- the European Free Alliance, comprising regionalist and nationalist parties such as the Scottish, Flemish, Basque, Corsican, Sardinian, Catalan, and Welsh nationalists.

A number of other (smaller) European political parties were created following the adoption of a system for financing such parties in 2004. These included:

- the European Left (which includes a number of Communist or former Communist parties);
- the European Democratic Party (which describes itself as a 'centrist political party in favour of European integration');
- the Alliance of European Conservatives and Reformists (AECR, including notably the UK Conservatives);
- the small European Christian Political Movement; and
- two separate Eurosceptic parties—the EU Democrats and the (now defunct) Alliance of Independent Democrats in Europe.

not have to support the EU itself. They also must publish their accounts and have them independently audited, as well as publish the names of any donors contributing more than €500. Parties may not accept donations of more than €12,000 from any single donor, nor accept anonymous donations. The money provided from the EU budget is for European parties; it may not be passed on to national parties.

The main parties are active in a growing number of areas. They organize regular congresses, composed of delegates from the respective national parties and involving their EP Group. Their leaders can hold 'summits' (often prior to European Council meetings) with fellow party members in the Commission, EP, and heads of government. They adopt common manifestoes for European elections. Their decision-making tends in practice to be by consensus among the national member parties, which means that the content of their policies tends towards the lowest common denominator. However, the incentive to achieve convergence can shape the positions of individual national parties.

What is the real impact of these parties? They are generally unknown to the public, except in the broadest sense that—for the Socialists, Liberals, Greens, and Christian Democrats—their voters may be aware that they are part of a larger European grouping and that they work together in the EP. Only a sophisticated minority of voters will actually be aware of the common manifestoes on which they stand in European elections. However, even without such an awareness, the elaboration of such manifestoes can lead to a degree of convergence around common positions of corresponding parties. The parties do certainly play a role in the 'division of spoils' in terms of securing prominent positions at European level, and not just within the EP. For example, it was quite clear at the time of the choice of Herman Van Rompuy as President of the European Council and Catherine Ashton as High Representative that these posts were to be shared between the EPP and the Socialists. Parties also play a role in the choice of President of the Commission, as we have seen earlier in the chapter. The further development of this role provides an opportunity for European political parties to become more visible, as well as offering the electorate a choice of personalities and not just of policies.

In short, European political parties do play a role, not just in representation but in policy formation and in the choice of some political office holders. That role remains limited and rather invisible to the bulk of the electorate. However, it has been developing and expanding, even if the process has been slow and very gradual.

Conclusion

The EU requires that its member states be democratic and respect fundamental rights (and even has a procedure for suspending a member state that ceases to fulfil this requirement). Whether these criteria are fulfilled by the EU itself is a more complex question. It has given rise not only to much debate, but also to many of the treaty amendments of the last 25 years.

We have seen that the EU system does fulfil fundamental democratic norms, but in a way that is more complex and less visible to the public than is the case at national level. Like any political system, it has its own idiosyncrasies. Inevitably, its detailed functioning is different from what people are familiar with within their own national system (themselves diverse). Those differences and complexity give rise to misunderstandings amongst concerned citizens, and can also be exploited by its opponents.

Nonetheless, the EU is unique in how far it goes to try to apply democratic principles at a level above the nation state. How successful it is, given how much of the governing of Europe it does, remains open to debate (see Habermas 2008). Nevertheless, there is no doubt that the debate itself is one of the features of the EU that make it so fascinating.

DISCUSSION QUESTIONS

1. How can democratic accountability be assured for those matters dealt with at European level? Should it be via national parliamentary scrutiny over their own government's negotiating position, or via the European Parliament, or both?

2. Does the relatively low turnout in European elections matter?

3. Are fundamental rights sufficiently protected at European level?

4. Should the European Commission emanate from a parliamentary majority in the EP?

5. Are referenda in individual member states an appropriate way to ratify EU treaties?

FURTHER READING

For detailed accounts of the EP, see Corbett et al. (2011) and Judge and Earnshaw (2008). Internal cleavages and voting patterns in the Parliament are covered by Hix et al. (2007) and Hix (2009), who also (2008) offers a comprehensive programme for democratic reform of the EU. For a critical appraisal of the EP's links with the public, see Hug (2010). For different evaluations of the democratic credentials of the EU and the challenges of transnational democracy, see Pinder (1999), Moravscik (2002), Siedentop (2002), Bogdanor (2007), and Hoeksma (2010). Corbett (2002) assesses the impact of having an elected parliament on the process of integration. For an interesting examination of alternative futures by a leading European intellectual, see Habermas (2008).

Bogdanor, V. (2007), *Democracy, Accountability and Legitimacy in the European Union* (London: Federal Trust for Education and Research).

Corbett, R (2002), *The European Parliament's Role in Closer EU Integration* (Basingstoke and New York: Macmillan, 2002).

Corbett, R., Jacobs, J., and Shackleton, M. (2011), *The European Parliament*, 8th edn. (London: John Harper Publishing).

Habermas, J. (2008), *Europe: the Faltering Project* (Cambridge and Malden MA: Polity).

Hix, S., Noury, A., and Roland, G. (2007), *Democratic Politics in the European Parliament* (Cambridge and New York: Cambridge University Press).

Hix, S. (2009), *What to Expect in the 2009–14 European Parliament: Return of the Grand Coalition?* (Stockholm: Swedish Institute for European Policy Analysis).

Hoeksma, J. (2010), *A Polity called EU: The European Union as a Transnational Democracy* (Amsterdam: Europe's World).

Hug, A. (2010), *Reconnecting the European Parliament and its People* (London: Foreign Policy Centre).

Judge, D. and Earnshaw, D. (2008), *The European Parliament*, 2nd edn. (London: Palgrave Macmillan).

Moravscik, A. (2002), 'Reassessing Legitimacy in the European Union', *Journal of Common Market Studies*, 40/4: 603–24.

Pinder, J. (1999), *Foundations of Democracy in the European Union* (Basingstoke and New York, and New York: Macmillan and St Martin's Press).

Siedentop, L. (2002), *Democracy in Europe* (Harmondsworth: Penguin).

WEB LINKS

Websites of the institutions: see Chapter 3.

- Voting Behaviour in the European Parliament: **http://www.votewatch.eu/**
- European People's Party: **http://www.epp.eu/**
- Party of European Socialists: **http://www.pes.org/**
- European Liberal Democrats: **http://www.eldr.eu/**
- European Green Party: **http://europeangreens.eu/**
- COSAC: **http://www.cosac.eu/en/cosac/**

Visit the Online Resource Centre that accompanies this book for additional material: **www.oxfordtextbooks.co.uk/orc/bomberg3e/**

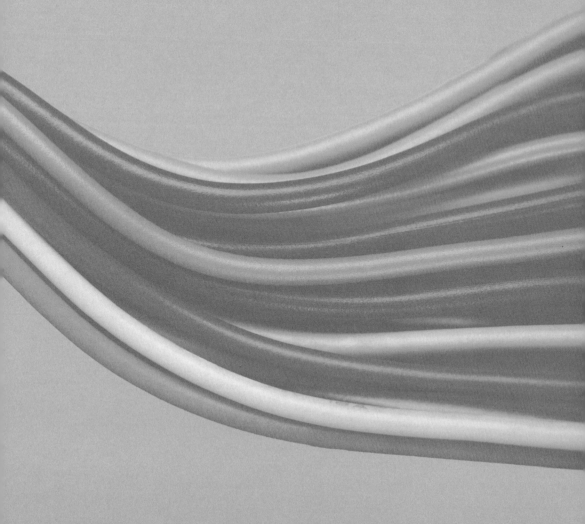

PART IV

The EU and The Wider World

CHAPTER 8

EU Expansion and Wider Europe

Graham Avery

▌ Summary

The European Union (EU) has expanded many times, and its widening continues. Enlargement demonstrates the success of the European model of integration, but poses fundamental questions. It has implications both for how the EU works (its structure and institutions) and for what it does (its policies). The expansion in the 2000s to include countries of Central and Eastern Europe showed how the EU's transformative power can promote stability, prosperity, and security. The EU has extended the prospect of membership to more countries, including the Balkans and Turkey. It has developed a 'neighbourhood' policy towards other countries, some of whom aim at future membership. The EU now operates on a continental scale: where will its final frontiers lie?

Introduction

The EU's process of expansion is interesting for students of European affairs because it goes to the heart of important questions about the nature and functioning of the EU. Why do countries wish to join? How does the EU decide its future shape and size? How should it interact with its neighbours? Enlargement is also ongoing: since the EU is committed to further expansion, past experience can help to guide future policy.

It is often said that enlargement is the EU's most successful foreign policy (see Chapter 10). It has indeed extended prosperity, stability, and good governance to neighbouring countries by means of its membership criteria, and this success gives enlargement a special place among the EU's external policies. But enlargement is much more than foreign policy: it is the process whereby the *external* becomes *internal*. It is about how non-member countries become members, and shape the development of the EU itself. In accepting new partners, and deciding the conditions under which they join, existing members define the EU's future composition and collective identity. In that sense, enlargement could better be described as 'existential' policy, since the EU determines its own nature when it makes choices concerning membership.

Widening versus deepening

The prospect of enlargement poses fundamental questions both for applicant countries and for existing members. Before applying, countries need to analyse how membership will affect them. What will accession (see Box 8.1) mean in political and economic terms? What will be the costs and benefits? What should be the country's long-term aims as a member? This kind of reflection raises questions of national strategy and even identity.

A recurrent theme in the development of the EU has been the tension between 'widening' of its membership and 'deepening' of the integration between its members. Each time the EU contemplates a further expansion, its members are compelled to address fundamental questions which do not present themselves to policy-makers in the normal course of events.

When considering *who* should be new members, the EU has to reflect on *what* it should do with them (what set of common policies?) and *how* to do it (with what institutional set-up?). Debates on the future of European integration regularly accompany enlargement, although for countries trying to join the EU these debates can be mystifying. To outsiders, the 'widening versus deepening' debate can seem introspective, and even a tactic for delaying enlargement.

But the potential impact of enlargement on the Union's capacity to act and take decisions is a very important question. Non-members apply to join the EU because

---

BOX 8.1   Key concepts and terms

Absorption capacity refers to the EU's ability to integrate new members into its system.

Accession is the process whereby a country joins the EU and becomes a member state.

Candidate refers to a country whose application for membership is confirmed by the EU but which is not yet a member.

Conditionality refers to the fact that accession is conditional on a country fulfilling the criteria for membership.

European Economic Area (EEA) is an arrangement which extends the EU's single market to Norway, Iceland, and Liechtenstein.

Screening occurs at the start of negotiations when the applicant and the Commission examine the *acquis* to see if there are particular problems to be resolved.

Transitional period is a period after accession when application of some of the *acquis* may be phased in or delayed.

Variable geometry, also known as multi-speed Europe, is the idea that not all EU member states should take part in every field of policy.

---

it is attractive, and one of the reasons why it is attractive is that it is effective in taking decisions and developing policies. To expand without safeguarding its effectiveness would be an error. Enlargement policy is thus linked with the wider debate on European integration; in fact, the accession of new members often provides an occasion for institutional reform.

Have successive enlargements weakened the EU? While it is true that the arrival of new members requires a period of 'settling in', it is often followed by the development of new policies and the strengthening of the institutional framework. For example, the EU's structural funds and a more ambitious cohesion policy resulted from the 1980s accession of Greece, Portugal, and Spain, poorer countries needing financial aid (see Chapter 5). Later it was feared that the accession of Austria, Sweden, and Finland, countries which had pursued neutrality or military non-alliance, would put a stop to the EU's Common Foreign and Security Policy (CFSP). But in practice they have viewed the CFSP's development more favourably than some of the older members.

From time to time 'old members' (those already in the EU) complain that it was easier to take decisions when the EU was smaller. That may be true (though crises were a regular feature of the EU even in its early days), but nevertheless it is plausible to suggest that successive increases in size have allowed the EU to develop more substantial and effective policies, internally and externally, than would have been possible with a smaller group. The process of widening has often accompanied or reinforced deepening: *more* has not necessarily led to *less*.

Enlargement as soft power

The success of enlargement in helping to drive political and economic change in Central and East European countries offers a good illustration of the EU's 'soft power' (Nye 2004; Grabbe 2006). The conditionality (see Box 8.1) or leverage of prospective membership encouraged policy-makers in those countries to pursue the basic reforms necessary for EU membership. External pressures—the 'demands of Brussels'—were a powerful factor during the pre-accession period.

Conditionality was not employed in earlier enlargements. When the Commission proposed in 1975 that Greece's membership should be preceded by a period of preparation, the idea was rejected by the EU's leaders. Later, Austria, Sweden, and Finland were able to join within two or three years of applying for membership.

Why was the principle of conditionality developed for the countries of Central and Eastern Europe? First, they were in transition from the Communist period and in search of western political and economic models, which required sustained external assistance and encouragement. Second, the existing members were apprehensive that taking in so many new countries without adequate preparation could impair the EU. It was enlightened self-interest, rather than altruism, that led the EU in 1993 to define the membership criteria for the countries of Central and Eastern Europe.

These membership requirements (referred to as the Copenhagen criteria, see Box 8.2) have become the standard template for enlargement. They require a wide-ranging assessment of a country's political, economic, and administrative standards, going further than any examination made by the EU of its existing members. This has led to the complaint that the Union demands higher standards of new members than it does of itself. Moreover, the leverage is effective only in the pre-accession period; after joining, an applicant country becomes a member like others. The EU does not apply its accession criteria to existing members, although potentially it can sanction them for failure to respect the EU's basic principles of democracy or human rights.

An institutional paradox

The enlargement process casts interesting light on the functioning of the EU's institutions. The mode of operation for enlargement is essentially intergovernmental in character. The Council adopts all decisions on enlargement by unanimity—though majority voting in EU decision-making has been extended in many areas, no one has

BOX 8.2	Criteria for membership

TREATY PROVISIONS

The Treaty on European Union, as amended by the Lisbon Treaty, states:

- Article 2:

The Union is founded on the values of respect for human dignity, freedom, democracy, equality, the rule of law and respect for human rights, including the rights of persons belonging to minorities.

- Article 49:

Any European state which respects the values referred to in Article 2 and is committed to promoting them may apply to become a member of the Union.

COPENHAGEN CRITERIA

The European Council at Copenhagen (1993) stated in its conclusions:

Membership requires:

1. that the candidate country has achieved stability of institutions guaranteeing democracy, the rule of law, human rights and respect for and protection of minorities
2. the existence of a functioning market economy as well as the capacity to cope with competitive pressure and market forces within the Union
3. the presupposition of the candidate's ability to take on the obligations of membership including adherence to the aims of political, economic and monetary union.

The European Council added:

4. The Union's capacity to absorb new members, while maintaining the momentum of European integration, is also an important consideration in the general interest of both the Union and the candidate countries.

ever suggested extending it to enlargement. Accession negotiations take place in an intergovernmental conference organized between the member states and the applicant state. The result is an Accession Treaty, signed and ratified unanimously between sovereign member states.

The roles of the European Parliament and the Commission in the intergovernmental process of enlargement are limited. The Parliament has the right to approve enlargement by consent (see Box 6.3), but only at the end of the negotiation process, when it can vote on an Accession Treaty on a yes/no basis, without being able to modify the text. During accession negotiations, Parliament is informed regularly, but has no seat at the table.

The Commission's status in accession negotiations is not the same as in external negotiations where it acts as spokesperson (such as trade, see Chapter 10). In accession conferences the Council Presidency, rather than the Commission, presents EU positions, even on matters where the Commission has competence. Formally the Commission is not the EU's negotiator, although it may be mandated by the Council to 'seek solutions' with applicants. Nevertheless, in practice the Commission plays an extremely influential role in the process of enlargement. Its role provides an illustration of the new institutionalist notion that influence can be exercised even in the absence of formal power. The Commission is better equipped technically than member states to monitor the progress of applicant countries in respect of the criteria for EU membership; its regular reports on each country provide the benchmarks for decisions on the conduct of enlargement. In matters where it has competence, the Commission has the sole right to present proposals to the Council for 'common positions' to be taken by the EU side. It is thus in a privileged position to act as interlocutor and intermediary with the applicant countries, and it can (and should) make proposals that reflect the views of the future members as well as existing members.

Within the Council enlargement is handled in the General Affairs Council, not the Foreign Affairs Council, and the EU's High Representative for foreign and security policy has no role in enlargement negotiations. When responsibility for foreign policy passed to the European External Action Service as a result of the Lisbon Treaty (see Chapter 10), enlargement policy remained with the Commission. This continuity illustrates that enlargement is not primarily foreign policy. It also shows that although enlargement is intergovernmental, the Commission plays a key role: in fact, it exercises more influence over applicant countries before rather than after they become members.

How the EU has Expanded

The first applications for membership were made by Britain, Denmark, and Ireland in 1961, soon after the European Communities came into existence. Although that first attempt was stopped when France's President Charles de Gaulle (twice) said 'No', the three tried again and joined in 1973. This first enlargement was followed by others (see Box 8.3) and more are in prospect (see Box 8.4). Over time the number of EU member states has quadrupled, its population has tripled, and its official languages have increased from four to 23. In fact there have been few periods in the life of the EU when it was not engaged in discussions with prospective members—a remarkable tribute to its magnetism.

But for countries wishing to join, the path to membership is not easy. Negotiations for accession are arduous (see Boxes 8.5 and 8.7): there is no guarantee that they will

BOX 8.3	Chronology of enlargement		
	Application for Membership	**Opening of negotiations**	**Accession**
United Kingdom	1967	1970	1973
Denmark	1967	1970	1973
Ireland	1967	1970	1973
Greece	1975	1976	1981
Portugal	1977	1978	1986
Spain	1977	1979	1986
Austria	1989	1993	1995
Sweden	1991	1993	1995
Finland	1992	1993	1995
Hungary	1994	1998	2004
Poland	1994	1998	2004
Slovakia	1995	2000	2004
Latvia	1995	2000	2004
Estonia	1995	1998	2004
Lithuania	1995	2000	2004
Czech Republic	1996	1998	2004
Slovenia	1996	1998	2004
Cyprus	1990	1998	2004
Malta	1990	2000	2004
Romania	1995	2000	2007
Bulgaria	1995	2000	2007

Notes

- The UK, Denmark, and Ireland first applied in 1961, but negotiations ended in 1963 after France vetoed their admission.

- Norway applied twice (1967, 1992) and completed negotiations (begun in 1970, 1993), but Norwegians twice said 'No' in referenda (1972, 1994).

- Switzerland made an application in 1992 but suspended it in the same year after the 'No' vote in a referendum on the EEA.

- A 'silent' enlargement took place in 1990 when the German Democratic Republic reunited with the Federal Republic of Germany.

- Morocco's approach to the EC in 1987—not a formal application—was rejected as it was not considered European.

end in agreement, or by a certain date, and the bargaining is one-sided. The EU insists that applicant countries accept all its rules (known as the acquis), and allows delays of application (transitional periods, see Box 8.1) only in exceptional cases. Meanwhile, as the EU's policies have expanded over the years, applicants, like athletes,

BOX 8.4	**Prospective members**		
	Application for membership	Candidate status	Opening of negotiations
Turkey	1987	1999	2005
Croatia	2003	2004	2005
Macedonia (FYROM)	2004	2005	
Montenegro	2008	2010	
Albania	2009		
Iceland	2009	2010	2010
Serbia	2009		
Bosnia-Herzegovina			
Kosovo			

Notes

- This list includes all countries currently considered by the EU to be in the enlargement process.

- When the EU decides that an applicant country has made sufficient progress, it may award it the status of 'candidate'. Until then, it has the status of 'potential candidate'.

- Kosovo is not recognized as a state by some EU members.

face a higher 'bar' that is more difficult to cross. But after all, they applied to join the Union, not vice versa. The EU has never invited others to join its club—in fact, it has tended to discourage them. In this sense, the EU's strategy for enlargement has been reactive rather than pro-active: it has grown mostly under pressure from its neighbours, not as a result of imperialist ambition.

Why countries want to join

Countries apply to join the EU because they think membership is in their political and economic interest. While opinions have differed, according to the country, on whether economics or politics were the most important factor, both have always counted. In the case of the United Kingdom (UK), its application was motivated by the prospective benefits of the common market for its trade and economic growth. But its leaders also understood that the original six members were on the way to creating a European system from which the UK could not afford to be excluded politically. It was natural for Ireland and Denmark, with their tradition of agricultural exports to the UK and the Six, to apply as well.

The applications from Greece, Portugal, and Spain were made in different circumstances. After getting rid of totalitarian regimes, these countries wanted membership

BOX 8.5   The path to membership

Start. A country submits an application for membership to the European Union's Council of Ministers.

1. The Council asks the Commission for an Opinion.

2. The Commission delivers its Opinion to the Council.

3. The Council confirms the applicant country's candidate status.

4. The Council decides to open accession negotiations, which are conducted in an intergovernmental conference between the EU member states and each applicant individually.

5. The Commission screens (see Box 8.1) the different chapters of the *acquis* with the applicant.

6. For each chapter in the negotiations the EU decides to open, the applicant presents a position; the Commission proposes a 'common position'; the Council approves it for presentation to the applicant.

7. After agreement is reached on a chapter, the EU decides whether to close it.

8. When all chapters are closed, the EU and the applicant agree on a draft Treaty of Accession (which may cover other applicants).

9. The Commission issues its Opinion on the Treaty.

10. The European Parliament gives its consent to the Treaty.

11. The member states and the applicant(s) sign the Treaty.

12. The signatory states ratify the Treaty according to national procedures (which may require referenda).

Finish. The Treaty of Accession comes into force, and the applicant becomes a member state.

BOX 8.6　　**Compared to what?**

EU and NATO—a double race to membership

After the end of the Cold War, most of the countries of Central and Eastern Europe wanted to join the North Atlantic Treaty Organization (NATO) as well as the EU. NATO is a transatlantic alliance created in 1949 in face of the perceived threat from the Soviet Union. Under Article 5 of the Washington Treaty, signatories commit themselves to mutual assistance: 'an armed attack against one or more of them in Europe or North America shall be considered an attack against them all'. NATO now has 28 members:

- two from North America (US and Canada);
- 26 from Europe:
  - 21 EU states (EU-27 minus Austria, Cyprus, Finland, Ireland, Malta, and Sweden); plus
  - Norway, Iceland, Turkey, Albania, Croatia.

Most other European states, including Russia, have an association with NATO but are not full members.

For the countries of Central and Eastern Europe, concerned about Russia's future intentions, NATO offered *hard security* in the military sense, including the US's nuclear 'umbrella'. The EU offered *soft security* through its political union (see Chapter 10). Even without a mutual defence clause this soft security was important, but the Central and East European countries considered the EU's nascent security and defence policy insufficient to guarantee their territorial integrity. Their accession to NATO in 1999 and 2004 preceded their joining the EU in 2004 and 2007. It was easier for these countries to join NATO for two reasons. First, NATO has simpler tasks and requirements than the EU. Its membership conditions mainly concern the organization and equipment of troops, while the EU has a wide range of political, economic, and administrative requirements. Secondly, NATO's leading member, the US, decided to push for its enlargement, much to the irritation of Russia.

The result of the double enlargement is that the membership of the two organizations now largely overlaps, which makes it easier for them to work together. But the NATO/EU relationship is not simple, and there remains a basic asymmetry. NATO, unlike the EU, includes the US. Moreover, NATO's role is now less focused on territorial defence and more on intervention in other regions. In these regions NATO still has the best military tools to deal with the *results* of insecurity, for example in Afghanistan. But the EU has the best civilian tools to deal with its *causes*, by promoting economic integration, prosperity, and good governance.

---

as a confirmation (and guarantee) of their return to democracy. The sense of being accepted back into the European family was as important to them as the prospect of access to the common market and the budget. Austria, Sweden, and Finland applied for membership despite having access to the common market through the European Economic Area (EEA; see Box 8.1). In their eyes, the EEA's economic benefits were compromised by the obligation to accept rules from Brussels without having a say

> **BOX 8.7   How it really works**
>
> **Joining the EU singly or together**
>
> The EU says it treats all applicant countries on their merits: the path to membership depends on individual progress in meeting the criteria, with no linkage between applicants. This principle is called 'differentiation'—there is no predetermined grouping of countries for accession. That is why accession negotiations are conducted by the EU with each applicant separately, which also gives it the possibility to play them off against each other ('divide and rule').
>
> The EU prefers an organized process of expansion, with intervals between enlargements. So, although each accession negotiation is separate, and a country can join singly (as Greece did in 1979) there are usually groups or waves of accession. Countries wishing to improve their chances in the race may be tempted to apply for membership prematurely in the hope of joining a good 'convoy'. For example, Macedonia applied soon after Croatia, but it did not succeed in opening accession negotiations.
>
> By creating competition between applicant countries the EU brings the market into the enlargement process. This 'group dynamic' (the wish to emulate others, and the fear of being left behind) helped to push the Central and East European countries forward to membership together. Applicants often demand a target date for membership, but the EU refuses to concede it until towards the end of negotiations since it considers that the promise of a date weakens the conditionality of the process.
>
> Accession negotiations are 'asymmetrical': the EU is always in the stronger bargaining position.

in deciding them. These countries also realized that the collapse of the Soviet bloc created a new political situation in Europe in which their traditional neutrality was less appropriate.

When the 10 countries of Central and Eastern Europe made the change from communism and Soviet domination, they turned to the EU not only for economic help but for membership. Like Greece, Spain, and Portugal, they wanted to rejoin the European family, and to consolidate their return to democracy. They also had further reasons. For their transition from central planning to market economy, the EU's system and standards offered a convenient 'template'. Uncertain of Russia's future role, they wanted EU membership for national security and as a back-up to NATO membership, which they pursued at the same time (see Box 8.6).

Recent enlargements

The collapse of the Soviet bloc in 1989 was a seismic shock, creating risks of instability in Europe. Civil war broke out in ex-Yugoslavia, and this strife could have occurred elsewhere if events had unfolded differently. But the countries of Central and Eastern Europe succeeded in charting a route to democracy, stability, and prosperity by making far-reaching economic, social, and political reforms. The prospect of EU membership served to guide them in a peaceful 'regime change' in which the process of Europeanization (adapting domestic politics to the EU's rules, norms, and policies) played a key role (see Chapter 4 and Grabbe 2006).

Faced with many new aspirants for membership by the early 1990s, the EU's first response was cautious. In its Europe Agreements (covering aid, trade, and political links with these countries) the EU refused to include the promise of membership. But at the Copenhagen summit in 1993 the EU accepted that the countries of Central and Eastern Europe could join when they fulfilled certain criteria for membership. These Copenhagen criteria (Box 8.2) were defined for the first time at that summit.

In the accession negotiations, which opened with six countries in 1998 and six more in 2000, the main problems (see Avery 2004) were:

- free movement of labour: the EU allowed old members to maintain restrictions on workers from new member states for up to seven years;

- agricultural policy: the EU insisted on a period of 12 years for introducing direct payments to farmers in the new member states; and

- money: the level of payments to new, much poorer members from the EU budget became a contentious issue.

But the negotiations in Brussels were less important than the preparation for membership in the applicant countries themselves. The 'conditionality' of the process created a framework in which the Central and East European countries were able to make the transition to democracy and market economy peacefully and on a durable basis. The economic consequences of enlargement were positive for both old and new member states, and created conditions for the European economy to face increased global competition. However, the influx of migrants from the new members caused social problems in some areas, and the persistence of bad governance (corruption, maladministration, weak judiciary) led to the realization that the accession criteria should have been applied more rigorously, particularly for Romania and Bulgaria. Nevertheless the enlargement to EU-27 was an extraordinary episode in the history of European integration, and it shifted the EU's scale of activity to a continental level. Whereas previous enlargements took place in a Europe divided between East and West, these enlargements helped to unite it.

The admission of the countries of Central and Eastern Europe has led to an interesting debate among political scientists. According to liberal intergovernmentalism, the EU-15 must have been guided in their decision to enlarge by the expected costs and benefits, and since enlargement proceeds by unanimity all member states must have reckoned that it was advantageous to them. But was that really so? In fact, some members were quite reluctant. According to the constructivist approach, which emphasizes the role of principles and values, it was the historic promise of peace and unity, rather than the material prospects, that created a 'rhetorical entrapment' which was the main driver of the decision (see Schimmelfennig and Sedelmeier 2005).

Prospective Members

We now review the countries which the EU officially considers as prospective members beyond the EU-27: Turkey, the Balkan countries, and Iceland. We also look at Norway and Switzerland, which have applied for membership in the past. Although the Treaty says any European state may apply to become a member (see Box 8.2), other countries are at present discouraged from applying, including those subject to the EU's Neighbourhood Policy (see below).

Balkan countries

In South-east Europe about 25 million people remain outside the EU:

- Albania: 3.6 million
- Bosnia-Herzegovina: 4.5 million
- Croatia: 4.5 million
- Former Yugoslav Republic of Macedonia (FYROM): 2.1 million
- Kosovo : 1.8 million
- Montenegro: 0.7 million
- Serbia: 7.3 million.

A glance at the map (Figure 8.1) shows that these countries—sometimes known as the Western Balkans—are surrounded by the EU. They are trying to make the political and economic reforms necessary to join, but have a difficult legacy of ethnic, social, and religious conflict. For most of the twentieth century the region was united in Yugoslavia, but the disintegration of that federation in the 1990s led to civil war and the intervention of the UN and NATO.

As a result ancient rivalries and fears lie just below the surface. There are basic problems of statehood— the question of Kosovo's international status is not fully resolved (its independence from Serbia is not recognized by all EU members, and its government is supervised by a European Union Rule of Law Mission—EULEX) while Bosnia is still under external tutelage: it is supervised by a UN High Representative who is also a EU Special Representative. Coupled with problems of poor governance, corruption, and criminality, the region suffers from a syndrome of political dependency on external actors. But reforms, and EU membership itself, require autonomy and a functioning democracy.

The countries are at different stages on the way to EU membership (see Box 8.4). The Stability and Association Process (SAP) package, which combines trade concessions and financial aid, has been a stepping-stone for all of them: Croatia concluded accession negotiations in 2011 with a view to accession in mid-2013. The others have either applied or intend to apply for EU membership.

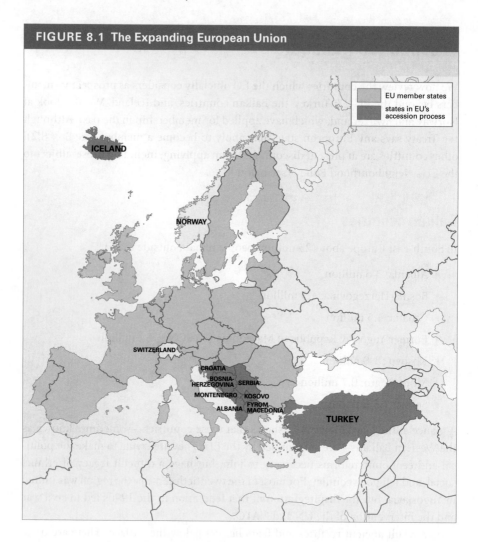

FIGURE 8.1 The Expanding European Union

Although the United States and Russia have influence in the region, the international community now sees it as Europe's main responsibility. At a summit at Thessaloniki in 2003 the EU's leaders recognized all the countries of the Western Balkans as prospective members. The region poses the biggest test yet of the EU's transformative power. Can conditionality and pre-accession instruments be used as successfully as they were in Central Europe? Can European integration provide a basis for the region's stability and prosperity by encouraging good governance and reconciliation between communities?

Turkey

Turkey's 'European vocation' was avowed as early as 1964 in its Association Agreement with the Community. Its application for membership dates from 1987. But as Redmond (2007) recounts, the path towards membership has been long, and remains difficult. Despite the fact that accession negotiations opened in 2005, Turkey's future membership is by no means assured.

Many of the arguments that were valid for preceding enlargements apply to Turkey. As Barysch *et al.* (2005) explain, its growing economy and young labour force would bring benefits for the single market. Although there would be costs for the EU's budget in the fields of agriculture and cohesion policy, the overall economic impact of Turkey's accession should be positive. Turkey has a big population: 78 million now, expected to grow to 90 million or more in future. In terms of income per head, it is much poorer than the EU average. Its position on Europe's southeastern flank gives it geostrategic importance in relation to the Middle East and the Black Sea region, and as a member of NATO it has played a key role in European security.

The majority of Turkey's population is Islamic, but it has been a secular state since the 1930s. Its efforts to conform to European standards of democracy, human rights, and rule of law are monitored closely by the EU. Progress has been made towards meeting the Copenhagen criteria, but more still needs to be done. Amongst the main problems are Turkey's treatment of its Kurdish minority, its restrictions on freedom of expression, and the political role of its military.

Many argue that by admitting Turkey, the EU would give a signal to other countries that it accepts Islam. To refuse Turkey would show that Europe is culturally prejudiced, and might lead to a reversal of Turkey's reforms, or even turn it against the West. Others reject this argument: just as religion is not a reason to say 'No' to Turkey, it is not a reason to say 'Yes'. Although Turkey's population is Islamic, it is not an Arab country, and it has a historic legacy of difficult relations with neighbours such as Armenia.

In foreign policy, Turkey's membership would be positive for the EU in many ways. For example, Turkey has more soldiers than any other European member of NATO. But it would also bring new problems and risks. With Turkey's accession, the EU's external frontiers would extend to Azerbaijan, Armenia, Iran, Iraq, and Syria, so it would be in direct contact with regions of instability.

Public opinion in the EU is influenced by fear of an influx of Turkish migrant workers, and the idea that Turkey is different—that it is not part of Europe in geographical or cultural terms. As a result Turkish membership is opposed by a number of political parties particularly in France, Germany, and Austria. It is also argued that the EU's decision-making system would have difficulty coping with Turkey, which would be the biggest member state.

Cyprus is a further thorn of contention. Since Turkey intervened militarily in 1974, the Turkish Republic of Northern Cyprus—not recognized by the rest of the international community—has been separated from the south by a UN peacekeeping force. Hopes of reuniting the two parts of the island were dashed by referenda in 2003 when the Greek Cypriots in the south said 'No' to a UN plan that was accepted by the north. As a result, the EU's enlargement of 2004 brought in a divided island. All these problems put a question-mark over Turkey's bid for EU membership. Some argue that, even if it does not finally become a member, Turkey has an interest in continued modernization in line with European criteria. But with an uncertain prospect of membership, the leverage for change in Turkey is less effective. There is a growing risk of crisis with Turkey in the accession negotiations, where progress has been slow and several chapters are blocked by objections from France and Cyprus.

Iceland, Norway, and Switzerland

Iceland applied for EU membership following a banking crisis which showed its vulnerability as a small country. It certainly fulfils the EU's basic criteria for membership. However, the common fisheries policy may be an obstacle in accession negotiations and the people of Iceland may not say 'Yes' in a referendum on the EU (see Avery *et al.* 2011).

It is sometimes forgotten that membership applications have been made by Norway and Switzerland (see Box 8.3). Oil-rich Norway negotiated and signed two Accession Treaties, but did not join after its people said 'No' twice in referenda. This divisive experience has made its politicians reluctant to reopen the question of EU membership. As a member of the EEA, it has access to the common market and participates in other EU policies. In fact, the EEA (which also includes Iceland and Liechtenstein) is the closest form of relationship that the EU has made with non-member countries.

Switzerland's application for EU membership was suspended when its citizens voted 'No' in a referendum on the EEA, and since then it has pursued its interests through bilateral agreements with the EU. While the French-speaking part of the population is broadly in favour of the EU, a majority of German-speakers are opposed. Switzerland's 'direct democracy' with frequent use of referenda could pose problems for its membership. However, small, rich countries like Switzerland and Norway are ideal applicants for the EU: if they decided to apply again, they would be accepted as candidates.

Wider Europe

European Neighbourhood Policy

With expansion to include Central and Eastern Europe, the EU encountered a series of new neighbours to the east. It already had a Euro-Mediterranean Partnership with countries to the south, and now it was obliged to rethink relations with the countries of Eastern Europe that were formerly in the Soviet Union. New EU members such as Poland and Hungary did not want to see their accession lead to the erection of new barriers to countries with which they have cultural, social, and economic links.

The result was the development of the European Neighbourhood Policy (ENP) covering 16 countries: Morocco, Algeria, Tunisia, Libya, Egypt, Israel, Jordan, the Palestinian

Authority, Lebanon, Syria, Armenia, Azerbaijan, Georgia, Moldova, Ukraine, and Belarus (see Figure 8.2). Its aim is to extend stability, prosperity, and security, and create a 'ring of friends' by developing political links and economic integration with the EU. Its main instrument is a series of Action Plans negotiated with each partner country and backed by financial and technical assistance. These plans cover political dialogue, economic and social reform, trade, cooperation in justice and security affairs, transport, energy, environment, education, and so on. They require the neighbours to take on European regulation and a large part of the *acquis*: the system is modelled, in fact, on the EU's Accession Partnerships with future members.

But the ENP lacks the big incentive of the enlargement process—the 'golden carrot' of accession. Its message is 'be like us' not 'be one of us'. For the East Europeans such as Ukraine, the fact that the policy is 'accession-neutral' has been a disappointment. Although it offers long-term benefits, it demands reforms that are difficult and costly, and does not fully satisfy participants' wishes in fields such as trade in agriculture or visas for travel to the Union. But it does provide increased financial aid and a closer political relationship.

The ENP is sometimes criticized as a 'one size fits all' formula for two groups of countries with different interests and problems—neighbours *of* Europe in the south, and neighbours *in* Europe in the east. But in practice Action Plans are tailored to fit the individual needs of the countries. Grouping the countries together strikes a necessary balance between the different geographical and political priorities of EU members such as Germany and Poland on the one hand, and Italy, France, and Spain on the other.

The diversification of ENP has continued, reflecting the different situations and interests of the countries concerned. On the initiative of France, relations with the countries of the EU's Southern neighbourhood were deepened through the creation in 2008 of the 'Union for the Mediterranean'. An initiative from Poland and Sweden led to the creation in 2009 of the 'Eastern Partnership' with six East European countries (Armenia, Azerbaijan, Belarus, Georgia, Moldova, and Ukraine). Although this Partnership remains accession-neutral, it provides improved political cooperation, further economic integration, and increased financial assistance. Partnerships then lead to Association Agreements, which in the past have been precursors of the accession process. However, despite the ENP's declared aims, in practice the EU has had limited success in exploiting it to promote democracy either in Belarus or in the Southern neighbourhood, where local rebellions against autocratic regimes obliged the Union to adapt the ENP to strengthen its conditionality.

The EU offered to extend its European Neighbourhood Policy to Russia, but the invitation was rejected. Russia has preferred to see itself as a 'strategic partner', and remains suspicious of the EU's links with countries such as Ukraine that it considers historically as part of its 'near-abroad'. With its invasion of Georgia in 2008 Russia demonstrated its capacity to influence events in its neighbourhood by the use of force, and that the EU's involvement with the East European neighbourhood does not extend to security.

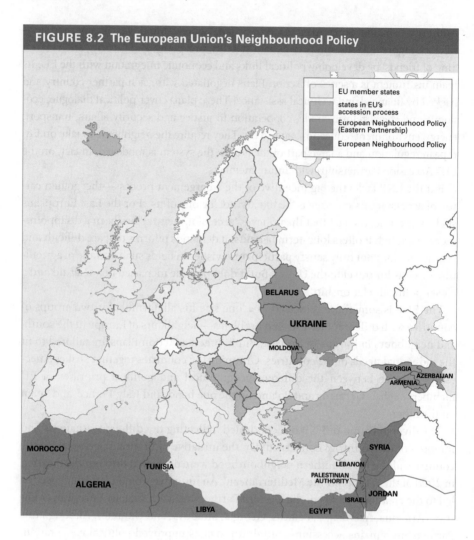

FIGURE 8.2 The European Union's Neighbourhood Policy

EU member states

states in EU's accession process

European Neighbourhood Policy (Eastern Partnership)

European Neighbourhood Policy

What Limits for the EU?

The EU has used the prospect of membership successfully to extend stability and prosperity to neighbouring countries. But is it realistic to continue without predetermined limits? Logically, the EU cannot expand indefinitely: it was not designed to be a world system of government, but an 'ever-closer union' of European peoples. How far can the European Union's expansion continue? Where should its final frontiers lie?

The EU can have different frontiers for different policies. This is already the case for the euro and Schengen (see Chapter 9). In this sense, the EU is already a multi-frontier system. But problems arise when its multi-tier potential is perceived as leading to a 'core-group', with some states having more rights than others. All members, and all applicants, want full rights in decision-making; there is no market for 'second-class' membership.

What is Europe?

The Treaty of Rome in 1957 said 'any European state may apply to become a member'. Subsequent Treaties have added a reference to values (see Box 8.2). It is sometimes suggested that the EU is based on shared values rather than geography. But if this argument were correct we would expect like-minded states in distant parts of the world—such as New Zealand—to be considered as future members. In fact geographic contiguity or proximity is a precondition for membership. The exception which proves the rule is France's overseas departments (such as Guadeloupe or Martinique) which are in the EU because they are part of French territory.

What are the geographical limits of the European continent? To the North, West, and South, it is defined by seas and oceans, but to the East there is no clear boundary. Although the Ural Mountains and the Caspian Sea are often invoked as natural frontiers, some geographers consider Europe as the western peninsula of the Asian landmass—a subcontinent rather than a continent.

In any case, different geographical, political, and cultural concepts of Europe have prevailed at different times. Asia Minor and Northern Africa were within in the political and economic area of the Roman Empire, but much of today's EU was outside it. Other historical periods are cited as characterizing Europe in cultural terms, such as the experience of the Renaissance or the Enlightenment. For some, the Christian religion is a defining factor. Such examples show how difficult it is to arrive at an agreed definition. The European Commission (1992) has taken the view that:

The term 'European' has not been officially defined. It combines geographical, historical and cultural elements which all contribute to the European identity. The shared experience of proximity, ideas, values and historical interaction cannot be condensed into a simple formula, and is subject to review by each succeeding generation. It is neither possible nor opportune to establish now the frontiers of the European Union, whose contours will be shaped over many years to come.

But is it so difficult to know which countries are considered European today? Another European organization, founded in 1949 before the creation of the European Communities, is the Council of Europe. It has a wider membership than the EU (see Box 8.8) and provides an important indication of the limits of Europe as recognized internationally. EU members are all signatories to the Council of Europe, and they can hardly refuse to consider the other signatories as 'European'. This suggests the following list of potential members of the EU:

- Albania, Bosnia-Herzegovina, Croatia, Kosovo, Macedonia, Montenegro, Serbia
- Turkey
- Iceland, Norway, Switzerland
- Armenia, Azerbaijan, Belarus, Georgia, Moldova, Ukraine
- Russia.

> ## BOX 8.8 Other Europeans
>
> Not all European states are in the EU. The other main intergovernmental organization in Europe is the Council of Europe which is mainly concerned with human rights, social and legal affairs, and culture. It has 47 members:
>
> - EU countries (27);
> - Albania, Bosnia-Herzegovina, Croatia, Macedonia (FYROM), Montenegro, Serbia;
> - Turkey;
> - Iceland, Norway, Switzerland;
> - Armenia, Azerbaijan, Georgia, Moldova, Russian Federation, Ukraine; and
> - Andorra, Liechtenstein, Monaco, San Marino.
>
> We should add two potential members: Belarus which would be accepted as a member if it became more democratic, and Kosovo which would be accepted if the problem of its international recognition was solved. However, looking at the list in relation to membership of the EU, we should leave aside the last four, which as mini-states have little interest in joining.

Of this list of 18, some are already considered by the EU as potential members. Could it eventually embrace all the others? Will the final limits of the EU be set at 45 countries?

An attempt by the EU institutions to decide in advance its ultimate limits—a decision requiring unanimity—would not give a clear answer. Member states have differing views on future membership. Those sharing borders with non-members often wish to include them in the EU for reasons of stability and security. Poland, for example, wants its neighbour Ukraine to be a member of the EU. But other states such as France have a more restrictive position, especially on the inclusion of Turkey. In fact, a discussion of the 'limits of Europe' can easily become a debate on 'should Turkey join?'

What are the prospects for countries such as Ukraine, which are presently in the framework of the EU's European Neighbourhood Policy? They are so far from meeting the Copenhagen criteria that EU membership is impossible for many years. So why try to decide 'Yes' or 'No' prematurely, particularly when 'No' could have undesirable consequences for both sides?

Russians consider their country to be European as well as Asian, and the idea of its membership of the EU has been mentioned by leaders on both sides. But could Russia, with its self-identity as a great power, accept the EU's *acquis*? Its geographic expanse and population of 140 million mean that Russia's joining the EU would be more like the EU joining Russia. But with its population declining towards 100 million by mid-century, and facing 1.3 billion Chinese, maybe Russia will one day look with more interest to the EU.

In this situation, prudence argues for keeping open the prospect of EU enlargement. Aspirant countries may be willing to modify their behaviour significantly in the hope of obtaining membership. To define the EU's ultimate borders now would demotivate those excluded, and diminish the leverage for those included. Thus a diplomatic policy of 'constructive ambiguity' seems likely to prevail.

Evaluating Enlargement

The pace of enlargement depends not only on the applicant countries but also on the attitude of the public and politicians in the EU. After its expansion to EU-27 the question of absorption capacity (see Box 8.1) has become an element in the debate. This notion, introduced at Copenhagen in 1993 (see Box 8.2), refers to the need to 'maintain the momentum of European integration'. It thus explicitly links future enlargement to the development of the EU's institutions, policies, and budget.

This brings us to the question, what is the purpose of enlargement? At the beginning of this chapter we saw that enlargement is not only foreign policy, but also a kind of existential policy, in the sense that each successive accession reconfigures the EU's composition. So what are the criteria for evaluating the success of enlargement policy? One cannot evaluate it by reference to the number of countries joining, or by the speed of their accession. The correct approach for evaluation is twofold: a first group of criteria applying to the period before enlargement—the 'pre-accession' period—and a second group to the period after accession, when applicant countries have become members of the EU.

The criteria for the pre-accession period are similar to those for foreign policy: enlargement policy is successful if it enhances security, stability, and prosperity both for the EU and for the neighbouring countries concerned. But a more important test of enlargement policy concerns the period after accession. Here the conditions for a successful result may be defined as the harmonious integration of new members (without disrupting existing members, or the functioning of the EU's institutions and policies) and the satisfactory continuation of the EU's development. Since there is no general agreement on the last criterion—what is a satisfactory development of the EU?—it is not surprising that opinions differ on the merits of enlargement. According to some, the supporters of expansion (typically, the British) want to weaken the EU, while according to others the opponents of expansion (typically, the French) want to safeguard acquired positions and advantages. Although these caricatures are both false, they show how attitudes to enlargement policy can differ widely within the EU (see Sjursen 2008).

What was the result of the increase from 15 to 27? It has not, as some feared, paralysed the EU's decision-making, which seems to work as well, or as badly, as it did in the past (see Chapter 3). Nor has it led to an increase in 'variable geometry' within the EU (see Box 8.1), as commentators predicted: most of the new members, unlike some old members, have joined the Schengen system, and many of them have joined the euro.

However, EU-27 is more complex and heterogeneous. In recent years 'enlargement fatigue' has also become a factor: public opinion in the EU, particularly among the 'old' member states, is more resistant to enlargement, which is sometimes blamed for problems arising from other causes such as globalization or the economic situation. Accessions may in future be subject more often to referenda in member states. Consequently the EU will be rigorous in applying its conditions for potential members, and cautious in making promises to others.

Conclusion

The expansion of the EU has been remarkable in its pace and impact. But after increasing its membership from 12 to 27 states and its population by a third in the period from 1995 to 2007, the EU will expand more slowly in future. In the medium term, it will limit its expansion to the countries of the Balkans and Turkey, whose accession is uncertain and in any case will not take place for many years. Iceland may join more rapidly, as would Norway and Switzerland if they applied for membership. In the longer term the EU may eventually accept other East European countries such as Ukraine, but in the meantime they remain in the framework of its Neighbourhood Policy. Thus the final limits of the European Union are likely to result from the course of events and successive political decisions, rather than from a strategic choice made in advance.

DISCUSSION QUESTIONS

1. Has the EU's enlargement to 27 members weakened its capacity for effective action? Has the 'widening' stopped the 'deepening'?

2. Turkey's application for membership dates from 1987: why is it so difficult for the EU to handle, and will it ever succeed in joining?

3. The EU's basic treaty says 'any European state may apply for membership': should it decide where its frontiers will ultimately lie?

4. The EU's Neighbourhood Policy aims at making a 'ring of friendly countries': can it be a substitute for joining the EU?

FURTHER READING

The enlargements of 2004 and 2007 are the subject of a voluminous literature, particularly on EU conditionality and reform in Central and Eastern Europe. The early stages of the process are covered in Mayhew (1998) and Torreblanca (2001), while the accession negotiations are described in Avery (2004). Schimmelfennig (2003) examines the expansion of NATO as well as the EU. Analyses of the theoretical aspects of enlargement can be found in Schimmelfennig and Sedelmeier (2005) while Sjursen (2006) comments on the EU's motives, Vachudova (2005) presents the 'realist' view and Schneider (2008) analyses the role of transitional periods. For conditionality and 'Europeanization' see Grabbe (2006) and Epstein and Sedelmeier (2009), and for a critique of the EU's handling of conditionality with Romania see Gallagher (2009). On neighbourhood policy, see Weber *et al.* (2007) and Whitman and Wolff (2010).

Avery, G. (2004), 'The Enlargement Negotiations', in F. Cameron (ed.), *The Future of Europe, Integration and Enlargement* (London: Routledge): 35–62.

Avery G., Bailes J.K., and Thorhallsson B. (2011), 'Iceland's Application for European Union Membership' *Studia Diplomatica*, Royal Institute for International Relations, Brussels, 64(1): 93–119.

Epstein, R. and Sedelmeier, U. (eds.) (2009), *International Influence Beyond Conditionality: Postcommunist Europe after EU Enlargement* (London: Routledge).

Gallagher, T. (2009), *Romania and the European Union: How the Weak Vanquished the Strong* (Manchester and New York: Manchester University Press).

Grabbe, H. (2006), *The EU's Transformative Power: Europeanization through Conditionality in Central and Eastern Europe* (Basingstoke and New York: Palgrave Macmillan).

Mayhew, A. (1998), *Recreating Europe: The European Union's Policy towards Central and Eastern Europe* (Cambridge and New York: Cambridge University Press).

Schimmelfennig, F. (2003), *The EU, NATO and the Integration of Europe* (Cambridge and New York: Cambridge University Press).

Schimmelfennig, F. and Sedelmeier, U. (eds.) (2005), *The Politics of European Union Enlargement: Theoretical Approaches* (London: Routledge).

Schneider C.J. (2008), *Conflict, Negotiation and European Union Enlargement* (Cambridge and New York: Cambridge University Press).

Sjursen, H. (ed.) (2006), *Questioning EU Enlargement: Europe in Search of Identity* (London: Routledge).

Torreblanca, J. I. (2001), *The Reuniting of Europe: Promises, Negotiations and Compromises* (Aldershot: Ashgate).

Vachudova, M. (2005), *Europe Undivided: Democracy, Leverage, and Integration after Communism* (Oxford and New York: Oxford University Press).

Weber K., Smith M. E., and Baun M. (eds.) (2007), *Governing Europe's Neighbourhood: Partners or Periphery?* (Manchester and New York: Manchester University Press).

Whitman, R. and Wolff, S. (eds.) (2010), *The European Neighbourhood Policy in Perspective: Context, Implementation and Impact* (Basingstoke and New York: Palgrave Macmillan).

 WEB LINKS

• The European Commission's websites provide information, official documents, and speeches on enlargement at **http://ec.europa.eu/enlargement/**. For Neighbourhood Policy the official sites are **http://ec.europa.eu/world/enp/** (including a useful interactive map and bibliography of academic research) and **http://www.eeas.europa.eu/enp/**.

- For regular analyses and updates on developments in both areas see the newsletter **http://www.euractiv.com/** and publications of the Centre for European Policy Studies **http://www.ceps.eu/** (especially its newsletter 'European Neighbourhood Watch'), the European Policy Centre **http://www.epc.eu/** and the Centre for European Reform **http://www.cer.org.uk/**.

 Visit the Online Resource Centre that accompanies this book for additional material: **www.oxfordtextbooks.co.uk/orc/bomberg3e/**

CHAPTER 9

The EU as a Security Actor

John Peterson and Sandra Lavenex

▮ Summary

At first glance, EU security policy seems limited by three powerful constraints. First, it is exclusively concerned with 'soft' security issues, such as immigration, transnational crime, and drug trafficking. Second, policy-making is dominated by sovereignty-conscious EU member states and national capitals. Third, security is not a major driver of European integration. We challenge all three of these assumptions. The EU is now involved in 'hard' security, especially counterterrorism but also military security. Second, policy-making is increasingly Brussels-centred. Third, while European integration has been driven primarily by economic cooperation, the safeguarding of Europe's (especially internal) security has emerged as a major *raison d'être* of the integration project.

Introducing European Security Policy

When we think about international security—questions of war and peace or conflict and cooperation—we tend to assume that the major actors are inevitably states or security alliances, such as NATO (the North Atlantic Treaty Organization). But the EU has assumed a more important security role over time, especially on matters concerning its own internal security. What was known until recently as Justice and Home Affairs policy has been one of the busiest areas of EU policy-making and legislation for most of the twenty-first century. Today, there are very few areas of security policy where the EU does not play a role, often working alongside other organizations. While traditionally and still primarily viewed as an economic actor, the European Union is very much in the security business.

EU activities that seek to promote security are diverse and spread between different policy areas. It is difficult to generalize about them. In fact, few in Brussels would recognize or understand what was meant by the term 'EU security policy'. More familiar would be the designations Common Foreign and Security Policy (CFSP), Common Security and Defence Policy (CSDP); formerly known as the European Security and Defence Policy), and what is officially known today as Police and Judicial Cooperation in Criminal Matters as well as issues related to immigration control: that is, *internal* EU security policy, which seeks to defuse or counter threats to security within the EU's own borders. Instead of 'security policy', scholars tend to focus on EU security 'governance' since it takes place in the absence of a single authority. The governance approach portrays the Union as a 'evolving, yet fairly stable policy-making system' (Norheim-Martinsen 2010: 1360; see also Kirchner and Sperling 2007).

The CFSP, created by the Maastricht Treaty in 1992, is meant to cover 'all aspects of foreign and security policy'. As we will see (in Chapter 10), it has often been criticized for its failure to be comprehensive or coherent. The CFSP certainly has not replaced national foreign or security policies in Europe or made them obsolete, even if they are shaped increasingly by Brussels-based cooperation. The EU plays no role in territorial defence and its Common Security and Defence Policy is central to no EU member state's national defence policy (Cooper 2004b: 189). It is safe to assume that no European army, marching under an EU flag, will ever be sent to fight on one side of any inter-state war in the lifetime of any reader of this book. Command of the spring 2011 military action to protect civilians in Libya from forces loyal to Moammar Gaddafi was controlled by NATO with the EU active only on the civilian front (for instance, by freezing Libyan assets). The EU thus is mostly a supplier of 'soft security' through (mostly) non-military policies that seek to defuse or prevent conflict. It is accepted wisdom (although increasingly subject to doubt) that the Union is not in the 'hard' security business: defence of the state via military power. But in an era when it is often argued that a 'new security agenda' has emerged (Cottey 2007: 32–57: see also Dannreuther 2007; Coker 2009), with threats that are more diverse and not always state-based, the EU is a policy factory. It is active in areas such as civilian and military crisis management, climate change, energy security, cybersecurity, and counterterrorism: all issues on which security policies have become more focused in general.

Meanwhile, internal security policy is the single policy area where the EU—perhaps ironically—has been most active since the mid-90s. The irony stems from the stubborn refusal of member states over the course of years to subject internal security policy to the Community method, whereby the Commission has a monopoly on the right to propose legislation and the European Parliament (EP) has the right to co-decide legislation or propose amendments, and Council can usually act by a qualified majority. Under the post-1992 'pillar system', internal security policy—as well as the CFSP—was mostly subject to intergovernmental methods, not requiring a Commission proposal nor agreement of the Parliament, and with nearly all decisions requiring the unanimity of all member states. Such cumbersome arrangements, however, proved inadequate to deal with policy problems arising from the abolition of checks at the EU's internal borders, including organized crime, drug and people trafficking, and unauthorized immigration. Over the course of a decade and a half, the EU spent far more time and effort debating internal security than on producing policy output.

The Lisbon Treaty abolished the pillar system. Qualified majority voting (QMV) was applied to key internal security policies, including police and judicial cooperation, with the EP given co-decision rights in many. Unanimity persists as the decision rule for most EU foreign and external security policy decisions. But hopes for a more coherent and effective CSDP were boosted by Lisbon's creation of a new High Representative, initially in the person of Catherine Ashton, whose (impossibly?) busy job description included 'steering . . . common defence policy' (Council 2009: 2), chairing meetings of European Defence Ministers (twice a year formally), and heading the European Defence Agency. In short, the EU has become a far more active security actor in recent years. Most signs point towards it becoming still more active in the post-Lisbon era.

To a casual observer, EU security policy reflects three dominant features. First, it is overwhelmingly concerned with 'soft' security issues, such as immigration, transnational crime, disease control, and drug trafficking. Second, EU member states are reluctant to see their sovereignty compromised on matters of security. As a result, concerns about sovereignty dominate EU policy-making. Third, European integration is primarily driven by economic, not security factors. Yet, all three of these assumptions are flawed. Through its CSDP, the Union has capacity to tackle 'hard' security issues, especially counterterrorism but also military security. Second, the EU uses mostly intergovernmental means to make security policy, but the Lisbon Treaty will subject much internal security policy to the Community method. Moreover, all forms of security policy are increasingly made in Brussels. Third, while the completion of the single market has long overshadowed the security dimension of European integration, the latter has emerged as a top priority in recent years, in particular given the project of creating an internal 'Area of Freedom, Security and Justice'.

How it developed

In a sense, security was the most important objective of the first steps in post-war European institution-building (see Weiler 1998). The European Coal and Steel Community, and later its Economic Community, were created above all to cure Europe of its bad habit of going to war every 35 years or so. Specifically, they sought to combine the economies—especially the war-making industries—of France and (then West) Germany. An early attempt to integrate European militaries—the European Defence Community—proved a step too far and was buried by France in 1954 (see Chapter 2). Thus, it took several decades before what became the EU was given any security policy role. Meanwhile, NATO became the main forum for military cooperation during the Cold War. Nevertheless, security has always been a fundamental goal of European integration.

Policy cooperation on internal security is rooted primarily in two intergovernmental frameworks initially created outside the (then) European Community: the 1976 Trevi framework to fight terrorism and drug trafficking and the 1985 Schengen Agreement that lifted internal border controls. These two domains were linked and brought into the newly-created European Union under the 1992 Maastricht Treaty. In defiance of proposals by the 1992 Dutch Council Presidency, internal security policy was not inserted into the Community pillar but instead formed a new intergovernmental 'third pillar' on Justice and Home Affairs. Given this awkward institutional structure, and the tendency of internal security ministry officials (unlike diplomats) to shun cooperation and guard jealously their national legal systems, the 1990s saw only a handful of specific actions agreed within the third pillar. As a partial solution, the 1997 Amsterdam Treaty mandated that migration policy would be made within the Community pillar, and that border controls, immigration, asylum, visas, as well as judicial cooperation in civil law matters could gradually become subject to Community rules with the possibility of applying QMV within five years. Still, slap-dash institutional compromises such as absorbing the Schengen Agreement into the EU's treaties, but with opt-outs for the UK, Denmark, and Ireland, suggested that internal security policy would continue to straddle the 'Community' and third pillar, and remain something of an institutional mess. The Amsterdam Treaty's section on internal security was widely thought to be one of the most complex treaties ever agreed.

In the construction of its cooperative framework for internal security, as in building the EU's defence policy, formal treaty reforms often have mattered less than informal learning by doing. Maastricht's pillar III gave an EU home to practical cooperation designed to open European borders but also to respond to concerns that the main beneficiaries could be terrorists or criminals by, *inter alia*, reinforcing the Union's external borders. The Amsterdam Treaty's (enormously complex) provisions for JHA sought to provide a stronger institutional base and also embraced the idea of making the EU an 'Area of Freedom, Justice, and Security'. Yet, this grand declaration by EU leaders did less to hasten new policies than pragmatic, ongoing cooperation on practical matters such as coping with different national laws on the prosecution of suspected criminals or fighting irregular migration (that is, cross-border movement that lacks legal authorization, as opposed to 'illegal' migration, which suggests an active breach of the law).

Similarly, the EU's external defence policy emerged mainly out of practical cooperation. On one hand, when it committed itself to (what became) the Common Security and Defence Policy, the Union still had yet to take on an independent military operation. The EU's failure to manage peacefully the break-up of Yugoslavia after 1991 led to broad consensus on the need for the Union to develop a military capability. The Maastricht Treaty, agreed as the Balkans burst into flames, contained vague language committing the EU to a 'common defence policy that might, in time, lead to a common defence'. However, a bilateral agreement preceded by ad hoc, practical cooperation between Europe's two major military powers—France and the United Kingdom (UK)—kick-started EU military cooperation. The 1998 St. Malo Declaration followed extensive operational cooperation between the French and UK militaries on the ground in the former Yugoslavia. With the Bosnian crisis a recent memory, and the Kosovo crisis still to come, EU heads of state and government formally launched (what became) CSDP at the 1999 Cologne summit.

Later the same year, two further EU summits under the Council Presidency of Finland marked turning points. Meeting in Tampere, European leaders tried to jump-start the Area of Freedom, Security and Justice. Tampere produced agreement on new criteria by which to measure progress, new institutions such as a European Police College and an agency in charge of the external border, Frontex, plus an extension of the powers of Europol, established in 1995 to facilitate the exchange of intelligence and coordination of criminal investigations between national police forces. A subsequent European Council in Helsinki was hailed as marking the moment when the EU finally 'came of age' as an international actor (Taylor 1999). Besides major decisions on enlargement and Turkey, the Helsinki summit also yielded decisive steps towards giving the EU an independent military capability, as well as civilian resources, to deal with crises on or near its borders. Helsinki was the moment when the Union went beyond conflict prevention between its own member states to take responsibility for crisis management in its own neighbourhood.

The 2001 Treaty of Nice was mainly concerned with preparing the EU for its next enlargement. It did little to advance internal or external security policy. However, the 2002–3 Convention on the Future of Europe agreed wide-ranging reforms of both security policy institutions and decision rules, most of which were accepted in the Constitutional Treaty. Its rejection by French and Dutch voters in referenda held in 2005 led to the new model Lisbon Treaty, with its multiple provisions to try to make both EU internal and external security policy more coherent and effective. Lisbon reasserted the fundamental security vocation of European integration by placing the target of an 'Area of Freedom, Security and Justice' second in a list of fundamental EU goals in Article 3 of the Treaty, just after a general commitment to peace and welfare, and preceding the goals of the single market or economic and monetary union. After Lisbon came into force, the key question became: could the EU finally deliver on its—still largely unfulfilled—potential as a security actor?

The basics

The European Union's emergence as a security actor has mostly been a post-Cold War phenomenon. Although the freeing of the internal market prompted intergovernmental cooperation on internal security in the 1980s (and even before), the EU itself focused overwhelmingly on economic—not security—policy prior to the fall of the Berlin Wall and collapse of the Soviet Union. Forty years of European integration did, of course, accomplish the primordial goal of eliminating the possibility of any future war between France and (West) Germany. Only later did post-Cold War geopolitical conditions enable the Union to achieve the same sort of rapprochement between Germany and Poland, an often-neglected but historically remarkable feat (Cottey 2007: 15). The EU thus must be seen as a different kind of security actor than the US or China or Russia. Its primary contribution to global security historically has been as a 'peace project' confined mostly to the European continent (Smith 2008: 171). Still, as a core area of a 'security community' (Deutsch *et al.* 1969) that extends to other modern democracies including the US and Japan and between whom war is unimaginable, the EU can claim to have made an important contribution to security ever since its origins.

The Union's post-Cold War transformation into a supplier of security policy has involved a gradual strengthening of powers, resources and institutions in two quite distinct policy domains. Its external security role is focused, above all, on preventing or managing crises on the EU's doorstep. Unlike other international organizations that are similarly tasked with conflict prevention such as the United Nations or OSCE (Organization for Security and Cooperation in Europe), the EU has both 'a considerable toolbox of policy instruments and, crucially, its own unique legacy as a successful exercise in conflict prevention' (Smith 2008: 170). Inside the toolbox are trade privileges (or sanctions), aid and various forms of political dialogue. When conflicts cannot be prevented, and turn into outright crises, the EU now has considerable resources for crisis management, including disaster relief, reconstruction aid, and even military force. Whether Lisbon's new and stronger machinery for foreign and security policy will make the Union a more effective external security actor is an open question. The tools are there, but they must be wielded more coherently for the EU to realize its potential as a security actor.

The EU's *internal* security regime involves a very different and very heterogeneous set of actors and institutions. Initially framed as a form of compensation—safeguarding internal security after the abolition of internal border controls—EU Justice and Home Affairs policies historically have linked very disparate issues such as asylum, migration, and organized crime, as well as cooperation on civil law matters (also arising from the consequences of the free circulation of citizens). The primary impetus for this cooperation was upgrading the EU's capacity to fight irregular migration, including the abuse of asylum systems and transboundary crime. However, questions relating to the rights of migrants and refugees as well as, to a lesser extent, criminal suspects, have gained more attention over time. The empowering of the EU's supranational institutions, in particular the Commission, the Parliament and, especially after Lisbon, the ECJ, has been key in this development (Lavenex 2006).

In parallel to this internal evolution, cooperation on the external dimension of migration and organized crime has become more prominent. Paradoxically, while policy substance thus has become blurred—in terms of the distinction between 'internal' and 'external' security policy (Rees 2008)—structures for making policies remain rigidly compartmentalized. The Union's external and internal security policies sometimes seem to be made on two islands between which there is little exchange or coherence. Yet, an increasingly important international task for the EU is reconciling its internal security policies with its external obligations. What were previously deemed 'soft' security issues, such as unauthorized migration and transnational crime, have risen to the top of the policy agenda and become infused with new urgency. The link between internal and external security cooperation became especially salient after the terrorist attacks in the US, Madrid, and London of 2001–5, and again in the context of the migration flows unleashed by the Arab Revolutions of 2011. Such events have acted as external shocks prompting a new impetus to European cooperation. To the surprise of many, the EU managed rapidly to reach ambitious agreements on a common definition of terrorism and a European arrest warrant in the immediate aftermath of 11 September 2001 (9.11). Events in the southern Mediterranean—especially in Arab states—in early 2011 stimulated a strengthening of the EU's external borders agency 'Frontex' (see below) and intensified calls for greater solidarity and burden-sharing between member states. However, EU internal decision-making soon reverted to its previously uneven pace. Again, the Lisbon Treaty's new provisions for decision-making on internal security, and its abolition of the pillar system, at least hold out the prospect of more effective, coherent, and timely internal security policies.

The EU and International Security

The EU's role in international security has expanded over time: by 2011 it had engaged in more than 20 missions on three different continents. Most—around two-thirds—were purely civilian missions, which channelled development aid or sent law enforcement officers or advisers to troubled regions, as opposed to military forces. An example trumpeted by the EU as a success has been its largest CSDP civilian mission: EULEX in Kosovo, which sent more than 2700 judges, prosecutors, and police to fight corruption, organized crime, and investigate war crimes between 2008–12. Working under the general framework of a United Nations Security

Council Resolution, EULEX was EU-led but included contributions from Norway, Switzerland, Turkey, Croatia, Canada, and the United States.

Other EU missions have involved sending military forces together with civilian delegations. Such mixed missions have not been without critics. Smith (2008: 179–82) goes as far as to argue that '[c]onflict-prevention policy exposes the weaknesses of the EU foreign policy system' since 'coordination between the military and civilian crisis management institutions within the Council . . . [is] poor', with the civilian side 'comparatively underdeveloped'. There is no question that the EU possesses more earmarked resources to promote security in troubled regions compared to other international organizations (see Box 9.1). What is equally clear is that EU missions often lack coherence.

The EU's contribution to international security also raises questions about whether the EU is truly a global actor (see Chapter 10) or merely one whose influence and activities are mostly confined to the European continent. In a purely

---

BOX 9.1   Compared to what? The EU as an international security actor

The EU is an alliance of states, so it naturally is a different kind of security actor than are other great powers. First and foremost, it has no role in territorial defence and no standing army. It would never enter into a security pact with non-EU states as, say, the US has done with Japan and the antipodean states (through the ANZUS—Australia, New Zealand—Treaty). Most (not all) EU member states are active members of NATO. In fact, most EU military operations have required extensive cooperation with NATO and use of its military assets.

Second, the Union is often portrayed as a 'civilian' power (see Chapter 10), which favours persuasion over coercion and primarily uses its economic and aid policies to try to achieve international peace and security. Other major international players—such as the US, China, and Russia—rely far more on their military power (or at least the threat of using it) to achieve their international objectives. In recent years, Manners (2002; 2008) has portrayed the EU as a 'normative power': that is, one with an active foreign and security policy that nonetheless influences international relations (IR) more because of what it is—a peaceful sub-system of IR—than what it does. In particular, by this view the EU is a supplier of 'human security': it influences others to embrace human rights generally and to eschew (for example) the death penalty. As a rule, it favours negotiated settlements instead the use of force.

Third and finally, the EU's external security interventions would be viewed by most students of international relations as modest and insignificant compared to those undertaken by other Great Powers. Security policy specialists tend to scoff at the notion of 'soft power'—the ability to get others to do what one wants them to do without coercion (see Nye 2004)—as a chimera in the hard-nosed, Hobbesian world of international politics. Whether or not they are right, none of the twenty-first century's Great Powers—again, the US, China, or Russia—would consider it a major security policy success story to have launched (say) a small, if successful, civilian mission in the troubled Indonesian province of Aceh.

European context, the EU again shows itself to be as or more important for what it is rather than what it does. Neutral or non-aligned European states find the EU provides them with a forum for security cooperation without requiring them to sign on to a mutual defence pact, as NATO does. In particular, Sweden, Finland, and Austria all have made significant contributions to EU security missions that would not have been politically possible if they were NATO missions (see Bergman and Peterson 2006). But with some exceptions (see Box 9.2), the EU's contribution to international security operations in Africa, the Palestinian territories, Iraq, Afghanistan, Indonesia, and Libya have been relatively small and incidental to much larger operations under the auspices of the UN, NATO, or the US.

The Common Security and Defence Policy

Given the CFSP's mixed record, as well as Europe's claims to be a civilian power, it might seem paradoxical to extend the EU system into the realm of defence. Most EU states have long accepted the supremacy of NATO on defence matters. Yet, the EU has taken small but decisive steps in recent years towards creating a CSDP. The 1999 crisis in Kosovo marked a turning point. Again, the EU appeared timid and weak as it had earlier in Bosnia. NATO took the lead in pushing both crises towards resolution, and the US military contributions dwarfed those of Europe. Thus, the EU made firmer Treaty commitments to security cooperation in response, first in Amsterdam but especially at Nice. In particular, the Treaty of Nice marked out the so-called Petersberg tasks—humanitarian and rescue missions, peacekeeping, and crisis management, including 'peacemaking' (the latter never clearly defined)—as basic EU foreign policy goals. A new Political and Security Committee of senior national officials was created and designated the linchpin linking CSDP to the CFSP. The EU was also given its own Military Committee and crisis management unit. Plans were agreed to enable deployment of a EU Rapid Reaction Force of up to 60,000 troops. After 2001, for the first time military officers were seen at work in the EU's Council building.

Sceptics argued that the real problem lay not with Treaty language or institutions but with Europe's weak and underfunded militaries. Military spending in most EU states declined sharply after the Cold War, leaving the US to extend its lead in the application of new technologies to military hardware. The target date for declaring the EU Rapid Reaction Force operational was delayed and then fudged. The American administration under George W. Bush initially refused European offers to contribute troops to the war in Afghanistan in 2001, in large part because there was almost nothing that US forces could not do more effectively on their own.

The CSDP has thus been restricted to modest missions. Its supporters insist that it has produced tangible achievements, such as the 2002 military intervention in the

BOX 9.2	Operation Artemis

The French-led 2002 intervention in Bunia (Democratic Republic of Congo) came in response to a UN request and was designed to keep a humanitarian disaster from escalating. Its main goal was to secure the region's only airport, which an anti-government rebel force threatened to take over. Under French command, Operation Artemis involved sending 1800 European soldiers to a remote and troubled region of Africa. It produced at least one dramatic result: Swedish military forces (a minority in a larger EU force in Bunia) engaged in actual combat and fired shots in anger for the first time in hundreds of years. The intervention was initially hailed as a success, as the airport was held and lives were saved, or so it was claimed. But Bunia became a source of considerable debate amongst students of CSDP (see Manners 2006; Howorth 2007: 236–7). Its scope was very limited and its benefits questionable.

Bunia region of Congo (see Box 9.2). Similarly, the EU claimed success in taking over from NATO command of a large peacekeeping force in Bosnia in 2004, but also was criticized for perpetuating a culture of 'dependency, helplessness, and disillusionment' in Bosnia and failing to 'coordinate complex civil and military matters' (see Manners 2006: 190–1). More recently the EU has launched small civilian missions (for policing and training) in Aceh (Indonesia), Gaza, and Afghanistan.

To its critics, CSDP has been viewed as a way for NATO's reluctant European members—especially the French—to create an alternative security alliance that distances the EU from the United States, and seeks to 'balance' against American hegemony. One leading scholar argues that CSDP 'is not quite a balancing project, but certainly an effort by Europeans . . . to develop an alternative security supplier' (Posen 2004: 12). Critics are often quick to add that the 'caveats' that have limited the capacity of European forces to contribute to the NATO effort in Afghanistan (for instance, giving some no more than the right to self-defence) has shown how weakly committed many EU states are to NATO.

However, the CSDP's detractors cannot deny that several developments in the twenty-first century cut against the grain of their argument. First, for the first time since the days of DeGaulle, France is now a full member of NATO's military command. Second, almost no one in EU security policy circles imagines that CSDP will morph into a collective security framework that replaces NATO, especially given swingeing cutbacks in European public expenditure following the post-2008 financial crisis. Third, multiple EU member states—particularly the UK but also France and Italy—have suffered significant casualties and loss of lives from their commitment of forces to Afghanistan, itself the scene of a conflict that few in Europe wanted when launched by the US in 2001. That conflict remained unresolved not least because of American neglect and the distraction of Iraq after 2003.

Whatever view one takes of CSDP, it has become a framework for combining European military assets at the 'hard' end of capabilities, through the so-called

European 'battle groups', in specialized areas such as jungle or desert fighting or coping with a chemical weapons attack (see Peterson *et al.* 2012). Each battle group includes at least 1500 combat troops drawn from multiple EU member states but with one designated as the 'lead nation'. A total of 15 battle groups were operational by 2010. Interestingly, a Nordic battle group initially formed by Sweden and Finland included troops contributed by Norway, despite its non-membership of the Union.

Meanwhile, the European Defence Agency (EDA) has sought to coax sorely needed cooperation between European defence ministries and arms makers, quietly but gradually, since its launch in 2004 (see Box 9.3). If there is one European economic sector where the internal market does *not* exist at enormous cost to European taxpayers, it is the arms sector. The EDA explicitly seeks to sustain the CSDP. Making post-Lisbon High Representative Catherine Ashton chair of its Steering Board, itself consisting of EU defence ministers, reflects determination to subject cooperation in defence production and spending to a new, higher level of political control. Defence cooperation may well be embraced to an extent previously unseen in Europe in response to post-recession cuts in public spending. Unprecedented operational military cooperation was embraced by Europe's two largest military powers, France and the UK, after the latter undertook large public expenditure cuts in 2010. More generally, CSDP remains an area with a large gap between ambitions and achievements, but it is also a continuing growth area for European integration.

Internal Security

One way to think about EU internal security policy is that it has developed in response to the vast disparity between political and legal integration in Europe. To illustrate the point, the Franco-German alliance has historically been viewed as one of the closest bilateral relationships between any two EU member states, and it has sometimes given considerable 'pulse' to the European project. Yet, until recently legal barriers complicated or even prevented cooperation on internal security policy between even these two closest of allies. When German prosecutors brought to trial four German residents who had planned to blow up a Christmas market in Strasbourg in late 2000, they had to drop a number of the charges—including those of belonging to a terrorist organization (of which these four people clearly were members)—partly because it was so hard to bring evidence and witnesses from France. It is possible, of course, to walk from the city centre of Strasbourg to Germany in about five minutes.

A recurrent feature of EU internal security policy is a preference for forms of cooperation that rely on coordination of national law enforcement systems, and which do

BOX 9.3	Key concepts and terms

Battle Groups: combine national military resources at the 'hard end' of European capabilities in specialized areas. The EU decided in 2004 to create 20 Battle Groups, which would be deployable at short notice for limited deployments.

CSDP stands for the Common Security and Defence Policy (formerly known as ESDP: the European Security and Defence Policy). It was created in 1999 to engage in the so-called 'Petersberg tasks' (named after a German castle where an earlier summit devoted to defence was held): humanitarian and rescue missions, peacekeeping, crisis management, and the vaguely-specified task of 'peacemaking'.

European Defence Agency (EDA) was created in 2004 'to support the Member States and the Council in their effort to improve European defense capabilities [particularly] in the field of crisis management and to sustain' the ESDP. It aims to move the EU towards more cooperation in arms production and procurement.

Frontex is the EU's agency for the management of its external border. It was created in 2005 to coordinate member states' operational cooperation in external border controls, provide training to national border guards, carry out risk analyses, organize joint control operations, and assist member states in migrant return operations.

Schengen or the 'Schengen Acquis' refers to two intergovernmental treaties concluded in 1985 and 1990 as well as the work of the Schengen Executive Committee, which provides for the abolition of controls at the internal borders of Schengen members. With the Amsterdam Treaty, the Schengen Acquis was integrated into EU. Not all EU states are members—the UK and Ireland have opt-outs—and the Schengen area includes Norway, Switzerland, and Iceland.

Soft security is a post-Cold War concept that refers to security that is obtained through non-military policy instruments (except in cases of peacekeeping) and does not involve territorial defence of the state. It is related to the ideas of 'human security'—defence of the citizen, as opposed to the state—and 'homeland security', obtained via policies designed to eliminate internal security threats.

not directly impinge on member states' sovereignty. Member states continue to favour integration via the horizontal networking of their domestic authorities rather than creating new supranational competences. Europol illustrates the point (see Box 9.4), as does Frontex: the EU's Agency for the Management of Operational Cooperation at its External Borders. Established in 2005, Frontex primarily coordinates national border guards with the aim of ensuring that the EU's tight border security standards are implemented (evenly) throughout the Union. Given the uneven burden carried by those (southern and eastern) member states that lie on the main

BOX 9.4   Compared to what: Europol

Europol is shorthand for the European Law Enforcement Agency. Some of Europol's found-ing fathers, in particular the former German Chancellor Helmut Kohl, hoped that Europol would develop into a future European FBI modelled upon the US Federal Bureau of Investi-gation. In reality, this comparison fails to stand up. Europol has no operational capacities of its own. Its officers have no direct powers of arrest. Europol is not a supranational policy force, it is only a coordination structure for national police forces in preventing and combating terrorism, drug trafficking, and other forms of organized crime. Over time, it has grown in size to the point where its staff included nearly 700 senior national EU police officers by 2011.

Its precursor, the European Drugs Unit (EDU), was created in the mid-1990s to fight the drugs trade, the trafficking of radioactive and nuclear substances, as well as vehicles and human beings. Europol was established by a Convention in 1995, although disagree-ments about the role of the European Court of Justice (ECJ) and the immunity of its staff delayed its entry into force for another three years. This legal basis, which posited Eu-ropol outside the Community framework and outside the control of the European Parlia-ment, was much debated. In 2010, Europol was reformed as a full EU agency, which gave the EP more control over its activities and budget.

Europol's main task is to support national law enforcement agencies by gathering, ana-lysing and disseminating information and coordinating operations in the fight against organized international crime. Europol's remit now extends beyond the EDU's to include the fight against currency forgery and terrorism. In 2002, and with 9/11 still a fresh memory, Europol was granted a limited operational role with the option of launching joint investiga-tion teams in which member state officials conducted, together with Europol staff, joint operations. Contact with national counterparts is primarily secured through the deployment of national liaison officers at the Europol headquarters in The Hague, including officers from associated third countries such as Australia, Canada, Columbia, Croatia, Iceland, Norway, Russia, Switzerland, and the US. Despite the existence of this network of now 124 liaison officers, member states have remained reluctant to share their criminal intelligence via Europol and its databases. Therefore, Europol's contribution to the fight against interna-tional organized crime is generally seen to have failed to meet expectations.

To its critics, Europol is neither transparent nor sufficiently accountable, and illustra-tive of how internal security policy has become gradually institutionalized over time (see Kostakopoulou 2006). Compared to its national counterparts, Europol does seem to oper-ate in a legal grey area with (for example) its officers enjoying a very strong form of legal immunity. However, it is probably easy to overestimate its reach and powers, particularly since it has been portrayed (often very inaccurately) in so many films, TV series and books—as is noted on Europol's own website. To its supporters, Europol is an important weapon in Europe's counterterrorism efforts: its investigations have led to the arrest of numerous individuals with links to Al Qaeda and other terrorist organizations since 2001.

In sum, Europol illustrates the choice by the member states to seek better coordina-tion of national law enforcement systems rather than by replacing them with new supra-national structures that could resemble a European FBI. This coordination is backed by joint professional training for national police officers, such as the joint curricula developed by the European Police College (CEPOL). As the problem of inadequate information-sharing via Europol shows, these bottom-up structures need time to develop, and require a strong degree of mutual trust between national law enforcement agencies.

migration routes to Europe, Frontex has been charged with the coordination of joint operations in which member states share personnel and equipment in the patrolling of a particular border area.

As in the case of Europol, Frontex has been hampered by a lack of necessary commitment and cooperation from member states. Such reluctance is perhaps not surprising given how politically-charged immigration has become. Still, irregular migration is clearly a shared European problem and several initiatives have been launched to render Frontex more operational. In 2007, Rapid Border Intervention Teams (RABITs) were introduced, with more than 700 personnel and a full range of technical equipment from aircraft to mobile radar units and heartbeat detectors, to provide rapid operational assistance for a limited period to member states facing a situation of 'urgent and exceptional pressure' at their external border. Frontex's budget and joint operations at sea and land borders have grown exponentially since its creation, so that by 2011, it had six permanent sea operations in the Mediterranean (so-called European Patrols Networks), and three land operations at the south-eastern and eastern borders. However, member states' lack of solidarity remains one of the main challenges to internal security cooperation. Joint operations have clearly diverted migration flows to new routes and travel itineraries have become increasingly risky for migrants' lives.

Greece became an illustrative case in 2010–11. It became a weak link in the EU's border controls after other entry points, such as Mediterranean sea routes, were mostly shut down. Frontex estimated that 90 per cent of irregular entrants to the EU crossed the Greek-Turkish border by this route, with 45,000 arriving in the first half of 2010 alone. Yet, in an illustration of how national capitals often flout EU rules, Greece's record of dealing with asylum seekers was so suspect that the European Court of Human Rights ruled in early 2011 that it was breaching asylum law. As a consequence, EU states stopped returning refugees to Greece who had first entered the Union by crossing the Turkish border, even though the 2003 Dublin Regulation required asylum seekers to request refugee status in their first country of entry. As one EU diplomat put it, 'Most interior ministries, given the chance, will take up any opportunity to rid themselves of potential refugees, especially if they can do so within European rules. That they would stop sending [asylum seekers] back to Greece just highlights how concerned they are' (*Financial Times*, 26 October 2010). This attitude again became salient in Europe's response to increasing immigration pressure following the 2011 revolutions in the Arab world, with calls by Italy and Malta for a redistribution of incoming refugees among the EU member states falling on deaf ears.

Member states' reluctance to pool internal security resources has been accompanied by a tendency to limit the scope of supranational legislation. This point was illustrated by the adoption, at the 1999 Tampere European Council, of the principle of mutual recognition in the area of criminal law (see Box 9.5) as opposed to new EU legislation. In short, the pressures for policy cooperation on internal security have intensified. But the hesitancy of member states to create truly common policies using traditional EU methods has remained mostly undiminished.

BOX 9.5	**Does law enforcement trump human rights?**

In contrast to operational cooperation between police forces and border guards, cooperation in the judicial sphere was initially slow to develop. Yet, since the 1999 Tampere European Council, it has been one of the most dynamic areas of JHA cooperation. The
cornerstone of this cooperation is the principle of mutual recognition of national laws and
judicial procedures—in contrast to harmonization via supranational law. The flagship example is the European Arrest Warrant (EAW), adopted just a few months after the terrorist
attacks of 9.11.2001. Under the EAW, national law enforcement authorities agree to arrest
and transfer a criminal suspect or sentenced person to another member state on the basis
of an arrest warrant issued by a judicial authority in that other state. Member states thus
began to recognize the judicial decisions of another member state, based on the criminal
law of that state, as mutually compatible with their own judicial system. Significant national differences in the exact definition of certain crimes or sentences made clear the
need for some form of harmonization—or legislative approximation—early on. However,
attempts to approximate laws on criminal proceedings and the rights of suspects ranged
from difficult to impossible due to member states' reluctance to accept European legislation in core areas of sovereignty. The EAW thus illustrates the 'tension between security
and freedom . . . constitutive of any liberal democracy' (Lavenex and Wagner 2007: 225).
In the EU's case, criminal law cooperation has tended to favour law enforcement at the
expense of the rights of individual citizens. This result may be partly due to the intergovernmental procedures by which these European rules have been adopted. As MacCormick
(2008: 172) observes:

. . . no parliament had any real say about the rules adopted in the [EAW] framework
decision—not the EP, which was only consulted, and not the national parliaments,
which did not even have to be consulted. The principle that a citizen's liberty should
be limitable only under laws agreed by his or her elected representatives had gone
out of the window. It could be argued that the EAW illustrates clearly that there was
a democratic deficit in the former intergovernmental pillar of JHA.

Theorizing the EU as a Security Actor

The theoretical perspectives applied throughout this book all shed light, albeit of
different hues, on EU security policy. Neofunctionalists could point to how functional pressures for cooperation have led both internal and external security policies
to become more Brussels-based over time. In particular, the abolition of controls
at the EU's internal borders, which was mainly economically motivated, engendered
a wide range of cooperation. It now extends to migration and police and judicial
cooperation deemed necessary for safeguarding internal security. Moreover, the Lisbon Treaty makes a serious move towards more qualified voting on police and judicial cooperation. Neofunctionalists would see the move as evidence that economic
integration has 'spilled over' and led to supranational policies and processes in areas
outside of economic policy *per se*.

For their part, liberal intergovernmentalists would argue that the dominant actors in both internal and external security policy remain national actors. To be sure, the EU has witnessed more security policy cooperation over time. But that cooperation is overwhelmingly between national officials and other kinds of actor—soldiers, police officers, or judicial experts—whose primary affiliation is to an EU member state. Intergovernmentalism thus endures even within (say) Europol or the EU battle groups.

In contrast, institutionalists would note how purely intergovernmental cooperation has become increasingly institutionalized over time, with new institutions such as the Political and Security Committee or Europol being created in recent decades. Path dependency is clearly visible in past choices on (say) the Petersberg tasks or the Amsterdam Treaty's enormously complex section on internal security. More specifically, these choices either shaped subsequent policies—such as the CSDP in the case of the Petersberg tasks—or were viewed as requiring repair, as Lisbon did in its 'clean up' of Amsterdam's internal security policy provisions.

Constructivists would highlight how constant interactions between both internal and external policy elites over the course of years has created both a new spirit and practice of cooperation amongst some of the most inward-looking and least predisposed officials to international collaboration. The steady pace of the communitarization of internal security policy has culminated in the Lisbon Treaty's provisions to subject most EU policies to the Community method. Meanwhile, constructivists would consider the development of the CSDP as evidence of how much policy cooperation is possible when governments and officials begin to seek common goals—such as the resolution of ethnic conflicts in Africa and the Balkans—because they share common ideas about the virtues of harmonious multiculturalism.

Finally, public policy specialists would note that EU security policy is highly technocratic, dominated by experts, and mostly made within specialized policy networks. Policy analysis that seeks to understand how policies emerge from interactions within networks bringing together security officials and law enforcement specialists operating from different levels of a multi-level system—incorporating the EU, national capitals, and other international organizations—is central to the 'governance' approach to EU security policy and European integration more generally. Governance via policy networks can lack transparency: EU internal security policies in particular have mostly been made in a process of shadowy bargaining between national officials that has often been considerably less than transparent. But both external and internal security policy networks have expanded to include more different types of actor over time. To illustrate, making internal security policies post-Lisbon will necessitate bargaining with members of the European Parliament, given their new powers to co-legislate with the Council, and therefore through more transparent procedures affording opportunities for NGOs to make their points. And soldiers now rub shoulders with diplomats in the Council building on Rue de la Loi in Brussels, as they never did in the past, with the EU's own Military Committee playing a key role in determining the scope and objectives of the EU's external security missions.

Conclusion

We have covered a very broad terrain in this chapter. Again, few EU officials would recognize the designation 'security policy' as an EU policy area. But all the actions we have discussed, say, to cut down on irregular immigration into the EU, stamp out corruption in Kosovo, or deliver humanitarian aid to Libya have something in common: they are framed in security terms. Moreover, as we have seen, recent years have witnessed a blurring of the boundaries between internal and external security, even if the policy-makers responsible for police and judicial cooperation on one hand and CSDP on the other have little to do with one another.

We also have seen that commonly accepted wisdoms about EU security policies have increasingly come into question. First, it has become more difficult to argue that the Union is exclusively concerned with 'soft' security issues: it has sent soldiers to multiple continents to try to keep or even 'make' peace, and its counterterrorism policy agenda is buoyant. Second, policy-making may still be dominated by the EU's member states and national actors more than in other areas of policy. But both external and internal security policies have become increasingly Brussels-centred. The policy areas covered in this chapter have been among those where European integration has proceeded the fastest and furthest in the two decades or so since the Maastricht Treaty gave birth to what we now know as the European Union. Third, these developments have re-emphasized the centrality of security in the general purpose of the European integration project. Police and judicial cooperation in the fight against irregular migration and transnational crime have progressed faster than the harmonization of judicial procedures or individual freedoms. The Union's CSDP may lack coherence, but the EU has, again arguably, reacted as best it could to the brutal wars of the 1990s in the Balkans or 2000s in Africa. The Union has grown into a vigorous security actor. It shows no sign of becoming any less so.

  DISCUSSION QUESTIONS

1. When what is now the EU was originally created, it was given no security role. Now the EU is very much *in* the security business. Why is this the case? What has changed?

2. What have been the main events since the 1980s that have encouraged or required the EU to develop new security policies?

3. Explain why the creation of the internal market and lifting of internal border controls within the EU gave impetus to create new internal security policies.

4. In what ways does EU internal security policy illustrate how concerns about national sovereignty limit the willingness of EU member states to create new common policies?

FURTHER READING

For a sharp, incisive treatment of twenty-first century security debates, see Dannreuther (2007). Cottey (2007) links these debates to European and EU security more specifically and Howorth (2007) offers what is, to date, the best and most comprehensive treatment of CSDP. Smith's (2008) volume on EU foreign policy has good sections on the Union's policy instruments, its conflict prevention efforts, and its fight against international crime. For an up-to-date treatment of internal security policy, see Lavenex (2010). A comprehensive analysis of EU asylum and immigration policies is given by Geddes and Boswell (2011). Kaunert (2011) gives a timely account of the dynamics towards supranational governance in JHA.

Cottey, A. (2007), *Security in the New Europe* (Basingstoke and New York: Palgrave).

Dannreuther, R. (2007), *International Security: the Contemporary Agenda* (Cambridge and Malden MA: Polity).

Howorth, J. (2007), *Security and Defence Policy in the European Union* (Basingstoke and New York: Palgrave).

Geddes, A. and Boswell, C. (2011), *Migration and Mobility in the European Union* (Basingstoke and New York: Palgrave).

Kaunert, Christian (2011), *European Internal Security: Towards Surpanational Governance in the Area of Freedom, Security and Justice* (Manchester and New York: Manchester University Press).

Lavenex, S. (2010), 'Justice and Home Affairs: Communitarization with Hesitation' in H. Wallace., M. A. Pollack, and A. R. Young (eds.), *Policy-Making in the European Union*, 6th edn. (Oxford and New York: Oxford University Press).

Smith, K. E. (2008), *European Union Foreign Policy in a Changing World*, 2nd edn. (Cambridge and Malden MA: Polity).

 WEB LINKS

• The best and most useful website for current research related to CSDP is that of the Paris-based Institute for Security Studies (**http://www.iss.europa.eu/**), which formally became an autonomous European Agency in 2002. The Council also maintains a comprehensive site on the CFSP at: **http://www.consilium.europa.eu/showPage.aspx?id=261&lang=en**. The European Defence Agency has its own website at: **http://www.eda.europa.eu/**; so do Frontex at **http://www.frontex.europa.eu/** and Europol at **http://www.europol.eu/** (a humorous list of portrayals of Europol in films and novels is available at: **http://www.europol.europa.eu/ataglance/Fictionalapperances/Fictional_apperances_of_Europol.pdf**). A comprehensive and critical databank on EU internal security cooperation is provided on **http://www.statewatch.org/**.

 Visit the Online Resource Centre that accompanies this book for additional material: **www.oxfordtextbooks.co.uk/orc/bomberg3e/**

The EU as a Global Actor

John Peterson

■ Summary

The European Union's ambitions to be a global power are a surprising by-product of European integration. Students of European foreign policy focus on EU trade, aid, and the Common Foreign and Security Policy (CFSP), but cannot neglect the extensive national foreign policy activities of its member states. On most economic issues, the EU is able to speak with a genuinely single voice. It has more difficulty showing solidarity on aid policy, but is powerful when it does. The Union's external policy aspirations now extend to traditional foreign and security policy. But distinct national policies persist and the EU suffers from weak or fragmented leadership. Debates about European foreign policy tend to be about whether the glass is half-full—with the EU more active globally than ever before—or half-empty, and mainly about disappointed expectations.

Introducing European Foreign Policy

One of the founding fathers of what is now the European Union (EU), Jean Monnet, once described European integration as a 'key step towards the organization of to-morrow's world' (quoted in Jørgensen 2006: 521). Nevertheless, Monnet and the other founders of the original European Economic Community (EEC) had little ambition to create a new kind of international power. In fact, the EEC was initially given explicit external powers only to conduct international trade negotiations, since a common market could not, by definition, exist without a common trade policy. Yet the Community's trade policy quickly produced political spillover: trade agreements with whom? What about sanctions against oppressive or aggressive states? Member states soon felt the need to complement trade policy (and the external aspects of other EC policies) with political criteria that they laid down in what was at first a separate, informal framework of 'political cooperation' and then later became a formal treaty objective of a common foreign and security policy.

The European Union now aspires to be a global power: that is, a major international actor that can, like the United States (US) or China, influence developments anywhere in the world, and draw on its full range of economic, political, and security instruments. It can be argued that 'foreign policy has been one of the areas in which European integration has made the most dynamic advances' (Tonra and Christiansen 2004: 545). Still, the EU is a strange and often ineffective global actor. Distinctive *national* foreign policies endure in Europe and show few signs of disappearing. The notion of 'European foreign policy', comprising *all* of what the EU and its member states do in world politics, collectively or not, has gained prominence (see Carlsnaes 2006; Hill and Smith 2011).

Debates about European foreign policy tend to be about whether the glass is half-full or half-empty. On one hand, the EU has used enlargement as a tool of foreign policy and dramatically transformed the regions to its east and south (see Chapter 8). The Union is an economic superpower. It is gradually developing a military capability for crisis management or humanitarian intervention (see Chapter 9).

On the other hand, the EU suffers from chronic problems of disunity, incoherence, and weak leadership. European foreign policy can be undermined by all manner of rivalries: between its member governments, between EU institutions, and between them and national foreign ministries. The EU was entirely sidelined during the 2003 war in Iraq because it could not come even remotely close to agreeing a common policy (see Peterson 2003/4). The Union stood accused of providing 'far too little leadership far too late' to the aborted 2005 effort to reform the United Nations (UN) (Laatikainen and Smith 2006: 21–2).

Sometimes, the same international event or issue can be used to defend either the half-full or half-empty thesis. Consider the call by the head of a leading non-governmental organization, Human Rights Watch, for the EU to 'fill the leadership void' on human rights post-Iraq, after the US was widely viewed as flaunting them. Here, we might see the Union as a beacon of hope for a more progressive, humane international order. Or, we might share the despair of the issuer of the plea at how the EU continues to 'punch well beneath its weight' on human rights (Roth 2007). The EU consistently fails to meet expectations while never ceasing to develop new ambitions.

How it developed

The EU's international ambitions have their origins in the 1960s. In particular, American disregard for European preferences in Vietnam and the Middle East presented the European countries with incentives to defend their interests collectively, and thus more effectively, in foreign policy. According to a logic known as the 'politics of scale', the whole—the EU speaking and acting as one—is more powerful than the sum of its parts, or member states acting individually (Ginsberg 2001).

By 1970, a loose intergovernmental framework, European Political Cooperation (EPC), was created to try to coordinate national foreign policies. Linked to the European Community, but independent of it, EPC was very much dominated by national foreign ministers and ministries. Member governments identified where their national interests overlapped, without any pretension to a 'common' foreign policy. The European Commission was little more than an invited guest, and the Parliament largely excluded.

Nonetheless, EPC fostered consensus on difficult issues in the 1970s and 80s, including the Arab–Israeli conflict and relations with the Soviet bloc (through what became the Organization for Security and Cooperation in Europe (OSCE); see Box 10.1). EPC also became the vehicle for the Community's condemnation of South Africa's apartheid system. Europe was mostly limited to saying things—issuing diplomatic *démarches*—as opposed to doing things via EPC. But increasingly it backed up EPC positions with European Community actions using economic aid or sanctions (which were applied to Argentina during the Falklands War).

EPC's perceived successes led to claims that Europe could become a 'civilian power' (see Galtung 1973). That is, the EC could emerge as an alternative to the two Cold War superpowers, uphold multilateralism, liberalism, and human rights as values, and be an advocate for peaceful conflict resolution. EPC was given treaty status and formally linked to the activities of the Community in the 1986 Single European Act.

Yet, the geopolitical earthquakes that shook Europe beginning in 1989 exposed EPC as weak and unable to foster collective action. The idea of strengthening foreign policy cooperation in a new 'political union' was given impetus by the dramatic transitions in Central and Eastern Europe, the Gulf War, the collapse of the Soviet Union, and war in Yugoslavia. Thus, the 1992 Maastricht Treaty grafted a new Common Foreign and Security Policy (CFSP, along with a new Justice and Home Affairs (JHA) policy) onto the existing Treaty of Rome, resulting in the European Union's then three-pillar structure. There is no question that the EU became far more active

> **BOX 10.1**   **Key concepts and terms**
>
> The **Common Foreign and Security Policy (CFSP)** was created by the 1992 Maastricht Treaty as a successor to the European Political Cooperation mechanism. It has been embellished by successive new Treaties and given (by the Treaty of Nice) a Brussels-based Political and Security Committee to prepare Foreign Ministers' meetings and (by Lisbon) a 'new look' High Representative and the EEAS.
>
> The **Cotonou agreement** was agreed in the African state of Bénin in 2000 and then revised repeatedly (lastly in 2010). It is the successor to the Lomé Convention and is claimed to be a 'comprehensive partnership' between former European colonies and the EU.
>
> The **European External Action Service (EEAS)** was created by the Lisbon Treaty and became active in 2010. It works under the authority of the High Representative and brings under one roof EU (Commission and Council) and national diplomats. One intended effect of the EEAS is to make the Union's missions in foreign capitals more like real embassies, with clout and resources.
>
> The **OSCE**—the **Organization for Security and Cooperation in Europe**—brings together 56 (as of 2011) states from Europe and beyond in what is the world's largest regional security organization. It claims to take a 'comprehensive approach to security', extending especially to human rights. The OSCE works on the basis of unanimity and its decisions are politically, not legally, binding. It thus is criticized as toothless, even though its predecessor—the Conference on SCE—was important in putting into motion the changes that led to the end of the Cold War.

internationally in the years that followed. There is considerable debate about whether it also became more effective.

The basics

The EU aspires to international power for two basic reasons. First, even the Union's largest states are medium-sized powers compared to, say, the US or China. All European states, especially smaller ones, seek to use the EU as a 'multiplier' of their power and influence. There is controversy about whether the Union is a truly global, as opposed to a regional power (Orbie 2008; Krotz 2009). However, its largest member states—France, UK, Germany, and Italy (the first two being members of the UN Security Council)—give the Union a 'pull towards the global perspective which many of the [other member states] simply do not have as part of their foreign policy traditions' (Hill 2006: 67). New EU military and civilian missions in Africa and Afghanistan, as well as the Balkans and Middle East, illustrate the point.

Second, the Union's international weight increases each time it enlarges or expands its policy competence. The twelve countries that joined after 2004 were all (besides Poland) small and (mostly) pro-American states with limited foreign policy ambitions. But EU membership allowed them to distance or defend themselves from the US on issues such as Russia or trade policy, while making the Union a potentially more powerful player on these and other international issues. Meanwhile, the EU has accumulated new foreign policy tools, beginning with aid programmes for Africa in 1963 and most recently a Common Security and Defence Policy (CSDP; see Chapter 9). It also has created, via the Lisbon Treaty, new figures to represent the Union externally: a 'permanent' European Council President and a High Representative for Foreign Policy who is also Vice-President of the Commission. Lisbon also gave birth to the European External Action Service (EEAS), potentially a nascent EU foreign ministry. But whatever institutions it creates, the EU is powerful internationally above all because it presides over the world's largest single market (including nearly 500 million consumers, or around 40 per cent more than the US).

Still, European foreign policy is hindered by three basic gaps. One is between task expansion, which has been considerable, and the integration of authority, which has been—at least prior to the Lisbon Treaty—limited. Before the creation of the EEAS, the total number of European diplomatic staff worldwide (EU plus national officials) was more than 40,000 diplomats in 1,500 missions. Yet, no minister or government could give orders to this huge collection of officials. No one claimed that the US—with around 15,000 staff in 300 missions—was weaker because it was so outnumbered (Everts 2002: 26). The new High Representative was given authority over the EEAS, which at least promised finally to give the Union an official who could direct the EU's own diplomatic corps, which often proved impossible in the past because of fragmented institutional structures in Brussels.

The gap between the EU's economic power and political weakness is a related but separate problem. Europe manages to defend its interests on matters of 'low politics'—economic, trade, and (less often) monetary issues—with a more or less single voice. External trade policy is made via the Community method of decision-making (see Chapter 3), which delegates considerable power to the Union's institutions and where Council acts by a qualified majority. The EU also has significant resources in aid and development policy, and has emerged as a potentially major power in international environmental diplomacy.

In contrast, the Union often fails to speak as one on matters of traditional diplomacy, or 'high politics', which touch most directly on national sovereignty, prestige, or vital interests, and where Council acts by unanimity. The CFSP created by the Maastricht Treaty was meant to cover 'all aspects of foreign and security policy'. However, there is no *single* EU foreign policy in the sense of one that replaces or eliminates national policies. In contrast to (say) EU trade policy, the CFSP relies overwhelmingly on intergovernmental consensus. It remains difficult to envisage member states ever delegating power to decide life and death questions, such as whether to contribute military force to a 'hot' war. In short, the gap between the EU's economic power and political weight endures largely because the Community system remains more efficient and decisive than the CFSP system.

A final gap is between the world's expectations of the EU and its capacity to meet them (Hill 1998). In the early days of the post-Cold War period, European foreign policy-makers often oversold the Union's ability to act quickly or resolutely in international affairs. Nearly two decades later, the rhetoric had muted but the EU still struggled to be a truly global, as opposed to a regional power in its European neighbourhood. Chris Patten (2005: 176), a former Commissioner for External Relations, was frank:

America is a superpower, partly because it is the only country whose will and intentions matter everywhere, and are everywhere decisive to the settlement of the world's problems. Europe can help to solve these problems, but there are only some parts of the world—like the Balkans—where our role (while not necessarily crucial) is as important as, or more important than, that of China in the case of North Korea.

These three gaps—between task expansion and integration, economic unity and political division, and capabilities and expectations—all contribute to a more general mismatch between aspirations and accomplishments. To understand its persistence, we need to unpack European foreign policy and consider it as the product of three distinct but interdependent systems of decision-making (White 2001):

- a national system of foreign policies;
- a Community system focused on economic policy; and
- the CFSP.

These systems remain distinct even if there is considerable overlap between them (see Table 10.1). To illustrate the point, the Lisbon Treaty essentially eliminated the pillar system and put all EU policies under the umbrella of a single institutional system. The 'EU system' now incorporates the CFSP as well as internal security policy. However, as Piris (2010: 260) notes, leaving aside the High Representative, 'the Lisbon Treaty confirms that CFSP remains clearly subject to different rules and procedures from the other activities of the EU. It therefore remains a second pillar as it was before.'

Overlaps between the EU's external policy systems are, however, rife. Europe is the world's largest foreign aid donor, but only when the disparate and largely uncoordinated contributions of the Union and its member states are added together. EU environmental policy is made via the Community method but it is often unclear who speaks for Europe in international environmental diplomacy, as was revealed—to the Union's cost—at the 2009 Copenhagen UN summit on climate change. Leadership of the CFSP sometimes falls to sub-groups of member states, as illustrated by the 'EU-3', with France, Germany, and the UK taking the lead on nuclear diplomacy towards Iran.

These overlaps reflect how high and low politics often blur together in the twenty-first century. Disputes arising from Europe's dependence on Russia for energy, or the tendency of Chinese exporters to flood European markets, can touch upon vital national interests and preoccupy diplomats and governments at the highest political levels. Meanwhile, the EU has begun work on a security and defence policy: the ultimate expression of high politics. Blurred boundaries between both policy realms and systems for decision-making make European foreign policy an elusive subject that is far more difficult to 'source' or study than (say) Indian, Mexican, or South African foreign policy.

TABLE 10.1 European foreign policy: three systems

System	Key characteristic	Location (or Treaty basis)	Primary actors	Policy example
National	Loose (or no) coordination	Outside EU's structures	National ministers and ministries	War in Iraq
Overlap	*Some coordination of national and EU efforts*	*Coordination with EU with nuances (in annexes to Treaty; no funds from Community budget)*	National ministers and ministries, Commission	*Cotonou agreement*
Community	EU usually speaks with single voice	Pillar 1*	Commission and Council	Commercial (trade) policy
Overlap	*Turf battles*	*Pillars 1 and 2**	*Council and Commission*	*Economic sanctions policy*
CFSP	'Common, not single' policy	Pillar 2*	High Representative; national ministers and ministries (especially of large states)	Nuclear diplomacy towards Iran

*Pre-Lisbon Treaty

A National 'System' of Foreign Policies

Distinctive national foreign policies have not disappeared from Europe, even if the EU has become a more important reference point. France uses the EU to try to enhance its own foreign policy leadership of a Europe that is autonomous from the US. Germany has wrapped its post-war foreign policy in a European cloak in order to rehabilitate itself as an international power. The UK views the EU as useful for organizing pragmatic cooperation on a case-by-case basis. Small states have considerably 'Europeanized' their foreign policies (Tonra 2001) and rely on the EU to have a voice in debates dominated by large states. But all EU member states conduct their own, individual, *national* foreign policy.

Whether or not national foreign policies in Europe form a true 'system', they are notable for:

- their endurance;
- their continued centrality to European foreign policy; and
- their frequent resistance to coordination.

The last observation points to what makes foreign policy different from other EU policies: the logic of foreign policy coordination differs markedly from the logic of market integration. Integrating markets mostly involves negative integration: sweeping away barriers to trade. Separate national policies can be tolerated as long as they do not impede free movement of goods, services, and people. Market integration typically has clear goals, such as zero tariffs or common standards. Progress can usually be measured and pursued according to timetables.

In contrast, it is plausible to think that a common foreign policy (analogous, for example, to the Common Agricultural Policy (CAP)) requires positive integration: new EU institutions and structures to replace national ones. Foreign policy often has a black or white quality: if all states do not toe the line when the EU condemns a human rights violation or imposes an arms embargo, then the Union cannot be said to have a policy at all. Foreign policy coordination is often difficult to tie to specific goals or timetables. Compare the two main policy projects of the Maastricht Treaty (see Smith 1997). Monetary union had a clear goal—the euro—a timetable for achieving it, and criteria for measuring progress. The CFSP was given no clear goal, nor any timetable or criteria for achieving it.

Defenders of Europe's system of foreign policy coordination, including Chris Patten (2001), concede that Europe lacks a *single* foreign policy. However, they insist that the EU usually has a *common* foreign policy through which its member states and institutions act collectively. Each plays to its strengths and contributes policy resources to a (more or less) common cause. Increasingly, all member states tend to respect common EU policies and procedures.

Critics counter-claim that the war in Iraq showed how the EU is easily marginalized on matters of high politics. Decisions on whether to support the war were almost entirely made in national EU capitals, not Brussels. Nation-states have long been primary sources of European foreign policy. They are likely to remain so.

The Community System

The Community system for foreign policy-making consists of three main elements: external trade policy; aid and development policy; and the external dimension of internal policies, not least the internal market.

Commercial (trade) policy

The European Union is a major trading power. It is the world's largest exporter and second largest importer. It accounts for more than one-fifth of all global trade, and claims a higher share than the US. The EU is sometimes portrayed as a purveyor of neoliberalism (which emphasizes the benefits of the free market and limited government interference; see Cafruny and Ryner 2003). Yet, all trading blocs discriminate against outsiders and more than half of all EU trade is internal trade, crossing European borders within a market that is meant to be borderless. EU member states are sometimes accused of acting like a protectionist club in which each agrees to take in the others' 'high cost washing', or products that are lower in quality or higher in price than goods produced outside Europe, ostensibly to protect European jobs (see Messerlin 2001).

In practice, the EU is a schizophrenic trading power, not least because it blends very different national traditions of political economy. Generally, its southern member states are less imbued with free-market values than those in the north or east. One consequence is that it is sometimes more difficult for the EU to agree internally than for it to agree deals with its trading partners. The power of the Commission in external trade policy is easy to overestimate (see Box 10.2). However, the EU does a remarkably good job of reconciling Europe's differences on trade. When the EU can agree, international negotiations become far more efficient. There is capacity in the Community system for shaming reluctant states into accepting trade agreements that serve general EU foreign policy interests. For example, in 2001 the Union agreed to offer the world's poorest countries duty-free and quota-free access to the EU's markets for 'everything but arms' (see Faber and Orbie 2009), which France firmly opposed but eventually agreed to accept. The deal was criticized for not doing enough to promote third-world development. But the EU generally claims that it offers the world's poorest countries a better deal than do most industrialized countries.

Europe increasingly finds itself facing fierce economic competition from emerging states such as China, India, and Brazil that have maintained much higher economic growth rates than the EU over recent years, even during the post-2008 recession. In the circumstances, EU trade policy has been accused of becoming aggressive, reactive, and defensive. The Union also shouldered much of the blame for the breakdown of the Doha Development Round of world trade talks, which floundered in 2008 mostly over its (and the US's) agricultural subsidies. With multilateral trade negotiations at an impasse, the EU has sought bilateral preferential trade agreements (PTAs): its PTA with South Korea in 2009 represented a breakthrough of sorts, since it involved a relatively large state and a high volume of trade. However, little progress was made in the pursuit of PTAs with India or the 10-state Asian group ASEAN (Association for South-East Asian Nations) even after the Union committed itself to these agreements in its 2007 strategy paper *Global Europe: Competing in the World* (Commission 2007).

An interesting question for students of European foreign policy is: how much is the EU's economic power used in the pursuit of its foreign policy objectives? The answer seems to be sometimes, but not often. The 2010 agreement to apply severe economic sanctions to Iran in response to its nuclear programme illustrates how the EU occasionally (in this case, after years of US cajoling) uses its economic power for political objectives. The same can be said for the PTAs the Union has agreed with developing countries and states on its borders as part of its Neighbourhood Policy (see Chapter 8). A striking example was the Libyan crisis of early 2011, when the EU rapidly adopted sanctions, travel embargoes, and asset freezes against the Gaddafi regime, even if there were visible misgivings among several governments about the military action. But EU trade policy structures and behaviour challenge the idea of Europe as a 'civilian power'. The Lisbon Treaty states that trade policy 'shall be conducted in the context of the principles and objectives of the Union's external action'. But responsibility is left in the hands of the Commissioner for Trade, not the High Representative. Damro (2010) characterizes the EU as 'Market Power Europe': that is, an EU that defends its economic interests aggressively in individual trade disputes with little regard for broader foreign policy objectives. An even less charitable portrayal is 'Parochial Global Europe' (Young and Peterson 2012): a trading power whose preoccupation with its own internal politics and policies, involving the staunch defence of its economic interests, hampers the Union's attempts to play a global role.

Aid and development

The EU and its member states spend around €50 billion annually on development aid, or over half of the global total. Aid and access to the Union's huge market are frequently combined, along with other policy instruments, as in the cases of the EU's free trade agreements with Mexico and South Africa. Market access or aid also may be part of political cooperation agreements designed to promote democracy or human rights. The EU's relations with its most important neighbours—such as Turkey, Ukraine, or Russia (see Box 10.3)—are usually conducted through complex package deals involving trade, aid, and political dialogue.

BOX 10.2   How it really works

Commercial (trade) policy

Trade policy is the most integrated of all EU external policies. The Commission negotiates for the EU as a whole in most cases. There is no specific Council of Trade Ministers, and effective oversight by member states (through the so-called Article 207 Committee of national trade officials) seems limited. The EP gained significant new powers from the Lisbon Treaty, with many measures adopted by co-decision, and its consent is now required for all trade agreements. Still, the Commission is clearly the lead institution and at first sight, its position often seems indomitable.

In practice, power is considerably diffused. Member governments defend their own economic interests robustly at all stages: when the Council defines the Commission's mandate for negotiations, during the negotiations themselves, and when the Council ratifies draft deals. The Treaty says that the Council can (with a few limited exceptions) decide by qualified majority. In practice, important external trade measures almost never pass without unanimity. Moreover, there seems little doubt that the post-Lisbon Parliament will be 'quite ready to make use of its right to reject an agreement', as it did in the case of a US–EU counterterrorism agreement in 2010 (Piris 2010: 287), or set conditions, as it did with the EU–South Korea PTA the same year. Thus, tensions between **intergovernmentalism** and **supranationalism** exist even at the heart of the Community system, even though the EU has a solid record of achievement in trade policy.

Increasingly, the EU seeks region-to-region agreements such as the EuroMed partnership with the countries of the Mediterranean, and the Cotonou agreement, a trade and aid accord between the EU and 79 African, Caribbean, and Pacific (ACP) states. Such package deals require links between different systems for making European foreign policy. For example, most aid to the ACP states is distributed via the European Development Fund (EDF), which member states finance directly and is not part of the EU's general budget.

The Union's aid policy has faced serious challenges in recent years. Evidence that EU aid programmes are not very effectively managed has contributed to 'donor fatigue'. The new wisdom—reflected in World Trade Organization (WTO) rules—is that poorer countries need trade more than aid. Trade is seen as helping poorer countries to grow from within in a sustainable way, while aid is often wasted, especially through corruption. The labelling of the twenty-first century's first global trading round as the Doha development agenda both reflected the new wisdom and focused global attention on the EU (and US) for their reluctance to open (especially) their agricultural markets to developing countries.

The world's poorest countries continue to insist that they need large injections of aid, and remain wary of the EU's new preference (driven by WTO rules as well as political choices) for creating free-trade areas. Large transfers of EU aid continue to flow to the Cotonou countries, most of which are in Africa. The EDF's budget, set at €13.8 billion for 2000–7, was increased to nearly €23 billion for 2008–13. Besides Africa, the Mediterranean and the Balkans are also priority areas for Community spending on development.

BOX 10.3   How it really works

The EU and Russia

The EU's relationship with Russia is a classic glass half-empty or half-full story. A pessimist would make much of the EU's dependence on Russia for energy, particularly since price disputes between Moscow and former Soviet republics in 2005–9 led to interruptions (or threats of them) in flows of Russian natural gas. The EU's concern for its energy security is often viewed as making it the weaker partner in its relationship with Moscow. One consequence, according to this view, is that the Union is reluctant to speak truth to power about the erosion of Russian democracy, the suppression of human rights in Chechnya, or even the 2007 cyber-war waged (apparently) by Russia on Estonia, an EU member state.

In practice, the EU and Russia are mutually and heavily interdependent. The EU relies on Russia to supply more than a quarter of both its oil and natural gas. But sales of raw materials to the EU account for most of Russia's hard currency earnings and fund nearly 40 per cent of Russia's federal budget. Around 60 per cent of Russia's export earnings come from energy, most of it in the form of sales to the EU. One former EU diplomat puts it bluntly: 'Europe should clearly work for a comprehensive partnership with Russia, but at the moment it is nonsense to suggest that this will be based on shared values' (Patten 2005: 178).

The point was illustrated at the 2006 Lahti EU summit held under a Finnish Council Presidency. Vladimir Putin was invited to participate, a first for a Russian President. By all accounts, the meeting was fraught and Putin bristled at any criticism of his government. When the President of the EP, Josep Borrell (a Spaniard), told Putin that the EU could not trade oil for human rights, Putin reportedly replied that corruption was rife in Spain. Putin also noted that mafia was an Italian word, not a Russian one. The French President, Jacques Chirac, enraged other EU delegations by arguing that morality should not be mixed with business in the EU's dealings with Russia.

Still, the (then) EU of 25—including former Soviet republics (such as Estonia) or satellites—delivered a more-or-less common message to Russia for the first time. The German Chancellor, Angela Merkel, insisted that she would continue to push Putin on human rights in Russia. So, perhaps the glass was half-full?

The Union has also become the world's largest donor of humanitarian aid through the European Community Humanitarian Office (ECHO), located within the Commission. It announced the largest contribution of any donor to humanitarian aid in Afghanistan within days of the start of the 2001 war. ECHO also contributed more relief than any other donor to areas affected by the 2004 Asian Tsunami and 2010 Pakistani floods.

The EU's good deeds are often marred by bad 'plumbing'. ECHO was slammed for its lax spending controls by the Committee of Independent Experts whose 1999 report sparked the mass resignation of the Santer Commission. For years, EU development funds helped prop up dictators who were overthrown in Egypt, Tunisia, and elsewhere in the 2011 Arab Spring. EU aid delivery certainly has become more efficient over time. But the Commission still has some distance to go before it escapes the memorable charge (made by a UK Minister for Development) that it is the 'worst development agency in the world' (Short 2000).

Externalizing internal policies

In a sense, the European Union has no internal policies: its market is so huge that every major decision it makes to regulate it (or not) has international effects. When the Union negotiates internal agreements on fishing rights or agricultural subsidies, the implications for fishermen in Iceland or farmers in California can be immediate and direct. The ultimate act of externalizing internal policies occurs when the EU enlarges its membership, as it did when it more than doubled in size from twelve to 27 member states after 1995.

A rule of thumb, based on a landmark European Court decision (see Weiler 1999: 171–83), is that where the EU has legislated internally, a corresponding external policy competence for that matter is transferred to it. The Community has frequently taken this route in environmental policy, and now participates in several international environmental agreements. Where internal lines of authority are clear, the EU can be a strong and decisive negotiator. The Commission has become a powerful, global policeman for vetting mergers between large firms. When the Union seeks bilateral economic agreements, whether with China, Canada, or Croatia, the Commission negotiates for the Union as a whole.

The Union's most important international task may be reconciling rules on its single market with rules governing global trade. The EU sometimes does the job badly, agreeing messy compromises on issues such as data protection or genetically modified foods that enrage its trading partners. External considerations can be a low priority when the Union legislates, and effectively treated as someone else's problem. Most of the time, however, the internal market has offered non-EU producers better or similar terms of access than they were offered before the internal market existed (Young 2002).

We have seen (in Chapter 9) that EU security policy has been subject to considerable criticism from both academics and practitioners. In contrast, EU enlargement has been widely hailed as the most effective tool of European *foreign* policy, in terms of exporting both security and prosperity (Nugent 2004; Smith 2005). But it has also produced enlargement fatigue and the European Neighbourhood Policy, a framework for cooperation with states on or near EU borders such as Ukraine or Russia which, in the Brussels jargon, do not have the 'perspective' of membership anytime soon (Dannreuther 2004; Weber *et al.* 2008). It is difficult to see how the powerful lure of actual membership could ever come close to being replicated by a policy that forecloses that possibility. Member states continue to tussle over how far the Neighbourhood Policy is a direct alternative, rather than a potential stepping stone to, EU membership (see Chapter 8). Neighbourhood Policy is another area where the EU struggles to meet expectations.

The Common Foreign and Security Policy

The gap between the Union's growing economic power and its limited political clout was a source of increasing frustration in the early 1990s. Thus, a distinct system of making foreign policy was created with the CFSP at its centre. This new system overlapped with but did not replace the Community system. Over time, it incorporated a nascent Common Security and Defence Policy (CSDP). Confusingly, the Common Foreign and Security Policy (CFSP) and CSDP are mainly labels for 'institutions that *make* [policies] but *are* not proper policies' in themselves (Jørgensen 2006: 509).

The CFSP unveiled in the Maastricht Treaty marked a considerable advance on the European Political Cooperation mechanism. But it still disappointed proponents of closer foreign policy cooperation. The CFSP gave the Commission the right—shared with member governments—to initiate proposals. It even allowed for limited qualified majority voting, although it was always clear that most actions would require unanimity. Compliance mechanisms in the CFSP were not made as strong as those in the first pillar, with the European Court of Justice mostly excluded. The CFSP (like the initial JHA policy) remained largely intergovernmental, even if links to the Community system were gradually strengthened.

Established habits of exchange between foreign ministries meant that member governments were able to agree a considerable number of common positions and joint actions in its early years (see Nuttall 2000: 184–8). Some measures, such as the 1993 Stability Pacts to stabilize borders in Central and Eastern Europe, or support for democratic elections in Bosnia (in the 1990s) went well beyond the usual EPC declarations. Nevertheless, critics scorned the CFSP's inability to deal with more complex or urgent security issues, above all the wars in ex-Yugoslavia (see Box 10.4).

The 1997 Amsterdam Treaty's main foreign policy innovation was the creation of a new High Representative for the CFSP (who also served as Secretary-General of the Council). The High Representative was meant to help give the EU a single voice and the CFSP a single face. After his appointment to the post in 1999, former NATO Secretary General Javier Solana at times proved a skilful coordinator of different actions and instruments, whether sourced in Brussels or national capitals. He fronted the Union's diplomatic efforts, in cooperation with NATO, to head off civil war in Macedonia in 2001, and had a leading role in nuclear dialogue with Tehran. However, the EU continued to be represented externally by its *troika*, with Solana joined by the Foreign Minister of the state holding the Council Presidency and the European Commissioner for External Affairs. In some cases, such as the Group of Eight summits, special formulae for representation involved a confusing mix of Commission and national representatives. Thus there,was never a clear answer to the legendary (and apparently apocryphal) question asked by the US Secretary of State, Henry Kissinger, in the 1970s: 'What number do I call when I want to speak to "Europe"?'

> **BOX 10.4   How it really works**
>
> **Making foreign policy decisions**
>
> Provisions in the Maastricht Treaty for **Qualified Majority Voting (QMV)** on foreign pol-icy seemed to mark a major change from European Political Cooperation. However, QMV was rarely used in the second (or third) pillar. The glass remained (at least) half-empty: rules on when QMV could be used were far more complex than in the first pillar, and nearly all important CFSP decisions required a consensus. Because it could not agree a unanimous position on Iraq (far from it), the EU was completely sidelined during the drift to war in 2003. It is difficult to identify any major foreign policy decision of the George W. Bush administration that was influenced by any CFSP decision, except perhaps a soften-ing in tactics for dealing with the Iran nuclear dossier. The CFSP's annual budget is in the range of a paltry €150 million. Looking to the future, foreign policy by unanimity seems impractical, even impossible, in an EU of 27 plus. Procedurally, it is clear how the CFSP works. Substantively, there is controversy about whether it works at all.
>
> But perhaps the glass is half-full. Each time the EU is faced with an international cri-sis, it tends to act more quickly, coherently, and decisively than it did in response to the last crisis. Following the terrorist attacks of 9/11, the EU agreed a raft of statements or decisions within days. Subsequently, the EU moved decisively—sometimes controver-sially so—and gave its consent to counter-terrorist agreements with the US on issues such as airline passenger records and container security (see Rees 2006). The EU's diplo-macy (through the 'EU-3') on Iran, its participation in the Middle East Quartet (on an equal footing with the US, Russia, and the UN), a range of actions in central Africa and the Balkans, and the Lisbon Treaty's new foreign policy machinery suggest, for optimists, a steady integration of European foreign policy.

But after the rejection of the 2004 Constitutional Treaty, the Lisbon Treaty as-signed that single number to a new EU High Representative, who would do the same job the Constitutional Treaty gave its EU Minister for Foreign Affairs (even if that title was rejected as too provocative). The new High Representative, Catherine Ash-ton in the first instance, combined the roles of the previous High Representative and the Commissioner for External Affairs. Ashton also served as Vice-President of the Commission and chaired EU Councils of Foreign Ministers, in perhaps the most au-dacious attempt ever to combine the supranational with the intergovernmental in one position. Doing so involves tricky compromises: for example, the High Representative has the (non-exclusive) right to propose CFSP initiatives without passing them through the entire College of Commissioners.

Ashton spent most of her first year (2010) in post navigating a minefield of insti-tutional bickering between the Commission, Council, and Parliament about the pre-cise composition of the EEAS. One upshot was to highlight how long it would take before the Service operated as a single—and single-minded—foreign service as na-tional EU foreign services do. Yet, many EU diplomats agreed that the EEAS offered a 'streamlined system for developing, deciding and executing European foreign policy. It should create new ideas and new synergies and enable the EU to act more decisively in international affairs' (Avery 2011: 2).

Theorizing the EU as a Global Actor

The expansion of the EU's foreign policy role confounds many international relations (IR) theorists, particularly those in the realist tradition. Most realists make two assumptions. First, power in international politics is a zero-sum commodity. Second, all alliances between states are temporary (see Mearsheimer 2001; Waltz 2002). On one hand, realists claim to be able to explain why the EU is often weak or divided on matters of high politics, such as Iraq or Russia. On the other hand, realists find it difficult to explain the EU's international ambitions and activities (see Box 10.5), or even why it does not collapse altogether. More generally, twenty-first century works of IR theory often barely mention the EU, or ignore it altogether (see Sullivan 2001; Elman and Elman 2003; Burchill *et al.* 2005).

One consequence is that research on European foreign policy 'has come to resemble an archipelago' (Jørgensen 2006: 507), which is only barely connected to the study of IR more generally. Consider intergovernmentalist approaches to European integration, which are themselves derived from liberal theories of international politics (see Moravcsik 1998). Intergovernmentalists assume that governments respond to powerful, domestic economic pressures. When governments agree economic policy deals that benefit national economic interests, they try to lock in those gains by giving EU institutions powers of enforcement. In contrast, governments face far weaker incentives to delegate foreign or defence policy powers to EU institutions, which explains why the EU's trade policy is far more integrated than the CFSP. Beyond that insight, however, intergovernmentalists have shown little interest in the EU's global ambitions. As such, what has been described as 'the most suitable theoretical tradition' for explaining European integration also seems to be 'currently running out of steam and relevance' to European foreign policy (Jørgensen 2006: 519).

In contrast, one of the oldest theories of European integration—**neofunctionalism**—may still have mileage, at least by proxy. Institutionalism, a theoretical cousin of neofunctionalism (see Haas 2001), focuses on how the EU produces habits that eventually mature into institutionalized rules of behaviour (see Smith 2003; 2004). For example, habits established through twenty years of foreign policy exchanges within EPC led to the CFSP. The EU often creates new roles or organizations—such as the High Representative or the Political and Security Committee—which develop their own interests, missions, and escape close intergovernmental control.

BOX 10.5   Compared to what?

The European Security Strategy

Equipping the EU with a military capability made it possible also to give the Union a *security strategy*: a set of principles that could guide foreign policy action and specify how ESDP might be deployed together with other EU policy instruments. The 2003 European Security Strategy (ESS) was agreed at a tumultuous time after the Union's sharp and bitter divisions over Iraq. It was possible to view the ESS as a step forward for the Union as a global actor (see Biscop 2005), but also impossible not to view it as partly, at least, a response to the 2002 US National Security Strategy (NSS; see Dannreuther and Peterson 2006).

The NSS was unveiled, with powerful symbolism, one year and one day after the terrorist attacks of 9/11. Many US allies were shocked by its endorsement of three principles: the need for shifting coalitions in a war on terrorism, the sanctity of unchallenged US military superiority, and the right to 'pre-empt' threats to American security unilaterally. The NSS was full of dark warnings about the nature of the terrorist threat and how the US would respond to it.

In contrast, the tone of the ESS was largely celebratory: extolling the achievements of European integration, while urging that European habits of cooperation needed to be exported. The ESS ended up being a much shorter document than the Bush administration's NSS. In places, it reads more like a set of ambitions than a genuine strategy (Heisbourg 2004). A report on its implementation in 2008 echoed the self-congratulatory tone of the ESS and but also admitted that Europe needed to be 'more capable, more coherent, and more active' to realize its potential (Council 2008: 2). On balance, there was just enough that was common to the two strategies—especially about the need for proactive policies to counter terrorism—to make it possible to think that the transatlantic alliance might be more durable than it sometimes appeared around the time of the Iraq war (see Anderson *et al.* 2008; Lundestad 2008).

Yet, the leading theory of European foreign policy has become constructivism (see Tonra and Christiansen 2004; Bretherton and Vogler 2006). Constructivists depart from realists and liberals in insisting that the interests and identities of EU member states are not fixed before they bargain with each other. Rather, they are 'constructed' through bargaining, which is a highly social process. Constructivists, in contrast to institutionalists, insist that ideas matter as much as (or more than) institutions in IR. Alexander Wendt (1992; 1999), perhaps the leading IR constructivist, portrays the EU as more than a temporary alliance because its member states assume a measure of common identity through shared ideas, including ones about the desirability of multilateralism, environmental protection, and so on. Many constructivists do not shy from questions about what the EU *should* do in foreign policy, insisting on the importance of a 'normative power Europe' that stands up for its values and principles (Manners 2002; 2008).

Arguably, however, constructivism sets the bar too low. Its proponents can become apologists for EU inaction or incoherence in global politics by always falling back on the argument that Europe remains 'under construction' as a global actor. As much as constructivists insist the glass is half-full, others—such as Toje (2010), who portrays the EU as a 'small power' analogous to Canada, Peru or Switzerland—argue that it remains half-empty.

Conclusion

When the former British Prime Minister, Tony Blair, urged that the EU should be-come a 'superpower but not a superstate' in 2000, he provoked little controversy outside of his own country. The idea that the EU should take a lead in expressing European power internationally has become almost a mainstream view (see Morgan 2005; Peterson *et al.* 2012). The EU has come a long way from humble origins in foreign policy. But it remains an odd global power, which has difficulty living up to its ambitions. It has increased its potential international power each time it has en-larged. Yet, EU foreign policy is only as good as the quality of the consensus amongst its members, and it is often of poor quality in an enlarged EU of 27+ member states.

One reason why assessments of European foreign policy vary so widely is because it is unclear how the EU's success should be measured. There is no question that the Union is far more active internationally than its founders ever imagined it could be. In several policy areas, especially economic ones, it is a global power. No other inter-national organization in history has even tried, let alone claimed, to have a 'common' foreign policy.

There were signs post-Iraq that foreign policy was being reclaimed by European national capitals, or groups of states acting together, even if none appeared to be giv-ing up on the CFSP altogether (see Hill 2004). The Lisbon Treaty's institutional re-forms may move the EU closer to a truly common foreign policy (see Rogers 2009). Consider the US Secretary of State, Hillary Clinton's, view: 'These are historic times for the EU. I expect that in decades to come, we will look back on the Lisbon Treaty and the maturation of the EU that it represents as a major milestone in our world's history' (21.1.11; http://euobserver.com/9/29322/?rk=1).

Or, Lisbon's effect might be, yet again, to raise expectations that cannot be met. How, for example, will coherence emerge from the constellation of a new European Council President, a new(-ly empowered) High Representative, and the Commis-sion President, as well as Commissioners for development and trade policy? The EU's interlocutors are often understandably confused about who to approach about what issue and how the CFSP actually works.

The future of European foreign policy will be determined largely by two factors: the EU's relationship with the US (see Toje 2009) and its ability to wield its 'soft power', or its power to persuade rather than coerce (Nye 2004; 2011). Whether the George W. Bush era marked a glitch or a watershed in transatlantic relations is an open question. The failure of hard (mostly) American military power to achieve US policy goals in Afghanistan or Iraq, let alone Iran or North Korea or the Middle East, rekindles questions about whether Europe's soft power might make it an alternative source of leadership in the twenty-first century (Rifkin 2004; Leonard 2005).

Alternatively, Europe's declining population and military weakness might foreclose such questions. One of the EU's top diplomats argues that Europe will never maximize its soft power until it invests far more in hard power (Cooper 2004a), a prospect that became increasingly remote in a climate of post-recession austerity as the second decade of the twenty-first century began. Yet, there is no question that the EU faces powerful incentives—especially as it loses economic ground to states such as China, India, and Russia—to become more united in foreign policy: As Howorth (2007: 22) argues, 'The pressures for the EU to speak to the rest of the world with a single voice will become intense. The refusal to make collective EU choices in the world of 2025 will be tantamount to an abdication of sovereignty.'

It is easy to see why debates about Europe as a global actor are so lively. The EU is likely to remain an often uncertain and hesitant global power but one that never stops trying to be more coherent and effective. It will no doubt continue to frustrate its partners, but sometimes show surprising unity, and fascinate—probably as much as it confounds—future students of international politics.

DISCUSSION QUESTIONS

1. Define 'European foreign policy'. Explain why this term has assumed wide usage amongst those who study the EU's international role.

2. Why are member states reluctant to entrust the Commission with responsibilities for the political side of foreign policy, while they have done so for important areas of economic external relations?

3. Why is the most effective way for the EU to promote development in the less-developed world increasingly seen as 'trade not aid'?

4. How best to characterize the EU as a global actor: Civilian power? Normative power? Market power? Small power?

FURTHER READING

The best single source text on Europe as a global actor is Hill and Smith (2011). Useful overviews include K. Smith (2008), Bindi (2010), and Toje (2010). Good historical treatments are available, told both from the points of view of a practitioner (Nuttall 2000) and an academic institutionalist (M. E. Smith 2003). The EU's neighbourhood policy is scrutinized in Weber et al. (2008) and its Security Strategy is the focus for Biscop (2005) as well as Dannreuther and Peterson (2006), who compare it to its US counterpart. The Union's contribution to the United Nations, as well as multilateralism more generally, is considered by Laatikainen and Smith (2006). On the idea of the EU as a 'civilian power', see Sjursen (2006).

Bindi, F. (ed.) (2010), *The Foreign Policy of the European Union: Assessing Europe's Role in the World* (Washington DC: Brookings Institution Press).

Biscop, S. (2005), *The European Security Strategy: A Global Agenda for Positive Power* (Aldershot and Burlington VT: Ashgate).

Dannreuther, R., and Peterson, J. (eds.) (2006), *Security Strategy and Transatlantic Relations* (London and New York: Routledge).

Hill, C. and Smith, M. (eds.) (2011), *International Relations and the European Union*, 2nd edn (Oxford and New York: Oxford University Press).

Laatikainen, K. V. and Smith, K. E. (eds.) (2006), *The European Union at the United Nations: Intersecting Multilateralisms* (Basingstoke and New York: Palgrave Macmillan).

Nuttall, S. (2000), *European Foreign Policy* (Oxford and New York: Oxford University Press).

Sjursen, H. (ed.) (2006), 'What Kind of Europe? European Foreign Policy in Perspective', Special Issue of *Journal of European Public Policy* 13/2.

Smith, K. E. (2008), *European Union Foreign Policy in a Changing World*, 2nd edn (Oxford and Malden MA: Polity).

Smith, M. E. (2003), *Europe's Foreign and Security Policy* (Cambridge and New York: Cambridge University Press).

Toje, A. (2010), *The European Union as a Small Power: After the Cold War* (Basingstoke and New York: Palgrave).

WEB LINKS

A good place to start researching the EU's external policy role is the website of the Paris-based Institute for Security Studies **http://www.iss.europa.eu/**), which formally became an autonomous European Union agency in 2002. Other specific areas of EU policy have their own, dedicated websites:

- External relations (general): **http://www.europa.eu/pol/ext/index_en.htm**
- Foreign and security policy: **http://www.europa.eu/pol/cfsp/index_en.htm**
- Humanitarian aid: **http://europa.eu/pol/hum/index_en.htm**
- Justice/home affairs: **http://www.europa.eu/pol/justice/index_en.htm**
- Trade: **http://europa.eu/pol/comm/index_en.htm**
- Development: **http://ec.europa.eu/europeaid/index_en.htm**

The Commission's site (**http://ec.europa.eu/index_en.htm**) has general information about EU foreign policy, but the websites of national foreign ministries often reveal more. On the EU's relationship with the US, see **http://www.eurunion.org/** and **http://www.useu.be/**. Web links on the EU's other important relationships include ones devoted to the Cotonou convention (**http://www.acpsec.org/**), EU–Canadian relations (**http://www.canada-europe.org/**), and the Union's relationship with Latin America (**http://aei.pitt.edu/view/subjects/D002022.html**). To see how the EU's aid policy has shifted towards promoting trade (instead of aid) see: **http://ec.europa. eu/development/icenter/repository/SEC_2010_0419_COM_2010_0159_EN.PDF**. The Brookings Institution (based in Washington DC) offers a 'scorecard for European foreign policy' at: **http://www.brookings.edu/reports/2011/0330_european_scorecard_ vaisse.aspx**.

 Visit the Online Resource Centre that accompanies this book for additional material: **www.oxfordtextbooks.co.uk/orc/bomberg3e/**

CHAPTER 11

Conclusion

John Peterson, Elizabeth Bomberg, and Richard Corbett

▌ Summary

The EU is exceptional, complex, and in important respects unique. This concluding chapter revisits three key themes that guide understanding of the EU, before returning to the question: how can we best *explain* the EU and how it works? We review some leading theoretical approaches, and identify what each approach claims is most important to explain about the EU, and why. Finally we confront the question: 'Where do we go from here'? Does knowing how the EU works give us clues about how it might work in the future?

Introduction

This book has offered a *basic* introduction to how the European Union works. A vast body of work has emerged in recent years to satisfy those who wish to know more. Much that has been written about the EU may seem confusing or obfuscatory to the curious non-expert. We—together with our co-authors—have tried to be simpler and clearer. For example, we have emphasized throughout how the EU works in practice, not just in theory. We have also tried to show that the EU is not so exceptional that it resists all comparisons.

Yet, it does not take much study of the EU before one is struck (or becomes frustrated) by how complex and ever-shifting it seems to be. Most of our 'compared to what' exercises have ended up drawing contrasts—some quite sharp—between politics and policy-making in Brussels and these same processes elsewhere. There are very few analytical 'bottom lines' about how the European Union works, except that it works quite differently from any other system for deciding who gets what, when, and how.

Three Themes

We have offered (see Chapter 1) three general themes as guides to understanding how the EU works. The first is experimentation and change. The European Union refuses to stand still: about the only thing that can be safely predicted about its future is that it is unlikely to remain static for long, even if change will usually be incremental rather than revolutionary. Second, EU governance is an exercise in sharing power between states and institutions, and seeking consensus across different levels of governance. Getting to 'Yes' in a system with so many diverse stakeholders often requires resort to informal methods of reaching agreement, about which the EU's Treaties and official publications are silent. Third and finally, the gap between the EU's policy scope and its capacity—between what it *tries* to do and what it is *equipped* to do—has widened. The EU has been a remarkable success in many respects, but its future success is by no means assured. We briefly revisit each of these themes below.

Experimentation and change

Every chapter in this book, each from a different angle, has painted a picture of constant evolution and change. Few could deny that the European Union has developed into more than an 'ordinary' international organization (IO). However, its development has not been guided by any agreed master plan. Rather, it has evolved through messy compromises struck after complex political bargaining between member states (see Chapters 2 and 4), institutions (see Chapter 3), organized interests (see Chapter 6) and competing visions.

One consequence is that when the EU changes, it usually changes incrementally. Radical reform proposals tend to be scaled back in the direction of modesty in a system with so many different kinds of interest to satisfy and where changes to the basic rules (the Treaties) need the agreement of every member state. The unsuccessful attempt to establish a Constitutional Treaty for the EU proves the point: although ratified by a large majority of member states, it proved a step too far, at least in terms of its symbolism, for all to accept. Yet, the Lisbon Treaty carried forward most of the institutional changes contained in the Constitutional Treaty while stripping out references to an EU flag, anthem and the provocative designation 'EU Minister for Foreign Affairs' (renamed, in the EU's familiar jargon, 'High Representative'; see Box 11.1).

However, apparently unexceptional acts of fine-tuning, such as slightly increasing the EP's power or sending an encouraging political signal to an applicant state, can sometimes gather momentum like a snowball rolling down a hill. Moreover, the EU's potential for fundamental change, as illustrated by the launch of single currency or dramatic decisions by the European Court of Justice (ECJ), cannot be denied. Perhaps because the EU is such a young political system, changes to its structure or remit are frequently debated and often enacted.

The more general point is that the EU is a fundamentally experimental union (Laffan *et al.* 2000). Nobody argues that it always works like a smooth, well-oiled machine. It has become far more difficult to shift it in any particular direction as its membership has more than doubled in the space of about a decade. Equally, almost no one denies that it is remarkably successful in coaxing cooperative, collective action out of sovereign states that regularly, almost routinely, went to war with each other a few generations ago. Increasingly, the Union is seen as a model or laboratory worthy, in some respects, of mimicry by other regional organizations in other parts of the world (Farrell 2007; Checkel 2007; see also Box 2.4).

Sharing power and seeking consensus

A second theme that cannot be avoided in studying the EU is that power is distributed widely—between states, institutions, and organized interests. At the same time, consensus and compromise are highly valued. Enormous efforts are often required to strike agreements that are acceptable to all who have a slice of power to determine outcomes. Just being able to agree is often viewed as an achievement in itself. Once sealed, EU agreements are almost always portrayed as positive sum—that is, bringing greater good to a greater number of citizens than did the previous policy. Of course, nearly every policy creates losers as well as winners. But the perceived need to preserve support for the Brussels system means that heroic attempts are usually made to avoid creating clear losers (or else to compensate them).

It follows that coming to grips with how the EU works does not just mean mastering the Treaties. The formal powers of institutions and member states, and formal

BOX 11.1   What's in a name? (revisited)

As we have seen, the terms used to refer to the EU's artefacts often stir up controversy. A word can have different connotations in different languages or cultural contexts. Examples include:

- **Assembly or Parliament?**
The designation of a European 'Parliament' was initially a term too far for some. The drafters of the original Treaties prudently used the term 'Assembly'. The Assembly decided to call itself a Parliament in the early 1960s. For a long time, some governments strictly avoided the term. However, in 1986, they agreed to amend the Treaty to introduce the name European Parliament.

- **Commission or Executive?**
Although many saw the Commission as an embryonic European government when what is now the EU was created, others did not. The authors of the Treaty thus shied away from even describing it as an executive. In French, it is often referred to as the *Commission exécutive* to distinguish it from *Commission parlementaire,* which is the French term for a parliamentary committee.

- **Constitution or Treaty?**
The Treaties are sometimes described as the EU's constitution, and the European Court of Justice has itself referred to them as a constitutional charter. However, the attempt to replace the Treaties by a single text formally described as a Constitution fell in 2005 when it failed to be ratified by France and the Netherlands. Arguments about that term featured in Dutch pre-referendum debates. Member states instead agreed to amend the existing Treaties without formally labelling them as a constitution.

- **Federal or supranational?**
The Schuman declaration, the basis for establishing the European Coal and Steel Community, referred to the ECSC as the first step towards a European federation. But this definition of the *finalité* of the Union has always been controversial. Definitions of 'federal' are highly divergent. The term supranational emerged instead.

- **Foreign Minister or High Representative?**
The merged post of Vice President of the Commission/High Representative was originally described as the EU Minister for Foreign Affairs in the unratified Constitutional Treaty. The term was dropped in the Lisbon Treaty, although it is still used informally in Brussels.

- **Representative or Ambassador?**
The heads of the EU's representations in third countries have ambassadorial status, and are commonly referred to as ambassadors, though they are officially just representatives.

- **Why 'President'?**
The EU gives the title 'President' to all kinds of functions that might have been named otherwise—at least in English. For Anglophones, it might make more sense to use 'Speaker' of the Parliament, 'Governor' of the Central Bank, 'Chairman' of the Council, and maybe 'Prime Commissioner'.

rules of policy-making, are not unimportant. But they do not come close to telling the whole story, since informal understandings and norms are crucial in determining outcomes. Most of our investigations of 'how it really works' have accentuated the importance of unwritten rules that have emerged over time and through practice, almost organically—as opposed to being mandated in formal or legal terms. These rules and norms have then been learned and internalized by EU policy-makers. For example, it is widely accepted in Brussels that formal votes in the Council should be avoided whenever possible, even if they have become more common—and perhaps more necessary—in a radically enlarged Union. Still, the idea that consensus should be the ultimate aim, and that long negotiations and manifold compromises are an acceptable price to pay for it, is powerfully engrained. These norms often matter far more than what the Treaties say about which state has how many votes, what constitutes a qualified majority, or where QMV applies and where it does not. The enlargements of 2004 and 2007 suggested that representatives of new states learn the rules of the game rather quickly. They were, for instance, able to lend their weight to a broad alliance supporting further liberalization of the services sector—not by threatening a blocking minority, but by constructively arguing their case.

Moreover, the EU is a uniquely multilevel system of governance. Even the most decentralized, federal nation-states—such as Germany or the US—have a government and an opposition. The European Union has neither. As such, it often suffers (not least in foreign policy) from a lack of leadership. Rarely does one institution or member state, or alliance thereof, offer consistent or decisive political direction. Instead, grand bargains to agree quasi-constitutional change, as well as many more mundane agreements, result from a unique kind of power-sharing across levels of governance, as well as between EU institutions and member states. It is this diversity and mix of actors—regional, national, and supranational, public and private—the wide dispersal of power between them, and the need always to try to increase the number of 'winners', yet without the paralysis of most international organizations, that make the European Union unique.

Scope and capacity

Third and finally, we have suggested that the EU's scope—both in terms of policy remit and constituent states—has grown much faster than its capacity to manage its affairs. Chapters 5 and 6—and perhaps especially Chapter 9—outlined the uneven yet unmistakable expansion of EU policy responsibilities. Chapter 8 focused on why, and with what consequences, the EU has continued to enlarge its membership and has tried to improve its relations to countries in its near abroad. Chapter 10 showed how the EU has evolved, almost by stealth, into a global power. With no agreed upon 'end goal', the EU has taken on new tasks and members, but without a concomitant increase in capacity, or tools and resources to perform its designated tasks. For instance, Chapter 3 highlighted the institutional limits of EU. Can the Commission, equivalent in size to the administration of a medium-sized European city, manage an ever larger and more ambitious Union? Perhaps its emphasis under the Presidency of José Manuel Barroso on a 'Europe of results' reflects, in part, a re-balancing of the traditional argument that certain problems require integration to solve them. Similarly, Majone (2005) argues that EU policies need to solve actual problems, as opposed to serving the political purpose of further political integration, which often seemed to be their primary goal in the past. Now that we have that integration, the EU must demonstrate that it is actually solving policy problems. But does it have the capacity to do so?

The Commission is far from alone in confronting a gap between scope and capacity. Can one Parliament adequately represent nearly 500 million citizens? Can 27 or more ministers sit around the Council table and have a meaningful negotiation? Crucially, the EU's political and geographic scope has increased with explicit support from its citizens being taken for granted, on the grounds that elected national parliaments and European parliaments supported it—an assumption challenged by referendum results on the Constitutional Treaty. Is it not risky to assume that the European Union can continue to take on ever more tasks and member states, while retaining its status as the most successful experiment in international cooperation in modern history? This gap between scope and capacity (institutional and political) raises broader questions about the EU's future.

Explaining the EU

While seeking above all to describe how the EU works, this book has also introduced—and tried to demystify—debates about what are the most important forces driving EU politics. Just as there is no consensus on the desirability of European integration, there is no consensus about what is most important about it. Social scientists disagree about what it is about the EU that is most important to *explain*. The position they take on this question usually reflects their own approach to understanding the EU: as an international organization (IO)? A polity in its own right? A source of constructed identity? Or a factory for public policies?

We have seen how theory can help us frame interesting questions, and help us determine what evidence is needed to answer them. If it is accepted that the European Union is exceptionally complex, then it stands to reason that there can be no one 'best' theory of EU politics. What a former Commission President, Jacques Delors, once called an 'unidentified political object' is a little bit like other IOs such as NATO or the United Nations, a little bit like federal states such as Germany and Canada, and a little bit like the other leading system for generating legally binding international rules: the WTO. But it closely resembles none of them. It makes sense in the circumstances to approach the EU with a well-stocked toolkit of theoretical approaches, and to be clear about what each singles out as most important in determining how it really works.

International relations approaches

International relations (IR) scholars bring important insights to the study of the EU. They can always be relied upon to ask hard, stimulating questions about the nature of power in international politics, and the extent to which cooperation is possible or durable in the absence of any 'international government'. In seeking answers to these questions, students of IR add value—in two principal ways—to debates about the nature and significance of European integration.

First, approaching the EU as a system within a system—a regional alliance in the wider scheme of global politics—encourages us to ask why European states have chosen to pool a large share of their sovereignty. For neofunctionalists, the answer lies in the way that the choices open to states become narrower after they decide to establish a common market and thus to increase their economic interdependence (Börzel 2005). EU institutions, in alliance with interest groups, guide and encourage 'spill-over' of cooperation in one sphere (the internal market) to new spheres (such as environmental policy). States remain powerful but they must share power with each other and with EU institutions and non-institutional actors in Brussels, as well as those in national and regional political capitals. For neofunctionalists, what is most important to explain about EU politics is how and why European integration moves inexorably forward. There are crucial differences between EU member states and ordinary nation-states in international politics, to the extent that European integration is largely irreversible.

For intergovernmentalists member states remain free to choose how the EU should work (Moravcsik 1998; Moravcsik and Schimmelfenig 2009). The Union is built on a series of bargains between its member states, which are self-interested and rational in pursuing EU outcomes that serve their economic interests. Of course, conflict may arise in bargaining between states, whose preferences are never identical. But, ultimately, the status quo changes only when acceptable compromises are struck between national interests, especially those of its largest states. The EU's institutions are relatively weak in the face of the power of its member states, which can determine precisely how much authority they wish to delegate to the Commission, Parliament, and Court to enforce and police intergovernmental bargains. For intergovernmentalists, what is most important to explain about the EU is how national interests are reconciled in intergovernmental bargains. European states are 'ordinary' states, whose national interests happen to be compatible often enough to produce unusually institutionalized cooperation. The EU 'occupies a permanent position at the heart of the European landscape' (Moravcsik 1998: 501) but only because member governments want it that way. Much about European integration remains reversible, and always will be.

A comparative politics approach

As the European Union's policy remit has expanded, many comparativists (at least those who study Europe) have found themselves unable to understand their subject—centrally, the state—without knowing how the EU works. In particular, new institutionalists, whose work has become deeply influential in the study of comparative politics as well as across the social sciences, have developed insightful analyses of how the EU works. Institutionalists view the EU as a system where cooperation is now normal and accepted. Policy-makers in Brussels have become used to working in a system where power is shared, in particular between its major institutions. Bargaining in the making of day-to-day, 'ordinary' EU policy is as much between institutions as it is between governments. Usually, it is contrasted with bargaining—viewed as primarily intergovernmental—in episodic rounds of Treaty reform. Yet, some analysts view institutionalism as better at 'capturing' and explaining negotiations than intergovernmentalism—even intergovernmental negotiations that alter the Union's Treaties (see Slapin 2008). A key determinant of actual outcomes in any EU negotiation is the extent to which 'path dependency' has become institutionalized and radical change is precluded.

Institutionalists share important assumptions with neofunctionalists, particularly about the need to view European integration as a continuous process (see Pierson 1996; 2004). But institutionalists tend to study the Union as a political system in itself, analogous to national systems, as opposed to a system of international relations. For them, institutions develop their own agendas and priorities, and thus load the EU system in favour of certain outcomes over others (Meunier and MacNamara 2007; Pollack 2009). The European Union is extraordinary, above all, because it has such extraordinary institutions.

A public policy approach

Studying EU politics without studying what it produces—actual policies—is like studying a factory but ignoring the product it manufactures. We have seen (especially in Chapter 5) that most EU policies are regulatory policies, many of them highly technical. We have also seen how resource-poor EU's institutions are, and how reliant they are on expertise and resources held beyond Brussels and/or by non-public actors. Advocates of policy network analysis insist that EU policy outcomes are shaped in important ways by informal bargaining, much of which takes place outside formal institutions or policy process (Peterson 2009). By the time that ministers vote in the Council or MEPs vote in plenary, legislative proposals have been picked over and scrutinized line-by-line by a huge range of officials, experts and, usually, lobbyists. Often, the proposal bears little or no relationship to what it looked like in its first draft. As we saw in Chapter 7, democratic controls are embedded in the EU more than in any other international organization. But policy network analysis assumes that most policy details are agreed in a world far removed from the political world of ministers and MEPs.

Moreover, the EU is distinctive in its lack of hierarchy: it has no powerful government to impose a policy agenda, so policy stakeholders bargain over what the agenda should be. No one actor is in charge, so they must work together and exchange resources—legitimacy, money, expertise—to realize their goals. For policy network analysts, what is most important to explain about the EU is its policies and who determines them. Making sense of policy outputs means investigating how sectoral networks are structured: are their memberships stable or volatile, are they tightly or loosely integrated, and how are resources distributed within them? The EU is, in effect, a series of different and diverse sub-systems for making different kinds of policy. What is common across the full range of EU activities is interdependence between actors: even those with the most formidable formal powers—the member states and EU institutions—are highly dependent on one another, and indeed on actors that have no formal power at all.

A sociological/cultural approach

What is the most important feature of the EU that requires explanation? For constructivists, it is how interests and identities are constructed. EU decision-makers are the same as anyone else: they are fundamentally social beings. But they are also different from most other political actors in that they interact intensively and extensively with actors whose national identity, language, and culture are different from their own. Brussels (along with Luxembourg and Strasbourg) is a truly multinational crossroads. There is no other political capital in the world that features a more diverse cultural mix. In a sense, Brussels is unlike the rest of Europe and one effect is to encourage a sort of disconnect between the EU and its citizens. But the European identity which often seems barely to register amongst a majority of citizens in Europe's heartlands is very much in evidence amongst those who are closely involved in EU politics and policy.

Again, it is worth reiterating that constructivism is not a substantive theory of regional integration comparable to intergovernmentalism or institutionalism (see Risse 2009). It is a philosophical, even 'metaphysical' position that insists that our social reality is constructed by human beings and reproduced in day-to-day practice. The main upshot is that we cannot explain how the EU works simply by calculating what is in the material interest of each member state, EU institution, or lobbyist and then assuming that Brussels is a vacuum in which those interests are unchanging, unaffected by the informal rules of the game, or untouched by how those at the centre of the EU system view themselves as part of a major collective, political endeavour. Of course, EU decision-makers are self-interested and egoistic. There is much about the European Union that does not work very well. But it produces far more collective action than any system ever invented, or 'constructed', for the reconciliation of multiple national interests. The insights of constructivism are inescapable and essential to explaining why.

There is no one approach with a monopoly of wisdom on EU politics. All shed important light on key features of how the EU works. All downplay, even ignore, factors that others argue are important—or can be in the right circumstances—in determining who gets what from the European Union. A first step in making sense of the EU is deciding what it is about this unidentified political object that is most important to explain.

Where Do We Go From Here?

When we ponder where the European Union may be headed, we have to remember where it has been. For over two decades, the Union has been either preparing, negotiating or ratifying a new treaty. In the 25 years after 1985, the EU modified its basic treaties five times. No Western nation-state has ever made so many major changes to its constitution, including hundreds of amendments, within a similar span. By way of comparison, the US Constitution has been subject to fewer than thirty amendments over nearly 225 years.

Agreeing to reform the EU's institutions, disagreeing on the details, and then agreeing to try to agree again in a future intergovernmental conference (IGC) has become routine. Meanwhile, the EU's policy remit has expanded, as has its membership (see Chapters 5 and 8). The Treaty of Nice (2001) marked an attempt to reform the EU's institutions to prepare the Union for enlargement. Its success in doing so was, to be charitable, limited (see Chapter 2). The institutional reforms mandated in the Lisbon Treaty may be more successful. Still, it will be many years before these reforms take full effect. Even given that prospect, it is difficult to argue that institutional development has kept pace with changes in the EU's policy remit and membership. So, where do we go from here?

Debating the future of Europe

Sometimes it seems as if a debate on the future of EU is 'much of the same old'. The debates of the 1950s dealt with many of the same challenges that the EU faces today. Institutional reform, enlargement, policy remit, money, and (more recently) foreign policy have always been on the EU agenda. The changes over the past 50 years might seem incremental in the short term. However, measured over time, the EU has actually experienced a radical metamorphosis from an institutionally weak and small club with a limited policy arsenal, separate currencies, and no foreign policy, to an institutional powerhouse of 27 members, an elected parliament, a plethora of policies, a single currency and an important role in world politics.

The first decade of the new millennium brought with it new themes to the European agenda. Peace, prosperity, and security remain the cornerstones of integration. But the agenda has shifted markedly towards economic reform, climate change, and energy. On one hand, the economic reform agenda resists simple solutions because an EU of 27 is far more economically diverse than ever before. And Europe was hit hard by the post-2008 global recession. On the other hand, there were signs of fresh life in the EU's economy as the second decade of the 2000s began, even given crises in the Eurozone. EU measures such as the liberalization of services and fresh efforts to extend the single market are two examples. The Union took a global lead on climate change by pledging to cut greenhouse emissions by at least 20 per cent by the year 2020 and encouraging the rest of the industrialized world to follow its lead. But it also was marginalized by emerging economy states at the 2009 Copenhagen climate change summit. The Union remained far from a common energy policy. At the same time, it at least encouraged European citizens to see connections between energy security and environmental protection.

After French and Dutch voters rejected the Constitutional Treaty, the EU went into a state of institutional hibernation. Following a reflection period of two years, the impasse was broken by the German Council Presidency in 2007. The member states—now numbering 27, 12 more than when the Treaty of Nice was agreed—were able to agree on the trimmed down Lisbon Treaty. The substance of the Treaty did not change radically, but all symbolic references in the constitution were dropped. The European Union's most fervent supporters lamented what they viewed as a missed opportunity to give the EU a secure constitutional foundation. A more optimistic view was that the EU was *finally* finished, at least for the foreseeable future, with major Treaty reforms and now ready to tackle other pressing issues, including economics, energy and the environment but also accession negotiations with Turkey, the financial system of the EU, Europe's relationships with Russia, China, and India, and the Union's ever expanding foreign policy agenda more generally.

How will it work?

We conclude with a few thoughts—we will not call them 'predictions'—about how the Union may evolve in the years to come. We have seen that there is no shortage of controversy concerning what is most important in determining how the EU really works. Be that as it may, it is useful to resort to models or visions of how the EU *should* work to stimulate thinking about different potential futures. These models are by no means mutually exclusive. On the contrary, the European Union has always been a hybrid of the:

1. *intergovernmental;*
2. *federal; and*
3. *functional.*

Intergovernmentalism denotes both a school of theory in the study of European integration and a descriptive term to describe an EU that is dominated by its member states. An intergovernmental outcome to the 2007 IGC would have meant a repatriation of competences, a weakening of the institutional triangle between the Commission, the Council and the European Parliament, and a return to unanimous decision-making—with many decisions taken outside the current institutional framework. Yet, the outcome was the opposite. The Lisbon Treaty extended qualified majority voting to some 30 new areas of policy. The pillar structure was collapsed. The EU was given a legal personality and all of its key institutions were strengthened (see Chapter 3). All member states realized that if the EU wanted to be a serious player on the international scene, strict intergovernmentalism was not an option. The experience of the Nice negotiations and the need for efficiency in an enlarged Union produced a new appreciation of methods of power-sharing that had worked in the past.

A fully *federal* Europe would have meant the adoption of something closer in form and substance to the Constitutional Treaty. Crucially, in symbolic terms, it would have been called a Constitution—at least in some EU states—and have included constitutional symbols such as the European anthem and flag, a president, and a foreign minister. But a truly federal EU, at least for ardent enthusiasts of the idea, would mean going beyond the Constitutional Treaty and giving the Union a more powerful central authority with wider competences. Supporters argued that a federal structure could be more transparent and democratic. Power-sharing in most federal regimes is governed by the subsidiarity principle (see Box 2.2), with powers formally divided in a way that brings government as close to the citizen as possible.

Put simply, most member governments and their publics remained unwilling to take a quantum leap to a federal state. The French and Dutch rejections of the Constitutional Treaty illustrate that point. Many of the hallmarks of a federal state—a large central budget funded through direct taxation, an army, or giving the power of constitutional amendment to the centre are unlikely.

To be sure, as the history of the European Union shows, there can be federalism without a federation. The euro and European Central Bank are nothing if not federative elements. Thus, we find another apparent contradiction: the idea of a federal Europe—a nightmare to Eurosceptics—is both a utopian pipe-dream and a practical reality in some areas of policy. But if it ever arrives, a United States of Europe will not arrive in the near future. In some ways, political agreement on the Lisbon Treaty, as an alternative to the Constitutional Treaty, was a setback to those who support a federal Europe.

A final, *functional* model of the future is a mix between the previous two. It is in essence what the Lisbon Treaty represents. After all, the Treaties are not just a compromise among governments but between different visions of the EU's future, including between intergovernmentalists and federalists. The functional model favours continuity in European integration and is sceptical of radical change. It embraces a largely functional path of integration, which is practical and utilitarian rather than decorative or symbolic. It accepts that the EU does not yet (and may never) operate in policy areas such as child care and most forms of taxation. It accepts that the Community method of decision-making, with powers shared between the EU's institutions, is inappropriate (at least initially) for some areas where European cooperation makes sense, including defence and border controls (see Chapter 9). The functional model might even accept a 'core Europe' in some areas of policy, as occurred in early eras with Schengen or the Eurozone, with some EU states forging ahead with cooperative agreements that others could not support, on the assumption that outsiders might become insiders later on (see Box 11.2). But the functional model also values power-sharing for its own sake. It

> ## BOX 11.2   Two-speed Europe?
>
> Debates about a 'two speed' Europe, with a vanguard of countries that integrate further, abound. The holding of Eurozone summits and the establishment of a 'Pact for the euro' with just 23 participating states in 2011 stimulated a further round of such discussions. Reality is more complex than the label 'two speed Europe' would suggest. In practice, a striking variety of speeds and configurations exist. Some examples include:
>
> - non-participation in defence cooperation: Denmark;
> - non-participation in all aspects of Schengen: Ireland and the UK (but participation of Norway, Iceland, and Switzerland from outside the EU);
> - no obligation to join the euro: UK and Denmark; no intention to join the euro soon: Sweden, Czech Republic;
> - right to opt-in (or not) to measures in the field of freedom security and justice: Denmark, Ireland, UK;
> - exemption from the single market rules regarding the acquisition of secondary residences on its territory: Denmark; and
> - exemption from the primacy of EU law regarding anything affecting abortion: Ireland.
>
> Thus, we certainly do not find any straightforward group of slow states, nor an *avant-garde* group of leading member states. Instead, there is a variety of *arrière-gardes*, in each case rather small and with a different configuration, sometimes a single country. The general unity of the Union remains largely intact, even if the growing number of special situations regarding the UK is frequently commented upon.

thus favours pragmatic cooperation that extends to all EU members based on strengthening the current institutional triangle between the Commission, Council, and EP—with the ECJ adjudicating disputes between them.

A basic assumption underpinning this model is that the EU—warts and all—has worked to further the greater good of European citizens. But form should follow function, not vice versa as in the federal vision. The functional model represents a path that has been followed from the earliest beginnings of European integration in the 1950s. It may well live on in the EU of the future simply because, in the past, it has worked: most say reasonably and some say remarkably, even if a minority says not at all.

Conclusion

The reality of European integration is naturally more complex than the simple models that we have just outlined. French EU policy illustrates this point. On some federal projects—such as the euro—France has been instrumental. At the same time France has given intergovernmentalists many reasons to be happy by putting a halt to further European integration: in 1954 by blocking the European Defence Community, in 1966 by refusing to move to QMV and in 2005 by rejecting the constitution. Yet, France has been a vocal advocate of the Common Security and Defence Policy, thus revealing its affinity for a Europe that is a more 'functional' global actor.

The EU has always been a combination of these three models. It is more than an ordinary international organization, but less than a state. It is likely always to be a multilevel system in which the supranational, national and regional co-exist. It is a unique and original way of organizing cooperation between states, whose governments (if not always their citizens) genuinely see themselves as members of a political union.

The EU of the future will probably remain an experimental system, always in flux, with plenty of scope to be reformed and competing ideas about how to do it. It will continue to be, above all, an exercise in seeking consensus and trying to achieve unity, where it makes sense, out of enormous diversity. As such, how it really works will never match any one vision of how it should work.

▌ APPENDIX: Chronology of European Integration*

1945 May	End of World War II in Europe
1946 Sept.	Winston Churchill's 'United States of Europe' speech
1947 June	Marshall Plan announced
	Organization for European Economic Cooperation established
1949 Apr.	North Atlantic Treaty signed in Washington
1950 May	Schuman Declaration
1951 Apr.	Treaty establishing the ECSC signed in Paris
1952 May	Treaty establishing the European Defence Community (EDC) signed
Aug.	European Coal and Steel Community launched in Luxembourg
1954 Aug.	French parliament rejects the EDC
Oct.	Western European Union (WEU) established
1955 May	Germany and Italy join NATO
June	EC foreign ministers meet in Messina to relaunch European integration
1956 May	Meeting in Venice, EC foreign ministers recommend establishing the European Economic Community (EEC) and the European Atomic Energy Community (Euratom)
1957 Mar.	Treaties establishing the EEC and Euratom signed in Rome
1958 Jan.	Launch of the EEC and Euratom
1961 July	The UK, Denmark, Ireland, and Norway apply to join the EEC
1962 Jan.	Agreement reached on the Common Agricultural Policy
1963 Jan.	French President Charles de Gaulle vetoes the UK's application; de Gaulle and German Chancellor Konrad Adenauer sign Elysée Treaty
July	Signing of Yaoundé Convention between EEC and 18 African states
1964 May	EEC sends single delegation to Kennedy Round negotiations on tariff reduction in General Agreement on Tariffs and Trade (GATT)
1965 July	Empty Chair Crisis begins
1966 Jan.	Empty Chair Crisis ends with Luxembourg Compromise
1967 May	The UK, Denmark, Ireland, and Norway again apply for EEC membership
July	The executive bodies of the ECSC, EEC, and Euratom merge into a Commission
Nov.	De Gaulle again vetoes the UK's application
1968 July	The customs union is completed 18 months ahead of schedule
1969 Apr.	De Gaulle resigns

July	The UK revives its membership application
1970 Oct.	Council agrees to create European Political Cooperation (EPC) mechanism. Luxembourg's Prime Minister Pierre Werner presents a plan for Economic and Monetary Union (EMU)
1972 Oct.	Meeting in Paris, EC heads of state and government agree to deepen European integration
1973 Jan.	The UK, Denmark, and Ireland join the EC
Oct.	Following the Middle East War, Arab oil producers quadruple the price of oil and send the international economy into recession
1975 Feb.	Lomé Convention (superceding Yaoundé Convention) agreed between EEC and 46 African, Caribbean, and Pacific (ACP) states
Mar.	EC heads of state and government inaugurate the European Council (regular summit meetings)
June	In a referendum in the UK, a large majority endorses continued EC membership
July	Member states sign a treaty strengthening the budgetary powers of the European Parliament and establishing the Court of Auditors
1978 July	Meeting in Bremen, the European Council decides to establish the European Monetary System (EMS), precursor to EMU
1979 Mar.	Member states launch the EMS
June	First direct elections to the European Parliament
1981 Jan.	Greece joins the EC
1985 June	The Commission publishes its White Paper on completing the single market
1986 Jan.	Portugal and Spain join the EC
Feb.	EC foreign ministers sign the Single European Act (SEA)
1987 July	The SEA enters into force
1988 June	EC and Comecon (East European trading bloc) recognize each other for first time
1989 Apr.	The Delors Committee presents its report on EMU
Nov.	The Berlin Wall comes down
1990 Oct.	Germany is reunited
1991 Dec.	Meeting in Maastricht, the European Council concludes the intergovernmental conferences on political union and EMU
1992 Feb.	EC foreign ministers sign the Maastricht Treaty
June	Danish voters reject the Maastricht Treaty
1993 May	Danish voters approve the Maastricht Treaty, with special provisions for Denmark
June	Copenhagen European Council endorses eastern enlargement
Nov	The Maastricht Treaty enters into force; the European Union (EU) comes into being
1994 Apr.	Hungary and Poland apply to join EU

1995 Jan.	Austria, Finland, and Sweden join the EU
1995 Mar.	Schengen Agreement implemented by seven EU member states
1995– 6	Eight additional Central and Eastern European countries apply to join the EU
1997 June	European Council agrees Amsterdam Treaty, which creates post of High Representative for the CFSP
Oct.	EU foreign ministers sign the Amsterdam Treaty
1998 Mar.	The EU begins accession negotiations with five Central and Eastern European countries, plus Cyprus
	UK and France agree St Malo Declaration on European defence
June	The European Central Bank is launched in Frankfurt
1999 Jan.	The third stage of EMU begins with the launch of the euro and the pursuit of a common monetary policy by 11 member states
Mar.	The Commission resigns following the submission of a report of an independent investigating committee; the Berlin European Council concludes the Agenda 2000 negotiations
May	The Amsterdam Treaty enters into force
Dec.	The European Council signals 'irreversibility of eastern enlargement'; recognizes Turkey as a candidate for EU membership
2000 Feb.	The EU begins accession negotiations with the five other Central and Eastern European applicant countries, plus Malta
Dec.	Meeting in Nice, the European Council concludes the intergovernmental conference on institutional reform
2001 Feb.	EU foreign ministers sign the Nice Treaty
June	Irish voters reject the Nice Treaty
2002 Jan.	Euro notes and coins enter into circulation
Feb.	Convention on the 'Future of Europe' opens
Oct.	In a second referendum, Irish voters approve the Nice Treaty
2003 Feb.	The Nice Treaty enters into force
June	The Convention on the Future of Europe promulgates a Draft Constitutional Treaty
Oct.	An intergovernmental conference opens to finalize the Constitutional Treaty
2004 May	Cyprus, the Czech Republic, Estonia, Hungary, Latvia, Lithuania, Malta, Poland, Slovakia, and Slovenia join the EU
June	The intergovernmental conference reaches agreement on the Constitutional Treaty
Oct.	National leaders sign the Constitutional Treaty in Rome
2005 May	French voters reject the Constitutional Treaty
June	Dutch voters reject the Constitutional Treaty
	The European Council launches a year-long 'period of reflection' on the stalled Constitutional Treaty
Oct.	The EU opens accession negotiations with Turkey

2006 June The European Council decides to prolong the 'period of reflection' and calls on Germany to find a solution to the constitutional impasse during the country's presidency in the first half of 2007

2007 Jan. Bulgaria and Romania join the EU

Slovenia adopts the euro

June European Council agrees mandate for new 'Reform Treaty' to replace Constitutional Treaty

July–Oct. Intergovernmental conference drafts the Reform Treaty

Dec. National leaders sign the new treaty in Lisbon (the Lisbon Treaty)

2008 Jan. Cyprus and Malta adopt the euro

June Irish voters reject the Lisbon Treaty

2009 Jan. Slovakia adopts the euro

Oct. In a second referendum, Irish voters approve the Lisbon Treaty

Dec. The Lisbon Treaty enters into force
The possibility of Greece defaulting on its soaring national debt causes its cost of national borrowing to soar and sparks crisis in the Eurozone

2010 Apr.–May Greece applies for emergency support and concludes a loan agreement with the EU and IMF

May EU leaders create the European Financial Stability Facility (EFSF) to make financial assistance available to troubled member states in the Eurozone.

Nov. Ireland agrees an emergency loan programme with the EU and IMF

2011 Jan. Estonia adopts the euro

Mar. EU creates a permanent mechanism to deal with sovereign bail-outs, called the European Stability Mechanism (ESM; operational in 2013)

May Portugal granted emergency loan assistance programme by the EU and the IMF

July Eurozone leaders agree a new loan assisatance programme for Greece.

*Compiled by Desmond Dinan and Andrew Byrne

■ GLOSSARY

Several of the terms below are defined and elaborated in more detail in the concept boxes of each of the chapters. Where this is the case, the box number is provided.

The EU also has its own official EU glossary which can be found at: http://europa.eu/scadplus/glossary/index_en.htm.

Absorption capacity (see Box 8.1) Refers to the EU's ability to integrate new members into its system.

Accession (see Box 8.1) The process whereby a country joins the EU and becomes a member state.

Acquis communautaire (see Box 4.1) Denotes the rights and obligations derived from the EU treaties, laws, and Court rulings. In principle, new member states joining the EU must accept the entire *acquis*.

Assent procedure (see Consent Procedure)

Asylum Protection provided by a government to a foreigner who is unable to stay in their country of citizenship/residence for fear of persecution.

Battle groups (see Box 9.3) Combine national military resources at the 'hard end' of European capabilities in specialized areas. The EU decided in 2004 to create 20 Battle Groups, which would be deployable at short notice for limited deployments.

Benchmarking (see Box 5.1) The use of comparison with other states or organizations with the aim of improving performance by learning from the experience of others.

Bicameralism (see Box 7.1) From Latin *bi*, two + *camera*, chamber. The principle that a legislature should comprise two chambers, usually chosen by different methods or electoral systems.

Cabinet The group of staff and advisers that make up the private offices of senior EU figures, such as Commissioners.

Candidate countries (see Box 8.1) Refers to a country whose application is confirmed by the EU but is not yet a member.

Charter of Fundamental Rights (see Box 7.1) Adopted by the Council at the Nice Summit in 2000 but (then)not legally binding, the Charter seeks to strengthen and promote the fundamental human rights of EU citizens. Given Treaty status by the Treaty of Lisbon.

Civil society (see Box 6.1) The collection of groups and associations (such as private firms and non-governmental organizations) that operate between the individual and state.

Co-decision procedure Under this decision-making procedure the European Parliament formally shares legal responsibility for legislation jointly with the Council of Ministers.

Cohesion policy Introduced after the first enlargement in 1973, its aim has been to reduce inequality among regions and compensate for the costs of economic integration.

Common Foreign and Security Policy (CFSP) (see Box 10.1) Created by the 1992 Maastricht Treaty as a successor to the European Political Cooperation mechanism. It has been embellished by successive new Treaties and given (by the Treaty of Nice) a Brussels-based Political and Security Committee to prepare Foreign Ministers' meetings and (by Lisbon) a 'new look' High Representative and the EEAS.

Common Security and Defence Policy (CSDP) (formerly known as ESDP: the European Security and Defence Policy) It was created in 1999 to engage in the so-called 'Petersberg tasks' (named after a German hotel where an earlier summit devoted to defence was held): humanitarian and rescue missions, peacekeeping, crisis management, and the vaguely-specified task of 'peacemaking'.

Community method Used especially in areas where common EU policies replace national policies (such as the internal market), the community method is a form of supranational policy-making in which the Union's institutions wield considerable power. Usually contrasted with the intergovernmental method.

Conditionality (see Box 8.1) Means that accession is conditional on fulfilling the criteria for membership.

Consent Procedure (see Box 6.3) Previously known as the **assent** procedure, requires the EP's approval in a simple yes/no vote on international treaties, the accession of new member states, and some other decisions. The EP cannot amend proposals subject to consent. For enlargement, the approval of an absolute majority of Parliament's members is necessary.

Constructivism (see Table 1.1) A school of thought drawing on cultural and sociological studies and emphasizing the non-rational 'social construction' of the collective rules and norms that guide political behaviour.

Consultation procedure (see Box 6.3) Decision-making procedure whereby the Council seeks the opinion of the European Parliament but need not heed that opinion.

Coreper (the Committee of Permanent Representatives) The most important preparatory committee of the Council, Coreper is composed of heads of the Permanent Representation (EU ambassadors) and their supporting delegations maintained by each member state in Brussels. (See also **Perm Reps**)

Cotonou agreement (See Box 10.1) Agreed in the African state of Bénin in 2000 and then revised repeatedly (lastly in 2010). It is the successor to the Lomé Convention and is claimed to be a 'comprehensive partnership' between former European colonies and the EU.

Demandeur (see Box 4.1) French term often used to refer to those demanding something (say regional or agricultural funds) from the EU.

Democratic deficit (see Box 7.1) Refers broadly to the belief that the EU lacks sufficient democratic control. Neither the Commission, which proposes legislation, nor the Council, which enacts it, is directly accountable to the public or national parliaments.

Demos From the ancient Greek, refers to 'the people', 'populace', or 'citizen body'.

Direct effect Established in the 1963 *van Gend en Loos* case, the doctrine has become a distinguishing principle of Community law. Under direct effect Community law applies directly to individuals (not just states) and national courts must enforce it.

Directive (see Box 5.1) The most common form of EU legislation. It stipulates the ends to be achieved but allows each member state to choose the form and method for achieving that end.

Directorates General (DGs) The primary administrative units within the Commission, comparable to national ministries or Departments. There are about thirty DGs, each focusing on a specific area of policy such as competition or trade.

Economic and Monetary Union (EMU) A package of measures designed to harmonize the economic and monetary policies of participating member states. It includes the free movement of capital and convergence of monetary policies. Its most visible element is a single currency—the euro—adopted in 1999 with notes and coins circulating in 2002. By 2011 17 member states were members of EMU.

Elysée Treaty (1963) A treaty of friendship signed between Germany and France signalling greater political cooperation.

Empty Chair Crisis (see Box 2.2) Protesting to the Commission's plans to subject more decisions to Qualified Majority Voting, French president De Gaulle pulled France out of all Council meetings in 1965 thereby leaving one chair empty.

Europe Agreements Signed in the early 1990s, these cooperation agreements between the EU and several east European countries were viewed as a first step towards accession. The agreements cover economic cooperation, cultural exchanges, and some foreign policy coordination.

European Convention on Human Rights (ECHR) (see Box 7.1) Formally the *Convention for the Protection of Human Rights and Fundamental Freedoms*, is an international treaty drafted in 1950 by the then newly formed Council of Europe. All (the now 47) Council of Europe member states are party to the Convention. Any person who feels his or her rights, as defined in the Charter, have been violated by a state can appeal to the **European Court of Human Rights**. Judgments finding violations are binding on the states concerned.

European Defence Agency (EDA) (see Box 9.3) Created in 2004 'to support the Member States and the Council in their effort to improve European defense capabilities [particularly] in the field of crisis management and to sustain' the CSDP. It aims to move the EU towards more cooperation in arms production and procurement.

European Defence Community (EDC) A French-inspired, American-backed proposal for a

European army. Tabled in 1950, the plan collapsed following its rejection by the French National Assembly in 1954.

European Economic Area (EEA) (see Box 8.1) An arrangement which extends the EU's single market to Norway, Iceland, and Liechtenstein.

European External Action Service (EEAS) (see Box 10.1) Created by the Lisbon Treaty and became active in 2010. It works under the authority of the High Representative and brings under one roof EU (Commission and Council) and national diplomats. One intended effect of the EEAS is to make the Union's missions in foreign capitals more like real embassies, with clout and resources.

Europeanization (see Box 4.1) The process whereby national systems (institutions, policies, governments) adapt to EU policies and integration more generally, while also themselves shaping the European Union.

Europol (see Box 9.4) The European Police Office designed to improve the effectiveness with which police forces across the EU could cooperate across national borders.

European Political Cooperation (EPC) The precursor to the Common Foreign and Security Policy (CFSP), the EPC was launched in 1970 as a way for member states to coordinate their foreign policies and speak (and sometimes act) together when national policies overlapped.

European Security and Defence Policy (ESDP): See CSDP.

Eurozone (see Box 5.1) The countries that are part of the Economic and Monetary Union (EMU). By 2011, 17 member states belonged to the Eurozone.

Federalism (see Box 5.1) Principle of sharing power and sovereignty between levels of governance, usually between central or federal level, and substate (state, provincial, Länder) level.

Free trade area (see Box 2.4) An area in which restrictive trading measures are removed and goods can travel freely among its signatory states. These states retain authority to establish their own tariff levels and quotas for third countries.

Frontex (see Box 9.3) The EU's agency for the management of its external border. It was created in 2005 to coordinate member states' operational cooperation in external border controls, provide training to national border guards, carry out risk analyses, organize joint control operations, and assist member states in migrant return operations.

GDP (gross domestic product) An index of the total value of all goods and services produced by a country, not counting overseas operations.

Globalization (see Box 1.5) The process by which the world becomes increasingly interconnected and interdependent because of increasing flows of trade, ideas, people, and capital.

GNP (gross national product) An index of the total value of all goods and services produced by a country, including overseas trade. Most common measure of a country's material wealth.

Governance (see Box 1.5) Established patterns of rules, principles, and practices that enable a community to be governed even without a government or ruler. The term is usefully applied to the EU because of its lack of identifiable government.

IGCs (Intergovernmental Conferences) Conferences bringing together representatives of member states to hammer out deals and consider amendments to the treaties, or other history-making decisions such as enlargement.

Integration, European (see Box 1.5) The process whereby sovereign European states relinquish (surrender or pool) national sovereignty to maximize their collective power and interests.

Integration, flexible Also called 'reinforced' or 'enhanced cooperation', flexible integration denotes the possibility for some member states to pursue deeper integration without the participation of others. Examples include EMU and the Schengen Agreement.

Integration, negative Integration through market-building and the removal of obstacles to trade. Less ambitious than positive integration.

Integration, positive Integration through the active promotion of common policies which effectively replace national ones.

Intergovernmentalism (see Box 1.5) Process or condition whereby decisions are reached by specifically defined cooperation between or among governments. Sovereignty is not directly undermined.

Internal market More than a free trade area, an internal market signifies the free trade of goods, services, people, and capital. Also known as the single market.

Legitimacy The right to rule and make political decisions. More generally, the idea that 'the existing political institutions are the most appropriate ones for society' (Lipset 1963).

Liberal intergovernmentalism (see Table 1.1) A theory of European integration which argues that the most important decisions taken concerning the EU reflect the preferences of national governments rather than supranational institutions.

Lobbying (see Box 6.1) An attempt to influence policy-makers to adopt a course of action advantageous (or not detrimental) to a particular group or interest.

Luxembourg Compromise (see Box 2.2) Agreed in 1966 to resolve the 'Empty Chair Crisis', this informal agreement established that when a decision was subject to Qualified Majority Voting (QMV), the Council would postpone a decision if any member states felt 'very important' interests were under threat.

Market (Box 5.1) A system of exchange bringing together buyers and sellers of goods and services.

Marshall Plan (1947) (see Box 2.2) A US aid package of $13 billion to help rebuild West European economies after the war.

Multilevel governance (see Box 1.5) A term denoting a system of overlapping and shared powers between actors on the regional, national, and supranational levels.

Neofunctionalism (see Table 1.1) A theory of European integration which suggests that economic integration in certain sectors will provoke further integration in other sectors, and can lead to the formation of integrated supranational institutions.

New institutionalism (see Table 1.1) As applied to the EU, a theoretical approach that suggests that institutions, including rules and informal practices, can mould the behaviour of policy-makers (including national officials) in ways that governments neither plan nor control.

Non-tariff barriers (see Box 5.1) Regulations, such as national standards, that increase the cost of imports and thus have the equivalent effect on tariffs.

Ordinary Legislative Procedure (see 'Co-decision')

OSCE (see Box 10.1) The Organization for Security and Cooperation in Europe brings together 56 (as of 2011) states from Europe and beyond in what is the world's largest regional security organization. It claims to take a 'comprehensive approach to security', extending especially to human rights. The OSCE works on the basis of unanimity and its decisions are politically, not legally, binding. It thus is criticized as toothless, even though its predecessor—the Conference on SCE—was important in putting into motion the changes that led to the end of the Cold War.

Path dependency The idea (developed especially by new institutionalists) that once a particular policy path or course of action is taken, it is extremely difficult to turn back because of the 'sunk costs' (time and resources already invested). Used to explain why even those policies that have outlived their usefulness remained unreformed.

'Perm Reps' Eurospeak for the Permanent Representatives (EU ambassador) and the Permanent Representations (similar to embassies) of each member state. Together the 'Perm Reps' from each of the member states make up Coreper.

Petersberg tasks (see Box 9.3) A series of security tasks designed to strengthen European defence capability and the EU's role as a civilian power. These tasks include humanitarian, rescue, and peacekeeping operations as well as tasks involving combat forces in crisis management.

Pillars (see Box 1.2) A shorthand term for describing the 'Greek temple' architecture created by the Maastricht Treaty, with the first pillar (the pre-existing European Community) and the second (foreign and security policy) and third (justice and home affairs) pillars together constituting the 'European Union'. The Treaty of Lisbon collapsed the EU's pillars into one institutional structure.

Police and Judicial Cooperation in Criminal Matters (formerly 'Justice and Home Affairs') Refers to EU actions designed to ensure internal security (that is, within the Union's borders), including those related to migration, drugs and people-trafficking, anti-terrorism, and organized crime. Most were contained within 'pillar III' following the 1992 Maastricht Treaty and until the 2009 Lisbon Treaty formally abolished the pillar system.

Policy networks (see Table 1.1) Clusters of actors, each of whom has an interest or stake in a given policy sector and the capacity to help determine policy success or failure. Scholars applying this notion argue that analysing such networks can reveal a great deal about day-to-day decision-making in the EU.

Public policy (see Box 5.1) A course of action (decisions, actions, rules, laws, and so on) or inaction taken by government in regard to some public problem or issue.

Qualified Majority Voting (QMV) (see Boxes 2.2 and 2.3) Refers to the most commonly used voting method in the Council of Ministers. Under this system each member state is granted a number of votes roughly proportional to its population.

Rapporteur (see Box 6.1) The Member of the European Parliament responsible for preparing a report in one of the Parliament's committees.

Schengen Agreement (see Box 2.2) An agreement stipulating the gradual abolition of controls at borders. By 2008, 15 EU member states were signatories as were Norway and Iceland. The UK and Ireland have not signed, and Denmark has opted out of certain aspects.

Schuman plan (see Box 2.3) A plan proposed by the French Foreign Minister, Robert Schuman, in 1950 to combine the coal and steel industries of Germany and France, thus making war between them impossible. It eventually became the basis for the European Coal and Steel Community, launched by the 1950 Treaty of Paris.

Single market (See internal market.)

Soft security (see Box 9.3) A post-Cold War concept that refers to security that is obtained through non-military policy instruments (except in cases of peacekeeping) and does not involve territorial defence of the state. It is related to the ideas of 'human security'—defence of the citizen, as opposed to the state—and 'homeland security', obtained via policies designed to eliminate internal security threats.

Sovereignty (see Box 1.5) Refers to the ultimate authority over people and territory.

Subsidiarity (see Box 2.2) The idea that action should be taken at the most efficient level of governance, but as close to the citizens as possible.

Supranationalism (see Box 1.5) Above states or nations. Supranationalism means decisions are made by a process or institution which is largely independent of national governments. The term supranationalism is usually contrasted with intergovernmentalism.

Tour de table (see Box 4.1) In the Council of Ministers a 'tour around the table' allows each delegation to make an intervention on a given subject.

Transparency (see Box 6.1) The process of making (EU) documents and decision-making processes more open and accessible to the public.

Venue shopping (see Box 6.1) The activities of an interest group searching or `shopping' for a decision setting most favourable or receptive to their policy claims.

The Glossary was compiled with the assistance of Louise Maythorne (University of Edinburgh) and Andrew Byrne (Universities of Köln and Edinburgh).

∎ REFERENCES

Allen, D. (2010), 'The Structural Funds and Cohesion Policy', in H. Wallace, M. Pollack, and A. Young (eds.) *Policy-Making in the European Union*, 6th edn. (Oxford and New York: Oxford University Press): 229–52.

Anderson, J., Ikenberry, G. J., Risse, T. (eds.) (2008), *The End of the West? Crisis and Change in the Atlantic Order* (Ithaca NY: Cornell University Press).

Armstrong, K. and Bulmer, S. (1998), *The Governance of the Single European Market* (Manchester and New York: Manchester University Press).

Aspinwall, M. and Greenwood, J. (1998), *Collective Action in the European Union: Interests, and the New Politics of Associability* (London: Routledge).

Aspinwall, M. and Schneider, G. (2000), 'Same Menu, Separate Tables: The Institutionalist Turn in Political Science and the Study of European Integration', *European Journal of Political Research*, 38/1: 1–36.

Avery, G. (2004), 'The Enlargement Negotiations', in F. Cameron (ed.), *The Future of Europe, Integration and Enlargement* (London: Routledge): 35–62.

_____ (2011), 'The EU's External Action Service: New Actor on the Scene', *EPC Commentary* (Brussels: European Policy Centre), http://www.epc.eu/documents/uploads/pub_1223_the_european_external_action_service_-_new_actor_on_the_scene.pdf.

_____ Bailes, J.K., and Thorhallsson, B. (2011) 'Iceland's Application For European Union Membership' *Studia Diplomatica*, Royal Institute for International Relations, Brussels, 64(1): 93–119.

Bache, I. (2008), *Europeanization and Multi-Level Governance: Cohesion Policy in the European Union and Britain* (Lanham MD: Rowman & Littlefield).

Bartolini, S. (2005), *Restructuring Europe: Centre Formation, System Building and Political Structuring between the Nation State and the European Union* (Oxford and New York: Oxford University Press).

Barysch, K., Everts, S., and Grabbe, H. (2005), *Why Europe Should Embrace Turkey* (London: Centre for European Reform).

Baun, M. and Marek, D. (2008), *EU Cohesion Policy after Enlargement* (Basingstoke and New York: Palgrave Macmillan).

Baun, M., Dürr, J., Marek, D., and Šaradín, P. (2006), 'The Europeanization of Czech Politics', *Journal of Common Market Studies*, 44/2: 249–80.

Bergman, A. and Peterson, J. (2006), 'Security Strategy, ESDP and the Non-Aligned States' in R. Dannreuther and J. Peterson (eds.), *Security Strategy and Transatlantic Relations* (London: Routledge): 147–64.

Bernhagen, P. and Mitchell, N. (2009), 'The Determinants of Direct Corporate Lobbying in the European Union', *European Union Politics*, 10/2: 155–76.

Best, E., Christiansen, T., and Settembri P. (eds.) (2008), *The Institutions of the Enlarged European Union: Continuity and Change* (Cheltenham and Northampton MA: Edward Elgar).

Bindi, F. with Cisci, M. (2005), 'Italy and Spain: A Tale of Contrasting Effectiveness in the EU', in S. Bulmer and C. Lequesne (eds.), *The Member States of the European Union* (Oxford and New York: Oxford University Press): 142–63.

Biscop, S. (2005), *The European Security Strategy: A Global Agenda for Positive Power* (Aldershot and Burlington VT: Ashgate).

Bogdanor, V. (2007), *Democracy, Accountability and Legitimacy in the European Union* (London: Federal Trust for Education and Research).

Booker, C. (1996), 'Europe and Regulation: The New Totalitarianism', in M. Holmes (ed.), *The Eurosceptical Reader* (New York: St. Martin's Press): 186–204.

Börzel, T. (ed.) (2005), 'The Disparity of European Integration: Revisiting Neofunctionalism in Honour of Ernst Haas', Special Issue of *Journal of European Public Policy*, 12/2.

Bretherton, C. and Vogler, J. (2006), *The European Union as a Global Actor*, 2nd edn. (London and New York: Routledge).

Buchan, D. (2010), *Eastern Europe's Energy Challenge: Meeting Its EU Climate Commitments* (Oxford: The Oxford Institute for Energy Studies).

Bulmer, S. and Lequesne, C. (2005a), 'The EU and its Member States: An Overview', in S. Bulmer, and C. Lequesne, (eds.), *The Member States of the European Union* (Oxford and New York: Oxford University Press): 1–24.

_____ _____ (2005b), *The Member States of the European Union* (Oxford and New York: Oxford University Press).

Burchill, S., Linklates A., Devetak, R., Donnelly, J., Paterson, M., Reus-Smit, C., and True, J. (2005), *Theories of International Relations* (Basingstoke and New York: Palgrave).

Cafruny, A. and Ryner, M. (eds.) (2003), *A Ruined Fortress? Neoliberal Hegemony and Transformation in Europe* (Oxford and Lanham MD: Rowman & Littlefield).

Caporaso, J. (2001), 'The Europeanization of Gender Equality Policy and Domestic Structural Change', in M. Green Cowles, J. Caporaso, and T. Risse (eds.), *Transforming Europe: Europeanization and Domestic Change* (Ithaca NY: Cornell University Press): 21–43.

Carlsnaes, W. (2006), 'European Foreign Policy', in K. E. Jørgensen, M. A. Pollack, and B. Rosamond (eds.), *Handbook of European Union Politics* (London and Thousand Oaks CA: Sage): 545–60.

Checkel, J. (1999), 'Social Construction and Integration', *Journal of European Public Policy*, 6/4: 545–60.

_____ (2004), 'Social Constructivisms in Global and European Politics; A Review Essay', *Review of International Studies*, 30/2: 229–44.

_____ (2006), 'Constructivism and EU Politics', in K. E. Jørgensen, M. Pollack, and B. Rosamond (eds.), *Handbook of European Union Politics* (London: Sage): 57–76.

_____ (2007) 'Social Mechanisms and Regional Cooperation: Are Europe and the EU Really All That Different?' in A. Acharya and A.I. Johnston (eds.), *Crafting Cooperation: Regional International Institutions in Comparative Perspective* (Cambridge and New York: Cambridge University Press).

Closa, C. and Heywood, P. S. (2004), *Spain and the European Union* (Basingstoke and New York: Palgrave).

Coen, D. (ed.) (2007) *Journal of European Public Policy,* special Issue on 'Empirical and Theoreticl studies in Ell Lobbying', 14/3.

_____ and Richardson, J. (eds.) (2007), *Lobbying in the European Union: Institutions, Actors and Issues* (Oxford and New York: Oxford University Press).

Coker, C. (2009), *War in an Age of Risk* (Cambridge and Malden MA: Polity).

Commission (2007b), *The Official EU Languages*. Available at: http://ec.europa.eu/education/policies/lang/languages/index_en.html.

_____ (2009a), *EU Budget 2008—Financial Report* (Bruxelles: Commission).

_____ (2009b), *26th Annual Report on Monitoring the Application of Community Law* (Bruxelles: Commission).

_____ (2009c), *General Budget of the European Union for the Financial Year 2009* (Bruxelles: Commission).

_____ (2010a), *EU 2010 Budget in Figures* (Luxembourg: Publications Office of the European Union) http://ec.europa.eu/budget/figures/2010/2010_en.cfm.

_____ (2010b), *EU Budget 2009—Financial Report* (Luxembourg: Publications Office of the European Union).

_____ (2011), *Frequently Asked Questions about DG Translation*, at http://ec.europa.eu/dgs/translation/faq/index_en.htm.

Cooper, R. (2004a), 'Hard Power, Soft Power and the Goals of Diplomacy', in D. Held and M. Koenig-Archibugi (eds.), *American Power in the 21st Century* (Oxford and Malden MA: Polity): 168–80.

_____ (2004b), Untitled in N. Gnesotto (ed), *EU Security and Defence Policy: the First Five Years (1999–2004)* (Paris: Institute for Security Studies).

Corbett, R. (2002), *The European Parliament's Role in Closer EU Integration* (Basingstoke: Macmillan).

Corbett, R., Jacobs, F., and Shackleton, M. (2010), *The European Parliament*, 8th edn. (London: John Harper Publishing).

Cottey, A. (2007), *Security in the New Europe* (Basingstoke and New York: Palgrave).

Council of the EU (2009) 'Treaty of Lisbon—Information Note', Brussels: Council General Secretariat, December 2009, available from: http://www.consilium.europa.eu/uedocs/cms_data/docs/pressdata/en/ec/111652.pdf.

Cowles, M. G. and Curtis, S. (2004), 'Developments in European Integration Theory: The EU as "other" ', in M. G. Cowles and D. Dinan (eds.), *Developments in the European Union II* (Basingstoke and New York: Palgrave): 296–309.

Damro, C. (2010) *Market Power Europe*, MERCURY e-paper, at: http://www.mercury-fp7.net/fileadmin/user_upload/E-paper_no5_final2_2010.pdf.

Dannreuther, R. (ed.) (2004), *European Union Foreign and Security Policy: Towards a Neighbourhood Strategy* (London and New York: Routledge).

_____ (2007), *International Security: the Contemporary Agenda* (Cambridge and Malden MA: Polity).

_____ and Peterson, J. (eds.) (2006), *Security Strategy and Transatlantic Relations* (London and New York: Routledge).

Daugbjerg, C. and Swinbank, A. (2007), 'The Politics of CAP Reform: Trade Negotiations, Institutional Settings and Blame Avoidance', *Journal of Common Market Studies*, 45(1): 1–22.

De Grauwe, P. (2009), *Economics of Monetary Union*, 8th edn. (Oxford and New York: Oxford University Press).

Deutsch, K. *et. al.* (1957), *Political Community and the North Atlantic Area: International Organization in the Light of Historical Experience* (Princeton NJ: Princeton University Press).

Dinan, D. (2004), *Europe Recast: A History of European Union* (Boulder CO and Basingstoke: Lynne Rienner and Palgrave).

_____ (ed.) (2006), *Origins and Evolution of the European Union* (Oxford and New York: Oxford University Press).

Donnelly, B. and Bigatto, M. (2008), 'The European Parliament and Enlargement' in E. Best, T. Christiansen, and P. Settembri (eds), *The Institutions of the Enlarged European Union: Continuity and Change* (Cheltenham and Northampton MA: Edward Elgar): 82–99.

Duchêne, F. (1994), *Jean Monnet: The First Statesman of Interdependence* (New York: Norton).

Egan, M. (2010), 'Political Economy' in M. Egan, N. Nugent, and W. E. Paterson (eds.), *Research Agenda in EU Studies: Stalking the Elephant* (Basingstoke and New York: Palgrave Macmillan): 216–55.

Eilstrup-Sangiovanni, M. (2006), 'The Constructivist Turn in European Integration Studies', in M. Eilstrup-Sangiovanni (ed.), *Debates on European Integration. A Reader* (Basingstoke and New York: Palgrave): 393–405.

Elman, C. and Elman, M. F. (eds.) (2003), *Progess in International Relations Theory* (Cambridge and London: MIT Press).

Epstein, R. and Sedelmeier, U. (eds.) (2009), *International Influence beyond Conditionality: Postcommunist Europe after EU Enlargement* (London and New York: Routledge).

Eurobarometer (2007), *Standard Barometer 67, First Results,* Spring 2007 (Brussels: European Commission). Available at: http://ec.europa.eu/public_opinion/archives/eb/eb67/eb_67_first_en.pdf.

Eurostat (2007), *Statistics in Focus. Population and Social Conditions,* 41/2007. (Luxembourg: Eurostat). Available at: http://epp.eurostat.ec.europa.eu/cache/ITY_OFFPUB/KS-SF-07-041/EN/KS-SF-07-041-EN.PDF

_____ (2010), *Regional Economic Accounts.* Available at http://epp.eurostat.ec.europa.eu/portal/page/portal/statistics/search_database.

Everts, S. (2002), *Shaping a Credible EU Foreign Policy* (London: Centre for European Reform).

Faber, G. and Orbie, J. (2009), 'Everything but Arms: Much More than Appears at First Sight', *Journal of Common Market Studies,* 47/4: 767–87.

Falkner, G. (2000), 'How Pervasive are Euro-Politics? Effects of EU Membership on a New Member State', *Journal of Common Market Studies,* 38/2: 223–50.

_____ , Treib, O., and Holzleithner, E. (2008), *Compliance in the Enlarged European Union* (Aldershot: Ashgate).

Farrell, M. (2007), 'From EU Model to External Policy? Promoting Regional Integration in the Rest of the World', in S. Meunier, and K. McNamara (eds.), *Making History: European Integration and Institutional Change at Fifty* (Oxford and New York: Oxford University Press): 299–316.

Gallagher, T. (2009), *Romania and the European Union: How the Weak Vanquished the Strong* (Manchester and New York: Manchester University Press).

Galtung, J. (1973), *The European Community: A Superpower in the Making* (London: George Allen & Unwin).

Garzon, I. (2006), *Reforming the Common Agricultural Policy: History of a Paradigm Change* (Basingstoke and New York: Palgrave Macmillan).

Geddes, A. and Boswell, C. (2011), *Migration and Mobility in the European Union* (Basingstoke and New York: Palgrave).

Gillingham, J. (1991), *Coal, Steel and the Rebirth of Europe, 1945–1955* (Cambridge and New York : Cambridge University Press).

_____ (2003), *European Integration, 1950–2003* (Cambridge and New York: Cambridge University Press).

Ginsberg, R. (2001), *The European Union in International Politics: Baptism by Fire* (Boulder CO and Oxford: Rowman & Littlefield).

Goergen, P. (2006), *Lobbying in Brussels: A Practical Guide to the European Union for Cities, Regions, Networks and Enterprises* (Brussels, D&P Services).

Goetz, K. H. (2005), 'The New Member States and the EU: Responding to Europe', in S. Bulmer and C. Lequesne (eds.), *The Member States of the European Union* (Oxford and New York: Oxford University Press): 254–84.

Grabbe, H. (2006), *The EU's Transformative Power: Europeanization through Conditionality in Central and Eastern Europe* (Basingstoke and New York: Palgrave Macmillan).

Grant, W. (2010), 'Policy Instruments in the Common Agricultural Policy', *West European Politics*, 33(1) : 22–38.

Green Cowles, M., Caporaso, J., and Risse, T. (eds.) (2000), *Transforming Europe: Europeanization and Domestic Change* (Ithaca NY: Cornell University Press).

Greenwood, J. (2003), *Interest Representation in the EU* (Basingstoke and New York: Palgrave).

Haas, E. (1958), *The Uniting of Europe: Political, Social, and Economic Forces* (Stanford CA: Stanford University Press).

_____ (1964), *Beyond the Nation-State: Functionalism and International Organization* (Stanford CA: Stanford University Press).

_____ (2001), 'Does Constructivism Subsume Neo-functionalism?' in T. Christiansen, K. E. Jørgensen, and A. Weiner (eds.), *The Social Construction of Europe* (London and Thousand Oaks CA: Sage): 22–31.

Habermas, J. (2008) *Europe: the Faltering Project* (Cambridge and Malden MA: Polity).

Hagemann, S. and De Clerck-Sachsse, J. (2007), *Decision-making in the Council of Ministers before and after May 2004*, Special CEPS Report (Brussels: Centre for European Policy Studies).

Hayes-Renshaw, F. and Wallace, H. (2006), *The Council of Ministers*, 2nd edn. (Basingstoke and New York: Palgrave).

Heisbourg, F. (2004), 'The "European Security Strategy" is Not a Security Strategy', in S. Everts *et al.* (eds.) *A European Way of War* (London: Centre for European Reform): 27–39.

Heisenberg, D. (2007), 'Informal Decision-Making in the Council: The Secret of the EU's Success?', in S. Meunier, and K. McNamara (eds.), *Making History. European Integration and Institutional Change at Fifty* (Oxford and New York: Oxford University Press): 67–88.

Henderson, K. (2007), *The European Union's New Democracies* (London and New York: Routledge).

Hill, C. (1998), 'Closing the Capabilities–Expectations Gap?', in J. Peterson and H. Sjursen, *A Common Foreign Policy for Europe? Competing Visions of the CFSP* (London and New York: Routledge): 91–107.

_____ (2004), 'Rationalizing or Regrouping? EU Foreign Policy since 11 September 2001', *Journal of Common Market Studies*, 42/1: 143–63.

_____ (2006), 'The European Powers in the Security Council: Differing Interests, Differing Arenas', in K. V. Laatikainen and K. E. Smith (eds.), *The European Union at the United Nations* (Basingstoke and New York: Palgrave).

_____ **and Smith, M.** (eds.) (2011), *International Relations and the European Union*, 2nd edn. (Oxford and New York: Oxford University Press).

Hix, S. (2009), *What to Expect in the 2009–14 European Parliament: Return of the Grand Coalition?* (Stockholm: Swedish Institute for European Policy Analysis).

_____ , **Noury, A., and Roland, G.** (2007), *Democratic Politics in the European Parliament* (Cambridge and New York: Cambridge University Press).

Hodson, D. (2010), 'Economic and Monetary Union', in H. Wallace, M. Pollack, and A. Young (eds.), *Policy-Making in the European Union*, 6th edn. (Oxford and New York: Oxford University Press): 157–80.

Hoeksma, J. (2010) *A Polity Called EU: The European Union as a Transnational Democracy* (Amsterdam: Europe's World).

Hoffmann, S. (1966), 'Obstinate or Obsolete: The Fate of the Nation-state and the Case of Western Europe', *Daedalus* 95/3: 862–915 (reprinted in S. Hoffmann (1995), *The European Sisyphus: Essays on Europe 1964–1994* (Boulder CO and Oxford: Westview Press)).

_____ (1995), *The European Sisyphus: Essays on Europe 1964–1994* (Boulder CO and Oxford: Westview Press).

Holmes, M. (ed.) (2001), *The Eurosceptical Reader*, 2nd edn. (Basingstoke and New York: Palgrave).

Hooghe, L. and Marks, G. (2001), *Multi-Level Governance and European Integration* (Lanham and Oxford: Rowman & Littlefield).

_____ **and** _____ (2003), 'Unraveling the Central State, But How? Types of Multi-Level Governance', *American Political Science Review*, 97/2: 233–43.

House of Lords (2006), *The Further Enlargement of the EU: Threat or Opportunity?* European Union Committee, Report with Evidence, HL Paper 273 (London: Stationery Office Ltd.). Available at http://www.publications.parliament.uk/pa/ld200506/ldselect/ldeucom/273/273.pdf.

Howarth, D. and Sadeh, T. (2010), 'The Ever Incomplete Single Market: Differentiation and the Evolving Frontier of Integration', *Journal of European Public Policy*, 17(7): 922–35.

Howorth, J. (2007), *Security and Defence Policy in the European Union* (Basingstoke and New York: Palgrave).

Hug, A. (2010), *Reconnecting the European Parliament and its People* (London: Foreign Policy Centre).

IMF (International Monetary Fund) (2010), *Direction of Trade Statistics Quarterly*, June 2010 (Washington, DC: IMF).

Jabko, N. (2006), *Playing the Market* (Ithaca NY: Cornell University Press).

Jeffrey, C. and Rowe, C. (2012), 'Social and Regional Interests: The Economic and Social Committee and Committee of the Regions', in J. Peterson, and M. Shackleton, (eds.), *The Institutions of the European Union*, 3rd edn. (Oxford and New York: Oxford University Press).

Jordan, A., Huitema, D., van Asselt, H., Rayner, T., and Berkhout, F. (2010), *Climate Change Policy in the European Union: Confronting the Dilemmas of Mitigation and Adaptation?* (Cambridge and New York: Cambridge University Press).

Jordan, A. and Schout, A. (2006), *The Coordination of the European Union: Exploring the Capacities for Networked Governance* (Oxford and New York: Oxford University Press).

Jørgensen K. E. (2006), 'Overview: the European Union and the World', in K. E. Jørgensen, M. A. Pollack, and B. Rosamond, *Handbook of European Union Politics* (London and Thousand Oaks CA: Sage): 507–25.

_____ , Pollack, M., and Rosamond, B. (eds.) (2006), *Handbook of European Union Politics* (London and Thousand Oaks CA: Sage).

Judge, D. and Earnshaw, D. (2002), 'No Simple Dichotomies: Lobbyists and the European Parliament', in *Journal of Legislative Studies*, 8/4: 61–79.

_____and _____ (2008) *The European Parliament*, 2nd edn. (Basingstoke and New York: Palgrave Macmillan).

Karakatsanis and Laffin, B. (2012), 'Financial Control: The court if Auditors and OLAF' in J. Peterson and M. Shackleton (eds.), *The Institutions of the European Union*, 3rd edn. Oxford and New York: Oxford University Press).

Kassim, H., Peters, B. G., and Wright, V. (eds.) (2001), *The National Co-ordination of EU Policy: The European Level* (Oxford and New York: Oxford University Press).

_____, Peterson, J., Bauer, M., Dehousse, R., Hooghe, L., Thompson, A., and Connolly, S. (2012), *The European Commission of the 21st Century: Decline or Renewal?* (Oxford and New York: Oxford University Press).

Kaunert, C. (2011), *European Internal Security: Towards Surpanational Governance in the Area of Freedom, Security and Justice* (Manchester and New York: Manchester University Press).

Kirchner, E. and Sperling, J. (2007), *EU Security Governance* (Manchester and New York: Manchester University Press).

Knill, C. and Liefferink, D. (2007), *Environmental Politics in the European Union* (Manchester and New York: Manchester University Press).

Kostakopoulou, D. (2006), 'Security Interests: Police and Judicial Cooperation' in J. Peterson and M. Shackleton (eds.), *The Institutions of the European Union*, 2nd edn. (Oxford and New York: Oxford University Press): 231–51.

Krasner, S. (1984), 'Approaches to the State', *Comparative Politics*, 16/2: 223–46.

Krotz, U. (2009), 'Momentum and Impediments: Why Europe Won't Emerge as a Full Political Actor on the World Stage Soon', *Journal of Common Market Studies*, 47/3: 555–78.

Laatikainen, K. V. and Smith, K. E. (eds.) (2006), *The European Union at the United Nations: Intersecting Multilateralisms* (Basingstoke and New York: Palgrave Macmillan).

Laffan, B. and O'Mahony, J. (2008), *Ireland in the European Union* (Basinstoke and New York: Palgrave).

_____ , O'Donnell, R., and Smith, M. (2000), *Europe's Experimental Union: Rethinking Integration* (London and New York: Routledge).

Lavenex, S. (2010) 'Justice and Home Affairs: Communitarization with Hesitation' in H. Wallace., M. Pollack, and A. Young (eds.), *Policy-Making in the European Union*, 6th edn. (Oxford and New York: Oxford University Press): 457–77.

_____ and Wagner, W. (2007), 'Which European Public Order? Sources of Imbalance in the European Area of Freedom, Security and Justice', *European Security*, 16/3–4: 225–43.

Lenschow, A. (2010), 'Environmental Policy', in H. Wallace, M. Pollack, and A. Young (eds.), *Policy-Making in the European Union*, 6th edn.(Oxford and New York: Oxford University Press): 307–30.

Leonard, D. and Leonard, M. (eds.) (2001), *The Pro-European Reader* (Basingstoke and New York: Palgrave).

Leonard, M. (2005), *Why Europe Will Run the 21st Century* (London and New York: Harper Collins).

Leonardi, R. (2005), *Cohesion Policy in the European Union: The Building of Europe* (Basingstoke and New York: Palgrave Macmillan).

Lewis, J. (2003), 'Institutional Environments and Everyday EU Decision Making: Rationalist or Constructivist?' *Comparative Political Studies* 36/1–2: 97–124.

Lindberg, L. (1963), *The Political Dynamics of European Economic Integration* (Stanford CA: Stanford University Press).

_____ and Scheingold, S. A. (1970), *Europe's Would-Be Polity: Patterns of Change in the European Community* (Englewood Cliffs NJ: Prentice-Hall).

Lindstrom, N. (2010), 'Service Liberalization in the Enlarged EU', *Journal of Common Market Studies*, 48(5): 1307–27.

Lundestad, G. (ed.) (2008), *Just Another Major Crisis? The United States and Europe Since 2000* (Oxford and New York: Oxford University Press).

MacCormick, N. (2008), 'Constitutionalism and Democracy in the EU' in E. Bomberg, J. Peterson, and A. Stubb (eds.), *The European Union: How Does it Work?*, 2nd edn (Oxford and New York: Oxford University Press): 159–76.

Majone, G. (1999), 'The Regulatory State and its Legitimacy Problems', *West European Politics*, 22/1: 1–13.

_____ (2005), *Dilemmas of European Integration: the Ambiguities and Pitfalls of Integration by Stealth* (Oxford and New York, Oxford University Press).

_____ (2009), *Europe as the Would-be World Power: The EU at Fifty* (Cambridge and New York: Cambridge University Press).

Manners, I. (2002), 'Normative Power Europe: A Contradiction in Terms?', *Journal of Common Market Studies*, 40/2: 235–58.

_____ (2006), 'Normative Power Europe Reconsidered', *Journal of European Public Policy*, 13/2: 182–99.

_____ (2008), 'The Normative Ethics of the European Union', *International Affairs*, 84/1: 45–60.

Martin, P. (2010), 'The US Supreme Court', in G. Peele, C. Bailey, B. Cain, and B. Guy Peters (eds.), *Developments in American Politics*, 7th edn. (Basingstoke and New York: Palgrave Macmillan).

Mayhew, A. (1998), *Recreating Europe: The European Union's Policy towards Central and Eastern Europe* (Cambridge and New York: Cambridge University Press).

McGuire, S. M. and Lindeque, J. P. (2010), 'The Diminishing Returns to Trade Policy in the European Union', *Journal of Common Market Studies*, 48(5): 1329–49.

Mearsheimer, J. J. (2001), *The Tragedy of Great Power Politics* (New York and London: Norton).

Messerlin, P. (2001), *Measuring the Costs of Economic Protection in Europe* (Washington DC: Institute for International Economics).

Meunier, S. and McNamara, K. (eds.) (2007), *Making History: European Integration and Institutional Change at Fifty* (Oxford and New York: Oxford University Press).

Milward, A. (1984), *The Reconstruction of Western Europe, 1945–51* (Berkeley: University of California Press).

_____ (1992), *The European Rescue of the Nation-state* (London and Berkeley: Routledge and University of California Press).

_____ (2000), *The European Rescue of the Nation-State*, 2nd edn. (London and New York: Routledge).

Moravcsik, A. (1993), 'Preferences and Power in the European Community: A Liberal Intergovernmentalist Approach', *Journal of Common Market Studies*, 31/4: 473–524.

_____ (1998), *The Choice for Europe: Social Purpose and State Power from Messina to Maastricht* (Ithaca NY and London: Cornell University Press and UCL Press).

_____ (2008) 'The Myth of Europe's Democratic Deficit', *Intereconomics: Journal of European Public Policy*, November/December: 331–40.

_____ and Schimmelfennig, F. (2009), 'Liberal Intergovernmentalism', in A. Wiener and T. Diez, *European Integration Theory*, 2nd edn. (Oxford and New York: Oxford University Press): 67–87.

Morgan, G. (2005), *The Idea of a European Superstate* (Princeton and Oxford: Princeton University Press).

Naurin, D. and Wallace, H. (2008), *Unveiling The Council of the European Union: Games Governments Play in Brussels* (Basingstoke and New York: Palgrave).

Nelsen, B. and Stubb, A. (eds.) (2003), *The European Union: Readings on the Theory and Practice of European Integration*, 3rd edn. (Boulder CO and Basingstoke: Lynne Rienner and Palgrave).

Neustadt, R. E. (1991), *Presidential Power and the Modern Presidents: the Politics of Leadership from Roosevelt to Reagan* (New York and London: Free Press), revised edition.

Norheim-Martinsen, P.M. (2010), 'Beyond Intergovernmentalism: the European Security and Defence Policy and the Governance Approach', *Journal of Common Market Studies*, 48/5: 1351–65.

Nugent, N. (ed.) (2004), *European Union Enlargement* (Basingstoke and New York: Palgrave).

Nuttall, S. (2000), *European Foreign Policy* (Oxford and New York: Oxford University Press).

Nye Jr., J. S. (2004), *Soft Power: The Means to Success in World Politics* (New York: Public Affairs).

_____, (2011), *The Future of Power* (New York: Public Affairs).

OECD (2010), *National Accounts—Volume IV—General Government Accounts* (Paris: OECD).

Orbie, J. (2009), *Europe's Global Role: External Policies of the European Union* (Farnham: Ashgate).

Panke, D. (2010), *Small States in the European Union: Coping With Structural Disadvantages* (London: Ashgate).

Papadimitriou, D. and Phinnemore, D. (2007), *Romania and the European Union* (London and New York: Routledge).

Patten, C. (2001), 'In Defence of Europe's Foreign Policy', *Financial Times*, 17 October. Available at: http://www.ft.com/.

_____ (2005), *Not Quite the Diplomat: Home Truths About World Affairs* (London and New York: Allen Lane/Penguin).

Peterson, J. (1995), 'Decision-Making in the EU: Towards a Framework for Analysis', *Journal of European Public Policy*, 2/1: 69–73.

_____ (2008), 'Enlargement, Reform and the European Commission: Weathering a Perfect Storm?', *Journal of European Public Policy*, 15/5: 761–80.

_____ (2009) 'Policy Networks', in A. Wiener and T. Diez, *European Integration Theory*, 2nd edn. (Oxford and New York: Oxford University Press): 105–24.

_____ (2012), 'The College of Commissioners', in J. Peterson and M. Shackleton (eds.), *The Institutions of the European Union*, 3rd edn. (Oxford and New York: Oxford University Press).

_____ **and Bomberg, E.** (1999), *Decision-Making in the European Union* (Basingstoke and New York: Palgrave).

_____, **Byrne, A. and Helwig, N.**(2012), 'International Interests: The Common Foreign and Security Policy', in J. Peterson and M. Shackleton (eds.), *The Institutions of the European Union*, 3rd edn. (Oxford and New York, Oxford University Press).

_____ **and Pollack, M.** (eds.) (2003), *Europe, America, Bush* (London and New York: Routledge).

_____ **and Shackleton, M.** (eds.) (2012), *The Institutions of the European Union*, 3rd edn. (Oxford and New York: Oxford University Press).

Pierson, P. (1996), 'The Path to European Integration', *Comparative Political Studies*, 29(2): 123–63.

_____ (2004), *Politics in Time: History, Institutions and Social Analysis* (Princeton NJ and Woodstock: Princeton University Press).

Pinder, J. (1999), *Foundations of Democracy in the European Union* (London and New York: Macmillan and St Martin's Press).

Piris, J.-C. (2010), *The Lisbon Treaty: a Legal and Political Analysis* (Cambridge and New York: Cambridge University Press).

Pollack, M. (2009), 'New Institutionalism', in A. Wiener and T. Diez, *European Integration Theory*, 2nd edn. (Oxford and New York: Oxford University Press): 125–43.

_____ (2010), 'Theorizing EU Policy-Making', in H. Wallace, M. Pollack, and A. Young (eds.), *Policy-Making in the European Union*, 6th edn. (Oxford and New York: Oxford University Press): 15–44.

Posen, B. (2004), 'ESDP and the Structure of World Power', *International Spectator*, 30(1): 5–17.

Puchala, D. J. (1972), 'Of Blind Men, Elephants and International Integration', *Journal of Common Market Studies*, 10/3: 267–84.

Quaglia, L. (2007), *Central Banking Governance in the European Union: A Comparative Analysis* (London and New York: Routledge).

Redmond, J. (2007), 'Turkey and the EU: Troubled European or European Trouble?' *International Affairs* 83/2 (London: Chatham House): 305–17.

Rees, W. (2006), *Transatlantic Counter-terrorism Cooperation: The New Imperative* (London and New York: Routledge).

_____, (2008), 'Inside-Out. The External Face of EU Internal Security', *Journal of European Integration*, 30/1: 97–111.

Richardson, J. (2005) (ed.), *European Union: Power and Policy-Making*, 3rd edn. (London and New York: Routledge).

Rieger, E. (2005), 'Agricultural Policy: Constrained Reforms', in H. Wallace, W. Wallace, and M. Pollack (eds.), *Policy-Making in the European Union*, 5th edn. (Oxford and New York: Oxford University Press): 161–90.

Rifkin, J. (2004), *The European Dream* (Cambridge: Polity Press).

Risse, T. (2009), 'Social Constructivism', in A. Wiener and T. Diez (eds.), *European Integration Theory*, 2nd edn. (Oxford and New York: Oxford University Press): 144–60.

Rogers, J. (2009), 'From "Civilian Power" to "Global Power": Explicating the European Union's "Grand Strategy" through the Articulation of Discourse Theory', *Journal of Common Market Studies*, 47/4: 831–62.

Rometsch, D. and Wessels, W. (1996), *The European Union and Member States: Towards Institutional Fusion?* (Manchester and New York: Manchester University Press).

Rosamond, B. (2005), 'The Uniting of Europe and the Foundation of EU Studies: Revisiting the Neofunctionalism of Ernst B. Haas', *Journal of European Public Policy*, 12(2): 237–54.

Roth, K. (2007), 'Europe must Pull its Weight on Human Rights', *Financial Times* 12 January. Available at: http://www.ft.com/.

Sandholtz, W. and Stone Sweet, A. (eds.) (1998), *European Integration and Supranational Governance* (Oxford and New York: Oxford University Press).

Sbragia, A. (2001), 'Italy Pays for Europe: Political Leadership, Political Choice, and Institutional Adaptation', in M. Green Cowles, J. Caporaso, and T. Risse (eds.), *Transforming Europe: Europeanization and Domestic Change* (Ithaca NY: Cornell University Press): 79–96.

Scharpf, F. W. (1999), *Governing in Europe: Effective and Democratic?* (Oxford and New York: Oxford University Press).

Schimmelfennig, F. (2003), *The EU, NATO and the Integration of Europe* (Cambridge and New York: Cambridge University Press).

Schneider C.J. (2008), *Conflict, Negotiation and European Union Enlargement* (Cambridge and New York: Cambridge University Press).

Settembri, P. (2007), 'The Surgery Succeeded. Has the Patient Died? The Impact of Enlargement on the European Union', Paper Presented at the Global Fellows Forum, NYU Law School, New York: 5 April 2007. Available at: http://centers.law.nyu.edu/jeanmonnet/papers/07/070401.html.

Short, C. (2000), 'Aid that Doesn't Help', *Financial Times* 23 June. Available at: http://www.ft.com/.

Siedentop, L. (2000), *Democracy in Europe* (Harmondsworth: Allen Lane/Penguin Press).

Sjursen, H. (ed.) (2006), 'What Kind of Europe? European Foreign Policy in Perspective', Special Issue of *Journal of European Public Policy* 13/2.

_____ (ed.) (2006), *Questioning EU Enlargement: Europe in Search of Identity* (London and New York: Routledge).

Slapin, J. B. (2008), 'Bargaining Power at Europe's Intergovernmental Conferences: Testing Institutionalism and Intergovernmental Theories', *International Organization*, 62/1: 131–62.

Smith, K. E. (2005), 'Enlargement and European Order', in C. Hill and M. Smith (eds.), *International Relations and the European Union* (Oxford and New York: Oxford University Press): 270–91.

_____ (2008) *European Union Foreign Policy in a Changing World*, 2nd edn. (Cambridge and Malden MA: Polity).

Smith, M. E. (1997), 'What's Wrong with the CFSP? The Politics of Institutional Reform', in P.-H. Laurent and M. Maresceau (eds.), *The State of the European Union Volume 4* (Boulder CO and Essex: Lynne Rienner and Longman): 149–76.

_____ (2003), *Europe's Foreign and Security Policy* (Cambridge and New York: Cambridge University Press).

_____ (2004), 'Institutionalization, Policy Adaptation and European Foreign Policy Cooperation', *European Journal of International Relations*, 10/1: 95–136.

Stakeholder.eu: the Directory for Brussels (2011) (Berlin: Lexxion).

Steunenberg, B. and Rhinard, M. (2010), 'The Transposition of European Law in EU Member States: Between Process and Politics', *European Political Science Review*, 2/3: 495–520.

Stolfi, F. (2008), 'The Europeanisation of Italy's Budget Institutions in the 1990s' *Journal of European Public Policy*, 15/4: 550–66.

Sullivan, M. P. (2001), *Theories of International Relations: Transition vs. Persistence* (Basingstoke and New York: Palgrave).

Taylor, S. (1999), 'Union Comes of Age in Helsinki', *European Voice*, 16 December, available from: http://www.europeanvoice.com/article/imported/union-comes-of-age-in-helsinki/39845.aspx.

Toje, A. (2009), *America, the EU and Strategic Culture: Renegotiating the Transatlantic Bargain* (London and New York: Routledge).

_____ (2010), *The European Union as a Small Power: After the Post-Cold War* (Basingstoke and New York: Palgrave).

Tonra, B. (2001), *The Europeanisation of National Foreign Policy: Dutch, Danish and Irish Foreign Policy in the European Union* (Aldershot and Brookfield VT: Ashgate).

_____ and Christiansen, T. (eds.) (2004), *Rethinking European Union Foreign Policy* (Manchester and New York: Manchester University Press).

Torreblanca, J. I. (2001), *The Reuniting of Europe: Promises, Negotiations and Compromises* (Aldershot: Ashgate).

Vachudova, M. (2005), *Europe Undivided: Democracy, Leverage, and Integration after Communism* (Oxford and New York: Oxford University Press).

Van Rompuy, H. (2011), 'Reassuring European Citizens: Democratic Checks and Balances in the Union', Keynote speech delivered at a seminar organized by the Ombudsman, 18 March 2011, http://www.consilium.europa.eu/uedocs/cms_data/docs/pressdata/en/ec/120024.pdf.

Wallace, H. (2000), 'The Policy Process', in H. Wallace and W. Wallace (eds.), *Policy-Making in the European Union*, 4th edn. (Oxford and New York: Oxford University Press): 39–64.

_____ (2005), 'Exercising Power and Influence in the European Union: The Roles of Member States', in S. Bulmer and C. Lesquene (eds.), *The Member States of the European Union* (Oxford and New York: Oxford University Press): 25–44.

_____ , Wallace, W., and Pollack, M. (eds.) (2005), *Policy-Making in the European Union*, 5th edn. (Oxford and New York: Oxford University Press).

_____ , Pollack, M., and Young, A. (eds.) (2010), *Policy-Making in the European Union*, 6th edn. (Oxford and New York: Oxford University Press).

Waltz, K. N. (2002), 'Structural Realism after the Cold War', in G. J. Ikenberry (ed), *America Unrivaled: the Future of the Balance of Power* (Ithaca NY and London: Cornell University Press).

Warner, C. M. (2007), *The Best System Money Can Buy: Corruption in the European Union* (Ithaca NY and London: Cornell University Press).

Weber, K. Smith, M. E., and Baun, M. (eds.), *Governing Europe's Neighborhood: Partners or Periphery?* (Manchester and New York: Manchester University Press).

Weiler, J. H. H. (1998), 'Ideas and Idolatry in the European Construct' in B. McSweeney (ed.), *Moral Issues in International Affairs* (Basingstoke and New York: Macmillan).

_____ (1999), *The Constitution of Europe* (Cambridge and New York: Cambridge University Press).

Wendt, A. (1992), 'Anarchy is What States Make of It: The Social Construction of Power Politics', *International Organization*, 46/3: 391–426.

_____ (1999), *Social Theory of International Politics* (Cambridge and New York: Cambridge University Press).

Wessels, W., Maurer, A., and Mittag, J. (eds.) (2003), *Fifteen Into One? The European Union and its Member States* (Manchester and New York: Manchester University Press).

White, B. (2001), *Understanding European Foreign Policy* (Basingstoke and New York: Palgrave).

Whitman, R. and Wolff, S. (eds.) (2010), *The European Neighbourhood Policy in Perspective: Context, Implementation and Impact* (Basingstoke and New York: Palgrave Macmillan).

Wiener, A., and Diez, T. (eds.) (2009), *European Integration Theory* (Oxford and New York: Oxford University Press) 2nd edn..

Woll, C. (2006), 'Lobbying in the European Union: From Sui Generis to a Comparative Perspective', *Journal of European Public Policy*, 13/3: 456–69.

Young, A. R. (2002), *Extending European Cooperation: the European Union and the 'New' International Trade Agenda* (Manchester and New York: Manchester University Press).

_____ , Pollack, M., and Wallace W. (eds.) (2010), *Policy-Making in the European Union*, 6th edn. (Oxford and New York: Oxford University Press).

INDEX